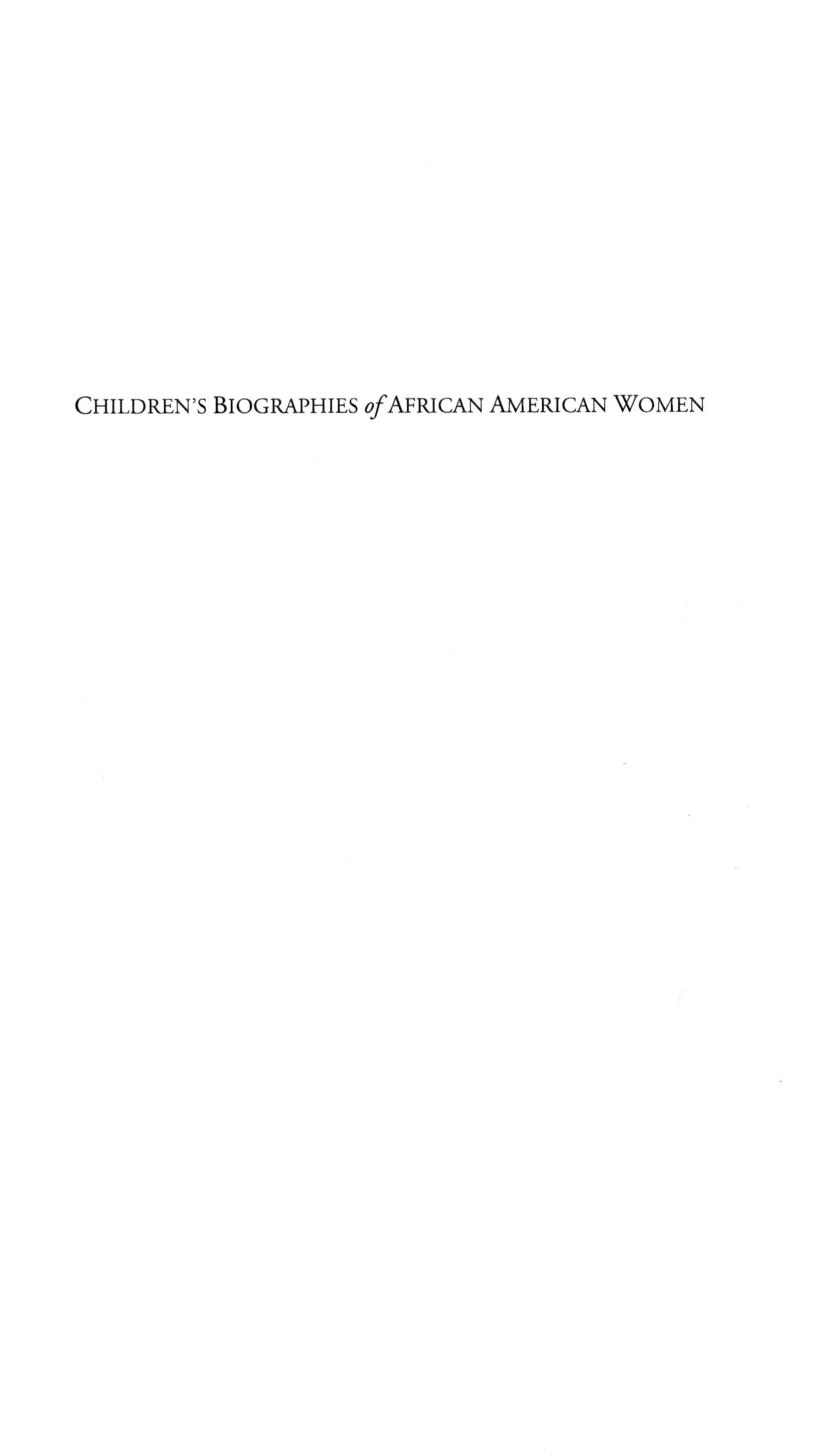

CHILDREN'S BIOGRAPHIES *of* AFRICAN AMERICAN WOMEN

CHILDREN'S BIOGRAPHIES *of* AFRICAN AMERICAN WOMEN

RHETORIC, PUBLIC MEMORY, *and* AGENCY

SARA C. VANDERHAAGEN

THE UNIVERSITY OF SOUTH CAROLINA PRESS

Published by the University of South Carolina Press
Columbia, South Carolina 29208

www.sc.edu/uscpress

Manufactured in the United States of America

27 26 25 24 23 22 21 20 19 18
10 9 8 7 6 5 4 3 2 1

Library of Congress Cataloging-in-Publication Data
can be found at http://catalog.loc.gov/.

ISBN 978-1-61117-915-6 (cloth)
ISBN 978-1-61117-916-3 (ebook)

For Chris

Contents

Acknowledgments

My experience of researching, writing, and revising this book leads me heartily to agree with this statement from the Book of Ecclesiastes: “Two are better than one, for they have a good return for their work.” I am glad to have this opportunity to thank all of those others who have helped me see a good return on my work.

First, I must acknowledge the institutions that supported this project, including Northwestern University and specifically Northwestern’s Alice Kaplan Institute for the Humanities. Other institutional support included that which I received as a DeKruyter Graduate Scholar in Communication from Calvin College and as a Harvey Fellow from the Mustard Seed Foundation. An Untenured, Tenure-Track Assistant Professor Summer Research Support Award from the Greenspun College of Urban Affairs at the University of Nevada, Las Vegas was likewise helpful.

I am also grateful for the support of Gerard Hauser, editor of *Philosophy and Rhetoric,* and Valeria Fabj, former editor of *Women’s Studies in Communication.* Sections of chapters 1, 4, 5, and 6 appeared in my essay “The ‘Agential Spiral’: Reading Public Memory through Paul Ricoeur,” *Philosophy and Rhetoric* 46:2 (2013): 182–206. This article is used by permission of the Pennsylvania State University Press. Sections of chapters 4–6 about Sojourner Truth appeared in my essay “Practical Truths: Black Feminist Agency and Public Memory in Biographies for Children” in *Women’s Studies in Communication,* which is reprinted by permission of the Organization for Research on Women and Communication (ORWAC). Reviewers at both journals enabled me considerably to strengthen my early ideas.

Many helpful readers have given their attention to this project. Faculty members at Northwestern University challenged and encouraged me as I developed the earliest version. Angela Ray has been a superb mentor. She supplied incisive criticism, offered compassionate counsel, and provided encouragement, each in its turn. She is an exemplary scholar and teacher and a valued friend. Keith Topper’s contributions enhanced my discussions of agency and memory and my application of Ricoeur. Bob Hariman encouraged me to reflect on the advantages and disadvantages of my reading strategy and, perhaps unwittingly, promoted my interest in philosophical hermeneutics (even though the field was, as he put it, “currently out of fashion”). Darlene Clark Hine read and applauded my early efforts at reading children's biographies about Sojourner Truth, and her expertise greatly enriched the project. I also thank Dilip Gaonkar for introducing me to Ricoeur and for offering unsolicited but appreciated insights about my individual scholarly identity. I am also grateful to the conference respondents, reviewers, and editors who read parts or all of the manuscript. Chuck Morris provided encouraging feedback on an early version of chapter 3. Leah Ceccarelli, Beverly Lyon Clark, Jessica Enoch, and the two anonymous reviewers at the University of South Carolina Press supplied astute, substantive feedback on the manuscript at various stages.

As a scholar with extroverted tendencies, I have depended upon the support and companionship of my colleagues and students. This project, in its infancy, was compassionately engaged by the members of a writing/support group: Tim Barouch, Jon Edwards, Rana Husseini, and Randy Iden. Since then, this project has also benefited from the constructive critique, smart conversation, sage advice, entertaining diversions, and laughter of Randall Bush, Donovan Conley, Matt deTar, Erika Engstrom, Jenny Guthrie, Cindy Koenig Richards, Kimberly Alecia Singletary, Patrick Wade, and all of my incomparable colleagues at UNLV. I also thank my UNLV mentors, David Henry and Denise Tillery, for their wisdom and friendship. My curiosity about and enthusiasm for the material in this book were invigorated by my students at UNLV, who asked me challenging questions about rhetoric, public memory, and African American history and taught me by sharing their perspectives.

While completing this work, I was nourished by a network of family and friends that spreads from Michigan to Chicago to Las Vegas. The following individuals have blessed me with gracious friendship, counsel and cheer, commiseration, and unflagging support: Jessica Bratt Carle; Katie DeVries; Kyla, Sean, Cora, and Emmet Ebels-Duggan; Becky Gelinas; Abram and Kristin Van Engen; Marissa, Matt, and Noah Metevelis; and Laura Verkaik. My families by marriage, birth, and adoption have also greatly influenced this work, including my mother- and father-in-law, Ginny and Rich Verkaik; my birthmother, Phoebe Dobrowski; and my extended birthfamily.

But this project and all that it represents would never have been possible without my parents, Ric and Julie VanderHaagen; my sister, Laura Gustafson, along with Sam, Bruce, Neil, and Luke; my daughter, Phoebe; and my husband, Chris Verkaik. My parents modeled lives of meaningful work, instilled in me a love of reading, and endured my overactive imagination and penchant for argument. My sister distracted me with arts and crafts and asked about my work even when she wasn't interested. My daughter, Phoebe—who arrived in the middle of this project—reminds me daily about the best way to approach the world and its people: with empathy, curiosity, and imagination.

Most of all, I thank and celebrate Chris. While I was writing the first version of this project, he worked outside the home so that I could pursue my research and writing without financial burden. Since the birth of our daughter, in 2013, he has worked inside the home, taking care of our family so that I could, again, be free to finish this book, among other things. He has been a compassionate listener, patient caretaker, worthy sparring partner, and strong companion. It is to Chris that I dedicate this book.

Chapter One

Locating Memories *and* Agents in Children's Biographies

> She had come to appreciate her own time and place, her very own role in the chain of events stretching from past to present.
>
> Catherine Clinton, *Phillis's Big Test*

> This is how the Aufklärer's own life gets its significance, by his or her taking a place, playing a role in this chain of progress.
>
> Charles Taylor, *Sources of the Self*

In her historical novel *Chains,* the 2008 recipient of the Scott O'Dell Prize for historical fiction for children and adolescents, Laurie Halse Anderson, gave voice to Isabel, a thirteen-year-old girl enslaved in New York City during the American colonists' struggle for independence.[1] The end of the novel finds Isabel in increasingly dire circumstances, having come under the ownership of a cruel mistress. This woman has sent Isabel's mentally unstable younger sister Ruth to a family plantation in Charleston, South Carolina, deceptively telling Isabel that Ruth has been sold away. Possibilities for Isabel's being sold to a more benevolent master evaporate. As the outlook grows bleaker, Isabel's "remembery" (as the narrator calls it) recalls a story imparted by her late mother: that of her contemporary, the poet and enslaved woman Phillis Wheatley. As Isabel's desire for freedom from bondage grows, she considers how she might achieve that goal: "Another picture hung itself in my mind, the poetry book in the stationer's shop. The one I'd been afraid to read. Miss Phillis Wheatley went free when her master released her. 'Twas on account of her fame, Momma said. Master Wheatley looked the fool for keeping a poetical genius enslaved in his household."[2]

Isabel claims she was "afraid" to read Wheatley because she feared that such reading about this exemplar from the past might provoke her to pursue her own freedom. In the text just previous to the quoted passage, Isabel thinks about her family, especially her sister Ruth, whom Isabel has been led to believe has been sold. She says to herself that "it didn't help to ponder things that were forever gone. It only made a body restless and fill up with bees all wanting to sting something."[3] Remembering people from the past makes Isabel want to do something—to lash out, whether at the system itself or at those people who kept the system running. After reflecting bitterly on her situation and her separation from her family, Isabel turns to Wheatley. She makes this shift as if someone else had put the image in her head—the picture of Wheatley's book had just "hung itself" in her mind. This recollection is followed by one of "other slaves who bought their freedom." So, Isabel ponders, one could earn freedom by being famous, like Wheatley, or one could buy freedom. Although Isabel imagines a world in which she could do the latter, she ultimately rejects the possibility, thinking, "It would never happen. Madam would not allow it. She was set on keeping my arms and legs dancing to her tune and my soul bound in her chains."[4] This final dismissal of the possibility of freedom envisions Isabel's owner in control. Isabel still cannot imagine herself as possessing the agency necessary to break those chains.

This fictional passage from a young adult novel exemplifies not only the power of memory but also its intrinsic connection with agency. Isabel tries to repress her memories—whether of people she has known or heard of—because she knows they will incite a desire to act, to do something about her enslavement, to make herself free. Just as she was taught to draw upon the stories and people of the past as resources for her action in the present, she models this process of appropriation for readers of Anderson's book. Isabel's story about remembering Wheatley illustrates how complex individual lives become distilled into memorable vignettes that can serve as publicly available resources for agency—as a model for an eighteenth-century enslaved girl such as Isabel or for a modern reader. In a broader sense, this passage draws attention to the potentially progressive power of remembering individuals like Wheatley, who have made themselves memorable through their own unlikely action.

This book examines a culturally significant set of texts located at the intersection between memory and agency: biographical narratives written for audiences of children and young adults. Although biographies for children have not been widely studied, they nonetheless serve as powerful vehicles for circulating the stories of historical figures and the values that animate those stories. By foregrounding the historical agent, biographical texts teach children about their own relationship with the past, the values of the present, and their responsibility to become the agents of the future. Biographies for young readers thus instantiate and perpetuate public memories, both to supply a source for models of judgment and action and to delineate an individual's role in an unfolding drama of action. I examine such texts as artifacts of public memory in order to show how biographies, often dismissed as conservative, should more accurately be understood as a complex rhetorical mix of conservative and progressive potential. This approach is important because much research on children's biographies has focused primarily on how they cover over trauma, sanitize messy people and events, and praise virtuous role models. Such work enables us too simply to dismiss—and, in so doing, fundamentally to misunderstand—the cultural and rhetorical work that children's biographies do. Framing biographies as rhetorical, commemorative artifacts reveals that their work is indeed persuasive and publicly significant.

My analysis focuses on a set of trade books, which are commercial, nontextbook works intended to be read by children for educational or recreational purposes. Within this category, I examine nonfiction biographies, biographical picture books, and longer fictionalized biographies. The audience of such texts includes a range of "children," from early readers to adolescents. By envisioning "children" broadly, I follow Karen Sánchez-Eppler, whose analysis in *Dependent States* treats childhood "not as a specific period of years but as a set of social conditions."[5] The ways in which creators of biographies understand this set of social conditions affect their assumptions about the purposes of history and the meaning of agency. These varied assumptions yield markedly different narratives about the same person during a particular historical moment, as well as subtle changes over time. In order better to compare and contrast these narratives, the majority of this book with the exception of chapter 3 examines biographies devoted to single individuals rather than collections of biographical sketches. This choice enables the analysis to delve more deeply into the details of each life, rather than remaining on the surface as many brief sketches are forced to do.[6] Because biographies for children devoted to individual African Americans have appeared regularly only since the mid-twentieth century, this study includes approximately seventy books published in the United States between 1949 and 2013.[7]

In order to highlight the uniquely progressive possibilities of this otherwise conservative genre, this book surveys biographies about three historically prominent African American women: the poet Phillis Wheatley, the activist and speaker Sojourner Truth, and the educator and politician Shirley Chisholm. The analysis focuses on black women because accounts of their lives and actions are often deployed as evidence of past progress or inspiration for future advancement.[8] While these women and their lives are complex, their stories are often treated as inherently progressive. Examining "progressive" lives rendered in the more conventional generic form of a biography for children discloses instructive instances of tension. I ask the following questions to discern these tensions: How do such texts present life stories that might be compelling to young readers in a particular time and place? How do these texts configure narratives in order to emphasize the actions, identities, and historical significance of these women? How do stories about these individuals then become historical examples for readers, part of a vast public repertoire for taking action and shaping identity? To answer these questions, I develop a critical tool adapted from the work of the philosopher Paul Ricoeur, which I call the "agential spiral." This concept highlights both the representation of agency within a narrative and the enactment of agency by those creating and consuming those narratives. Most significant, it shows how biographies propel public commemoration and action by connecting agents across time. Ultimately, I argue that African American biographies for children use traditional means to serve progressive ends and, in so doing, reveal tensions surrounding race and gender and conflicts concerning the rhetorical form and public role of biography itself.

Three Lives: Wheatley, Truth, and Chisholm

Phillis Wheatley is believed to have been born in West Africa around 1753 or 1754. At about the age of seven, the girl who would later become Phillis Wheatley was taken from her home, put on a ship to North America, and sold as a slave in Boston. She was purchased by a local family, the Wheatleys, who named her Phillis. According to many sources, the family treated Phillis kindly, encouraged her to learn, and connected her with important contemporaries. She eventually discovered that she loved to write. Her biographer Vincent Carretta has explained that she wrote her first poetry when she was "not yet a teenager."[9] In 1773, when Wheatley was about twenty, she published her first and only collection of verse, *Poems on Various Subjects, Religious and Moral.* Around that time, she became free from slavery. She later corresponded with General George Washington, married a free black man, bore three children, and wrote more poetry. But she died young, at the age of thirty or thirty-one, in 1784.[10] Shirley Graham (later Du Bois) wrote the first stand-alone biography of Wheatley, *The Story of Phillis Wheatley: Poetess of the American Revolution,* first published in 1949, almost two hundred years after Wheatley's birth.[11]

The child who would become Sojourner Truth was born around 1797, just a few years after Wheatley's death. Isabella Baumfree, as she was known then, spent most of her early years enslaved in upstate New York's Ulster County, which was populated primarily by Dutch farmers and landowners.[12] Isabella was sold away from her parents around the age of nine. She was sold from owner to owner until she claimed her freedom from John Dumont in 1826, one year before state law freed most enslaved adults in New York in 1827. In the decade that followed, she came into increasing contact with the public world outside Ulster County, encountering everything from generous abolitionists and surprising legal victories to New York City squalor and cult involvement.[13] In 1843, these experiences converged at a spiritual turning point in which Isabella answered God's call to head east to "lecture"—as Truth's *Narrative* reported, to exhort "the people to embrace Jesus, and refrain from sin."[14] Isabella Baumfree then adopted the name "Sojourner Truth" and began to travel around the country speaking at religious gatherings, women's rights conventions, and abolitionist meetings. During her travels, she encountered other nineteenth-century notables, including Frederick Douglass, William Lloyd Garrison, Abraham Lincoln, Elizabeth Cady Stanton, Susan B. Anthony, and Harriet Beecher Stowe. She died in Battle Creek, Michigan, in 1883, in a home near two of her daughters. About fifty years later, in 1938, the prominent Harlem Renaissance writer Arthur Huff Fauset penned the first full-length biography of Truth, *God's Faithful Pilgrim.*

This study's twentieth-century subject, Shirley Chisholm, was born in Brooklyn, New York, in 1924. After spending her early years with her grandmother in Barbados, she returned to her parents' Bedford-Stuyvesant neighborhood in 1934. She attended Brooklyn College, where she majored in sociology, joined political clubs, and honed her debate skills. Although she had wished to become a teacher, racial discrimination forced her to find employment at a day-care facility. While she worked as an educator in New York, she became involved in local politics and eventually won a place in the New York State Assembly in 1964. In 1968 she became the first African American woman elected to the United States Congress, and she launched an unsuccessful bid for the presidency in 1972. The first biography about the congresswoman was written by Susan Brownmiller in 1970, well before Chisholm's death in 2005.

These three women lived very different lives during very different times. Wheatley's claim to fame rests primarily on her contributions to American literature. Truth's achievements lay in the realm of speech and social activism. Chisholm's accomplishments were primarily in education, policy, and politics. Wheatley and Truth experienced enslavement; Chisholm did not. Two of the women, Wheatley and Chisholm, received excellent educations, especially for African American women during those periods. Truth, on the other hand, had no formal education and never learned to read. Wheatley's short life witnessed the Great Awakening and the American Revolution. Truth lived through the religious upheavals of the Second Great Awakening, the abolition of slavery throughout the United States, the Civil War, and the early fight for woman suffrage. Chisholm experienced the Depression, the Second World War, the civil rights movement of the twentieth century, and the women's liberation movement. Such differences supply meaningful points of contrast to the analysis of these women's biographies.

Yet these women's lives and memories about them also exhibit similarities that illuminate the rhetorical dynamics of biographies more broadly. Reading the lives of Wheatley, Truth, and Chisholm foregrounds the issues of agency, exemplarity, intersectionality, and temporality. First, all three women have become important historical figures who represent the potential for agency during times when the burden of a racist, sexist society was even greater than it is in the twenty-first century. In particular, as published writers and public speakers, these women represent the historical possibilities for rhetorical agency, which I follow Karlyn Kohrs Campbell in defining as "the capacity to act . . . to have the competence to speak or write in ways that will be recognized or heeded by others in one's community."[15] Wheatley, Truth, and Chisholm are three African American women whose rhetorical actions left distinct marks on the historical record, which often serve as justification for writing biographies about them. Second, because they have become historically prominent, they have been strongly relied upon as examples of black women's achievements and potential. In this way, their life narratives have become sites for the construction of not only American public memory but also specifically black American public memories. Although these sets of memories overlap, they also diverge at key moments. Third, although these figures are all black women, each of them also uniquely exhibits additional intersecting identities of educational level, language, religion, and class.[16] The challenge of representing these complex identities in a way that is accessible to contemporary young people forces authors and editors to make choices that illuminate cultural tensions surrounding those identities. Some biographers highlight blackness over femaleness, whereas others foreground educational attainment over social position. Finally, memories of these women have changed over time, as their narratives were reworked in light of new historical information, to serve the purposes of political activism, or in order to make them palatable or accessible to different audiences.[17] In the cases of Wheatley and Truth, these memories were revised most dramatically by others, whereas Chisholm took a more visible role in shaping her story. Because historical circumstances severely constrained the women's power, the question of how and whether they embodied agency often also affected their narratives.[18] For all of these reasons, many different versions of these narratives circulate throughout American public culture, providing fodder for shared memories of these women. Whether writing in 1949 or 2009, each new biographer reframed each subject's agency and legacy in ways that reflected the political demands, literary practices, and imagined audiences both of a common public culture and of a particular moment.

Juvenile Biography as a Vehicle for Public Memory

In their important study of how everyday Americans use the past, the historians Roy Rosenzweig and David Thelen concluded that the responsibility of adults to pass on to their children an understanding of history is "probably the most central issue for any culture."[19] Respondents in the study "envisioned a participatory culture in which their children could sort out how and why individuals in the past had tried to make a difference in their worlds, how and why they had made things better and worse."[20] These respondents wanted their children not only to be able to understand history but also to shape it. Historical understanding is "passed on" to children through family, museums, commemorative sites, school pageants, textbooks, and teachers. Whether in a museum or a book, children often encounter the past through story. Dianne Johnson, a scholar of children's literature, noted that African American communities have long used stories to transmit an appreciation of the past: "Reading, writing, and sharing Afro-American literature is one way to pass 'it'—history, mutual respect, cultural and social awareness—on. And passing it on helps to ensure the future survival of our communities. To be successful, this process must begin with the youngest members of our communities."[21] As recreational reading and as a supplement to textbooks, the stories in biographies have played a significant role in teaching children and young people to understand those individuals who "tried to make a difference," to use the phrase of Rosenzweig and Thelen's respondents. Children's biographies are intended—whether explicitly or implicitly—to educate children about how to understand the past and how to appropriate it, using the texts of historical lives. For this reason, the typical children's biography attempts to tell a story that facilitates both emotional engagement and knowledge acquisition. Juvenile biographies are meant to "instruct and inspire," to be "entertaining and informative."[22] Although the goals of entertainment and education or character development and knowledge expansion are not inherently at odds, they blur the lines between a *story* and an *explanation,* which professional historians have long striven to keep separate.[23]

This vexing combination has led many scholars to dismiss—or, at the very least, to treat only superficially—these "didactic" texts. Critics have rightly observed that biographies possess the ideological power to shape readers' understanding of self and society.[24] Scholars such as Rob Wilson have criticized the genre of biography as "a supreme technology of Western selfhood" that uncritically promotes individualism and self-help.[25] Timothy Cook's examination of Newbery Award recipients in the twentieth century has shown that children's biographies—indeed, children's literature in general—actively promote potentially restrictive "American" images of selfhood and agency.[26] The children's literature scholar Perry Nodelman expressed disappointment with this state of affairs, lamenting, "Unfortunately, many biographies intended for children have been composed to accomplish an obviously propagandistic purpose: to provide acceptable role models for young readers."[27] Even Marc Aronson, who views biography as a valuable tool for developing historical understanding, also bemoaned juvenile biographies' traditional focus on teaching "some supposed moral lesson."[28] Although many scholars have opined about the problems of juvenile biography, only a few have examined its actual features. Gale Eaton's *Well-Dressed Role Models: The Portrayal of Women in Biographies for Children,* for example, is the only book-length scholarly study of biographies for children. However, Eaton's book focused more on describing than on critically analyzing various biographies. Though constituting only one chapter in *Making Americans: Children's Literature from 1930 to 1960,* Gary Schmidt's critical discussion of the popular midcentury biography series Childhood of Famous Americans demonstrated the "complex vision of culture" that he believed characterized children's books in the United States at that time.[29] Only a handful of essay-length studies engage biographies from a critical perspective, including analyses of biographies about women, Barack Obama, and jazz greats.[30]

Some children's literature scholars have espoused Nodelman's strong opinion about "propagandistic" biographies, others have expressed reservations accompanied by a call for reform, and yet others have enthusiastically endorsed biographies as a "lost" pedagogical art.[31] Biographies for children may be deemed propagandistic or progressive (or both), but they all reconstruct stories from the past for use by the public in the present. These texts are also produced by the interaction of elite interests (for example, educational institutions and publishers) and the interests of those with less power (for example, some parents and teachers, children). Thus, they illustrate John Bodnar's conceptualization of "public memory," which he defined as the space of contestation between memories that serve either "the concerns of cultural leaders or authorities" or "an array of specialized interests." Bodnar described the former as "official" memory and the latter as "vernacular." He went on to explain that, in the case of vernacular memories, "defenders of such cultures are numerous and intent on protecting values and restating views of reality derived from firsthand experience in small-scale communities rather than the 'imagined' communities of a large nation."[32] Bodnar's explanation is particularly relevant here because it acknowledges the rhetorical negotiations required by narratives that serve both specific communities and the official interests of the United States as a nation. Because of biographies' unique admixture of education and entertainment, persuasion and pleasure, and official and vernacular memories, they are powerful vehicles for the circulation of public values and public memories. As such, they should be closely studied as rhetorical artifacts, not dismissed as either unimportant or not rich enough for analysis.

Biographies for children about African Americans function rhetorically in part because they are intentionally *addressed* to audiences defined by shifting cultural discourses of childhood and identity. By being addressed, these audiences are in turn rhetorically constituted by the texts. The children's literature scholar Peter Hunt clarified the addressivity of children's literature with the phrase "texts for children." He explained that, in order for this phrase to work, "the meanings of all three words have to be highly flexible."[33] "Texts" can take many different forms of communication, including media and performance. "For" can reflect the intentions of the author, refer to the classificatory needs of a publisher or librarian, or be assumed by parents, teachers, or children themselves. The idea of "children" depends on the highly variable concept of "childhood," which has been, at different times, nonexistent, a Rousseauesque ideal of romantic innocence, a time of simplicity and subordination, or an object of nostalgia. Karen Sánchez-Eppler explained that "these large-scale cultural transitions in the meaning of childhood do not have clear boundaries, and in the negotiation of these new understandings there is much variation on the basis of class, region, gender, and race."[34] Although the meaning of childhood varies significantly according to historical context, scholars generally agree that these meanings powerfully shape texts intended for children.[35] Acknowledging the complexity of this field, I adopt the pragmatic description of Nodelman, who identified "children's literature" as "the body of texts . . . produced by professional publishing houses—writing for young people by adults."[36] Nodelman's definition draws attention to three rhetorically salient features of this literature: first, it is defined primarily by its imagined audience; second, its identity is constrained by certain conditions of production; and third, its producers exercise certain intentions for this literature, whether or not these intentions are ultimately realized in the audience's reading.[37]

As Sánchez-Eppler pointed out, constructs of race and gender—whether circulating in the broader culture, expressed by an author, or envisioned in readers—influence the conception of childhood manifested in children's texts. This book thus focuses, in part, on the important subset of American children's literature that is by, about, and/or for African Americans. Although the history and criticism of children's literature have been dominated by Western white English speakers, twenty-first-century children's literature is increasingly written by and about people of color. Children's literature by and for African Americans, in particular, has grown since the mid-twentieth century.[38] The education scholar Rudine Sims Bishop defined African American children's literature as "books written by African Americans, focused on African American people and their life experiences, and primarily intended for children up to age fourteen." Bishop recognized the diversity within black communities, yet she also explained how creators' similar experiences of oppression have led to the production of a body of very deliberate literature: "Because of the historical circumstances from which it has emanated, much of African American children's literature has been purposeful, intended to serve functions that have not been expected of the larger body of American children's literature. A number of Black authors and artists have articulated the goals and objectives they wish to achieve with their children's books, and the philosophical ideas and ideological stances that underlie those books or motivate them to write for children."[39]

The creators' identities and purposes figure more prominently in defining the boundaries of African American children's literature than in mainstream literature for white children. In addition to a more prominent creator influence, African

American texts for children often feature specific content intended to challenge or displace racist narratives about black identity and experiences. Whereas audience functions as the key element in defining children's literature more generally, creator and content also play critical roles in defining African American children's literature. Therefore, I treat all three of these elements in my analysis. Unfortunately, the number of book-length critical works examining this body of texts is limited. The few monographs written since the mid-1990s have focused broadly on literature by and about African Americans, rather than on biographies or even nonfiction, specifically.[40] I aim in this book to contribute to the growing research on African American children's literature, even as the work remains grounded in the field of rhetorical studies.

Joining Public Memory and Agency

This book examines biographies for children using a rhetorical approach that attends to the pedagogical, persuasive, and public functions of texts as situated within particular contexts. The approach enacted here assumes, as do Carole Blair, Greg Dickinson, and Brian Ott, that "what most clearly distinguishes rhetoric from other critical protocols (cultural studies or literary criticism, for example) is that it organizes itself around the relationship of discourses, events, objects, and practices to ideas about what it means to be 'public.'"[41] Biographies for children are public in the straightforward sense of being accessible to large numbers of people and used in settings marked as public, such as education. But they are also public in two more complex ways. First, biographies must make an individual life story legible beyond that individual life and, in so doing, emphasize the "public relevance of private life," as Michael Warner put it.[42] Second, biographies for children purport to provide resources for virtuous action in a contingent world, where knowledge is limited and timeliness is essential. As thinkers dating back to ancient Greece have argued, rhetoric is the native art to such a world.[43] Although the contingent nature of the public sphere persists, the nature of the contingencies changes. This is why new biographies will continue to be published about the same figures, as the needs of the present demand new presentations of old lives.

Two critical concepts central to rhetorical studies animate my analysis: public memory and agency. I view biographies for young readers as both an influential practice of public memory and a potent source of messages about what it means to possess and exercise agency. By examining juvenile biographical texts using these concepts, I am able both to develop a rhetorical reading of an underexplored body of powerful public texts and to advance our understanding of the concepts of public memory and agency. I treat these concepts both separately and by joining them in the term "exemplar" and the critical concept of the "agential spiral." In so doing,

I posit that the very idea of public memory emphasizes the role of human agents in creating, interpreting, and circulating narratives about the past.

"Public memory," in this analysis, conceptualizes the rhetorical function of historical interpretation and representation. By describing it as "rhetorical," I mean that public memory is a situated interpretation of the past, oriented toward the persuasion and constitution of particular, though not always definite, audiences—Americans, Las Vegans, African Americans, schoolchildren, and the like. The phenomenon is "public" insofar as it is a communal process of interpreting shared history. The phenomenon is a form of "memory" insofar as it provides an alternative or supplement to professional history and, as such, does not always conform to the standards of professional history. I view public memory as an actively reinterpreted resource for action in the present and future, negotiated by public discourse. By approaching public memory in this way, this analysis follows the work of rhetorical scholars such as Carole Blair, Greg Dickinson, and Brian L. Ott; Kendall R. Phillips; and Bradford Vivian.[44] Yet it also advances this work by focusing specifically on how agency is performed and represented within public memories.

I use "public memory" as a hermeneutic term rather than a label for a category of objects. Employed as a critical lens, public memory foregrounds the ways in which individuals or groups interpret and represent the past in order to act in the present. Reading a text as "public memory" attends first to the markers of temporality appearing in the text. How does the text construct the relationship between present and past? Are historical figures construed as alien or accessible? Interpreting a text as one that reflects or shapes public memory also involves examining its public features. How are historical figures related to contemporaneous communities and movements? How are isolated actions related to the historical events that have been granted public meaning? Using public memory as a hermeneutic also involves inquiring how texts create an emotional investment in the past. Does having a sense of belonging in the present depend on a particular interpretation of the past? How do representations of the past activate particular affective structures? How are these structures tied to the production of shared meaning? Finally—and fundamentally, for this study of texts about black women—this critical approach attends to the ways that power shapes interpretations and representations of the past. It assumes that discourse about the past has important political and ethical implications for the present. Most significant, this book uses public memory as a hermeneutic in order to show how agency is enacted and represented in historical narratives and what these representations may mean to people in the present.

Shifts in both academic and public discourses about the past motivate my use of "public memory" as an interpretive term. Directly and indirectly, public discussion about public memory, or at least some historical practice separate from "history," reflects a growing sense among members of the late twentieth- and early twenty-first-century U.S. public that they should be active participants in shaping the historical narratives that circulate in their nation and neighborhoods. Ongoing debates over public school history textbooks, Confederate memorials and flags, and historically inspired films such as *Selma* demonstrate the American public's investment in the representation of the past. Participation in such debates further illustrates the belief that the task of historical representation can no longer be left to elites. This perspective depends upon the view that public or popular history is not simply a collection of petrified facts but a living account of the past with implications for the present. The idea that there is something called "memory" that should be recognized as a legitimate representation of the past also reflects the increased importance of narrating one's own history and identifying one's connection with the past. Participants in public debates ask, What does this past mean for us in our everyday choices and actions? In considering this question, participants in such discussions implicitly recognize a close relationship between memory and agency. These discussions assume that how one remembers events or people or histories directly affects how one acts in society. People regularly look to the past as a resource for understanding how to act in the future.

Since the late 1980s, the popularity of the term "memory" in the academic realm has grown along with the acceptance of the idea that the human world—and its history—is not simply given but is instead constructed by humans through language. The creation of a field called "memory studies" accompanied the linguistic turn that wrought dramatic changes across the humanist disciplines, both in subjects studied and methods used.[45] In 2001, the historian David Gary Shaw even claimed that "language" had surpassed all other concepts to become "the dominant revolutionary theme of the twentieth century."[46] In addition to opening the door to memory, the turn toward language during the late twentieth century fostered a renaissance in the field of rhetorical studies. Widespread emphasis on the influence of discourse in public life placed a high demand on the rhetorician's analytic skills and increased interest in her work. Moreover, the linguistic turn, which rode in on the coattails of structuralism, increased scholarly attention to contingency, contextuality, and the power of language to shape common worlds, all concepts central to the tradition of rhetoric.[47] Because memory studies has emphasized how the use of strategic, often politically loaded language profoundly shapes our understanding of the past, rhetorical analysis supplies a vital tool for understanding this public process.

In this book, I draw upon the usage of the concept of public memory in two disciplines: first, in rhetorical studies and, second, in historical studies, the field arguably most affected by the resurgence of the idea of memory. Although scholars approach memory in different ways and apply it to a vast array of objects, its usages in the two disciplines do possess some common features, particularly when contrasted with the concept of history. A survey of work in the fields of rhetoric and history reveals that several elements are implicitly at play when a scholar chooses to use the term "memory" or "public memory." First, use of the term "memory" indicates both affectivity and activity. That is, it marks an affective investment and active involvement in representations of the past, whether for the critic, the historical subjects in question, or addressees. Second, scholars invoke the concept of memory to describe the fluid, continuous nature of the practices involved in historical representation, to open them beyond the confines of a fixed text. Scholars often employ "memory" to describe phenomena that are both practical and textual. Third, "memory" is typically considered public, both in the sense of being common and in the sense of being visible and (supposedly) accessible to all. As such, memory is often treated as inherently democratic.[48] Fourth, use of the term "memory" suggests a concern with the past that connects individual and collective agents. That is, the slippage between "memory" and its pluralized counterparts, "collective memory" and "public memory," points to the term's applicability to different registers of scale. Unlike "history," which tends to connote a singular past, "memory" can apply to both individuals and groups in a way that foregrounds multiple interpretations.

The increased attention to memory signals an assumption that individual human agents should be central in the construction and selection of histories. That is, thinking of one's relationship to the past in terms of public memory foregrounds the question of agency. But, even more than memory, the concept of agency has been much debated among scholars. This is particularly true in the fields of rhetorical studies and history, where scholarship traditionally has been guided by a "great man" approach that, often problematically, constructs historical significance in terms of recorded, recognizable individual action. In a 2001 issue of *History and Theory,* the historian David Gary Shaw succinctly articulated the stakes attached to the idea of agency in his field: "If you believe in agency, which may these days have logical and rhetorical similarities to believing in God, then it is a time of reorganization and ferment. . . . We should hope that we are in a 'leadership domain,' in which our choices—and that means our words—can make a crucial difference."[49] Shaw painted agency as a quasi-theological concept, not only something one "believes in" but also something whose existence through belief can change one's understanding of the world. A 2005 essay by the rhetorical scholars Christian Lundberg and Joshua Gunn sounds a similar note, arguing that the notion of the human agent is typically shielded from criticism and meaningful interrogation because of its centrality to rhetorical studies.[50]

The polysemous nature of the term "agency" complicates this situation. As the rhetorical scholar Karlyn Kohrs Campbell observed, "The term 'agency' is polysemic and ambiguous, a term that can refer to invention, strategies, authorship, institutional power, identity, subjectivity, practices and subject positions, among others."[51] In this sense, agency is a concept not unlike memory. These two overdetermined concepts communicate myriad and sometimes conflicting values, whether expressed or unexpressed, held by their users.[52] By foregrounding the concept of agency in this study, I throw in my intellectual lot with scholars who believe that human agency is possible, observable, and rhetorically meaningful. Nonetheless, like Campbell, I recognize that agency is constrained, constructed, and complicated. But, significantly, this study does not simply assume that agency exists prior to language; rather, it examines the many ways that agency is understood, represented, and potentially produced through specific texts.

In the field of rhetorical studies, the concept of rhetorical agency typically describes the capacity of the rhetor to engage in action through speech that intends (consciously or not) to affect the world around them. When an individual or group or discourse "speaks," she, they, or it activates power by harnessing it through what we call "agency." The majority of rhetorical scholars see agency, in this sense, as "a fundamental property of rhetoric."[53] Likewise, rhetorical practice—the processes of invention and production, symbolic action, and strategic language use—is a critical function of human agency.

Agency, in the sense of being part of rhetorical practice, is performed, but it is also represented. Narratives about people from the past, then, are a prevalent mode of representing agency. Charles Taylor's history of the origins of modern selfhood, *Sources of the Self,* usefully explains the ideas of agency that pervade contemporary Western societies and thus ground approaches to biographical narrative.[54] Taylor's analysis of the puzzle of modern identity and the meaning of action produces three conclusions that are particularly pertinent to this book. First, modern individuals understand, develop, and express their agency and sense of identity primarily through telling stories about themselves. As Taylor put it, moderns emphasize "self-narration" to a degree unprecedented in history.[55] This emphasis on self-narration makes storytelling and, through it, the human experience of historical time central features of the self-understanding of human agents. Although I examine stories that people tell about historical others rather than about themselves, Taylor's insight remains useful because it emphasizes the ways that story deeply affects individual identity in the modern era.

Second, the narration of modern selfhood requires individuals to connect their actions to some larger secular historical movement. Such connections became a critical component of giving meaning to one's life when Enlightenment naturalism broke down the idea of "sacred time," a cyclical vision of divinely ordained time in which humans found their meaning.[56] The declining belief in sacred time also changed cultural perceptions about what constituted meaningful historical narrative, both for groups and for individuals. Rather than a cyclical narrative of ascent and decline, history became a story of progress toward human perfection, of a struggle from "blindness" to clear vision.[57] The recent emphasis on memory as means of conceptualizing an alternative to history suggests that nonhistorians have recognized the significance of establishing a connection with this story of progress through shared representations of the past. Indeed, Rosenzweig and Thelen's survey of how Americans engage the past indicates that "the metaphor that best captured what mattered to them [respondents] in the past could be elicited by the concept of *connection.*"[58] As the discourse on public memory illustrates, this connection must possess an expressly affective dimension. The intensified affective investment in the past, which can be noted in the process and products of public memory, can be seen as an effort to make this connection between individual humans and a shared narrative.

Third, Taylor connected the question of human agency to the precarious status of what he called "moral sources." Taylor explained that the behaviorist, "naturalist" bent among modern thinkers promoted the view that the agent can and should act independently and objectively. He showed how this ambition, which stems from the "cosmological revolution of the seventeenth century," has dramatically and negatively affected the modern understanding of the human agent by ignoring the essential fact that such agents "exist in a space defined by distinctions of worth," or spaces of value.[59] That is, Taylor stated that the various discourses locating the self in moral space have ultimately produced a disjuncture between the exceedingly high moral *standards* of modern life—such as universal justice, benevolence, toleration, and so on—and the lack or disavowal of or disagreement about moral *sources.*[60] In Taylor's view, this gap creates significant problems for modern individuals who are attempting to live up to high moral standards without the necessary framework. Thus, he recommended bringing moral sources back into the conversation, since a recovery of sources will uniquely "open us to something which empowers."[61] Not only must we have access to "something which empowers"; we must be opened to the very idea of being "empowered" in this way. How might this objective be accomplished? Taylor answered that when a "publicly accessible cosmic order of meanings is an impossibility," as it is in contemporary life, any discourse on moral sources or action must be articulated in the language of personal resonance, as an index to personal vision.[62] In the creation of public memory, this means that, in order for a shared representation of the past to resonate ethically, it must be addressed to the individual in some meaningful way. This representation must appeal individually to the self-conception of an addressee, as well as to the cultural narratives that animate that self-conception.

Taylor's discussion, like many others in rhetoric and philosophy, assumes that agents are adults. However, because this book examines *children's* biographies, it is crucial to consider how the creators of such texts either represent or enable a kind of agency unique to their young audience. Allison James noted that, in 2009, child agency had become a central concern of scholars in the field of childhood studies, as many had shifted toward "seeing children as social actors."[63] A growing number of scholars recognize that children exercise agency, even if in a sense different than their adult counterparts. My analysis of biographies for children acknowledges that the intended readers exercise some control over their own lives. At the same time, I follow scholars such as Robin Bernstein and Marah Gubar in recognizing that the agency of children—like that of adults—is both enabled and constrained by certain texts and practices. Bernstein, for instance, has shown how children perform the scripts of childhood provided to them by toys and texts while at the same time contributing to those scripts in creative ways.[64] In a related vein, Marah Gubar has outlined a balanced approach to childhood agency that avoids the extremes of what she called the "difference model" and the "deficit model."[65] She proposed, instead, a "kinship model" of childhood, which treats children and adults as fundamentally alike yet acknowledges the need to distinguish between the two groups. This model, Gubar explained, generates the following theory of agency: "Children, like adults, have agency, even if aspects of the aging process are likely to limit the form or degree of agency that they have." Gubar's formulation also acknowledges the role that texts play in shaping social visions of childhood and representations of agency for children. Significantly, her model dovetails with the conceptualization of rhetorical agency elaborated earlier, insofar as it draws attention to the ambiguity of agency, whether exercised by adults or children. Gubar explained, "Rather than assume that adults are full-fledged autonomous agents and then attempt to discern how children fail to live up to that standard, a kinship-model adherent is more likely to note that all human beings begin life in a compromised position, a state of dependency in which key decisions about who we are and how we live our lives are being made for us, affecting how we conceive of ourselves and the world around us. Even if we pick up many skills and abilities as we age that enable us to function more independently, we never fully outgrow that originally compromised state. So, the issue of how much agency a person has is always, at some level, a messy one."[66] My reading of biographies for children also recognizes that individuals—whether biographees, creators, or child readers—exercise varying degrees of agency, in different ways, at different times. While these biographical texts can manifest discourses of childhood and agency in simplistic ways, responses of "children" as "agents" are anything but simplistic.

Agency is both performed and represented in biographical texts written for young people. The creators of these texts adapt and deploy the life stories of Phillis Wheatley, Sojourner Truth, and Shirley Chisholm in order to provide an index to readers' personal vision and, in so doing, offer "something which empowers." What this "something" is and how it "empowers" are also explored. Twentieth- and twenty-first-century biographies of Wheatley, Truth, and Chisholm exemplify the challenges of providing stories that empower while also instructing young people how to understand the past historically. More obviously—and often less reflectively—than adult biographies, these texts for young people situate their subjects' actions within an interpretive framework intended to give meaning—whether singular, multiple, or even contradictory—to those actions. The framework is typically governed by the values of the present and frequently employed not only to teach readers about historical understanding but also to equip them with resources for action in the present and future.

My analysis is aided by the concept of the "exemplar," which bridges the concepts of public memory and agency. Approaching biographical subjects as exemplars highlights not only an epistemic but also an ethical relationship between the reader and the past. The concept draws attention to the ways that life stories from the past can function as "moral sources." Although the idea has fallen out of favor, the exemplar has a rich history stretching back to ancient Greece. The concept of the exemplar originated as a pedagogical tool to train students of rhetoric for judgment and action. In ancient Greece, Isocrates taught his students both to imitate exemplary individuals and to use their speeches in order to persuade others. Such practices aligned with Isocrates's belief that the praise and imitation of excellent individuals most effectively promoted the development of good character and prudent action.[67] Aristotle developed the idea of the rhetorical example as an important tool that operated through inductive reasoning processes, which he believed were particularly useful for persuading the uneducated masses.[68] During the Renaissance and early modern periods, the exemplar became a mainstay in epistolary practice, and it remained a critical justification for the writing of literary and historical texts.[69] The convention remained widespread until Romantic ideals of originality and self-expression took hold in Europe, eventually inserting a wedge between two previously inseparable ideas: imitation and invention. The idea of invention fit well in a new paradigm that favored future progress over the lessons of past traditions; the practice of imitation seemed unsuited to the innovative thinking and acting required by modernity.[70] These developments troubled the notion of exemplarity, and it lost favor as a rhetorical and literary device in Western cultures, because of a belief that following models implied slavish copying. Although providing "exemplars" of moral character has fallen out of favor in much of contemporary American culture, the veneration of "heroes" and "role models" persists. This book's analysis of biographies about black American women presents notable exceptions to this trend, particularly in marginalized communities where exemplars still do the important work of countering negative stereotypes and providing models of resistance.

Reading Public Memory through the Agential Spiral

Though not always explicitly, agency has figured significantly in the study of public memory, as scholars have explored the ways that human agents—whether individual or collective—strategically and publicly negotiate the *construction* of the past. However, most scholars have not yet closely examined how the *interpretation* of agency and the *representation* of the human agent might also fundamentally shape texts and practices of public memory. I argue further that the appropriation of meaning from historical narratives like those found in children's biographies depends upon how a text represents agency and situates the agent within historical frameworks. One must therefore consider how historical narratives are rhetorically constructed *by* particular agents, whether individual or collective, *in* particular contexts, *for* particular audiences. Historical narratives should be read as strategic responses to contingent circumstances, addressed to some people and not others; this is how I approach biographies for children.

This book focuses on how memories are deployed rhetorically to connect agents across time and thereby perpetuate meaningful public action, building on previous work by employing the "agential spiral" as a critical framework for reading biographies.[71] The agential spiral focuses critical attention on the process in which different agents (or groups of agents) rhetorically reconstruct the past so that it can be productively appropriated by other agents. The key agents are, generally, those acting in history, those interpreting and stabilizing historical narratives, and those reading about or otherwise consuming these narratives. I have adapted this idea from the philosopher Paul Ricoeur's concept of "threefold mimesis." His *Time and Narrative* "pivots," as he said, around the idea of threefold mimesis in order to demonstrate how narrative represents human action by emplotting it in a framework of temporality. These narratives, in turn, lead to action in the real world: the reader "takes up through doing something—the act of reading—the unity of the traversal from $mimesis_1$ to $mimesis_3$ by way of $mimesis_2$."[72] But, as Gary Schmidt reminded us, "children's literature is not simple mimesis" but a complex process of interpretation and appropriation.[73] The image of an agential *spiral* accounts for this complexity by highlighting the simultaneously constraining and empowering potential in biographical narrative.

Ricoeur argued that human actions from the past are rendered intelligible through "emplotment" in a narrative, a term he adapts from Aristotle's *Poetics*.[74] The emplotment of these actions reflects the period in which the narrative is composed and the audience toward which it is oriented, including the audience's cultural values and understanding of the human person.[75] In this sense, historical narrative serves conservative purposes by reinforcing existing beliefs. However, as a representation of human action in time, narrative can also produce potentially progressive outcomes through mimesis. Mimesis, as Ricoeur described it, is both the representation and the imitation of human action.[76] Ricoeur was careful to point out that the mimesis that he had in mind was not mindless copying. "There is no doubt that the prevalent sense of mimesis is the one instituted by its being joined to *muthos,*" Ricoeur observed. "If we continue to translate mimesis by 'imitation,' we have to understand something completely contrary to a copy of some preexisting reality and speak instead of a creative imitation."[77] The imitation takes place at two key points in a circular process: at the initial moment when a writer or historian reconstructs the actions into a narrative and at the moment when the reader of this narrative is urged to "take up" the action by imitating it in the real world. The representational moments of mimesis, on the other hand, occur at three points in this process. Ricoeur called these $mimesis_1$, $mimesis_2$, and $mimesis_3$. Each of these moments is characterized by a distinct kind of figuration. As Ricoeur explained, his hermeneutic inquiry seeks to understand "the concrete process by which the textual configuration mediates between the prefiguration of the practical field and its refiguration through the reception of the work."[78] Prefiguration aligns with $mimesis_1$, configuration with $mimesis_2$, and refiguration with $mimesis_3$.

In order to understand how historical texts for children both inform and entertain, I look at how these texts bear the marks of agency in the moments of prefiguration, configuration, and refiguration. These moments can be described with specific reference to the relevant agent. First, the agent of history is the historical personage or group that acts in history and whose acts are represented and/or judged. Second, the agent of historical production is the historian, memoirist, museum curator, or community group that promotes a certain version of the past and fixes it so that it may be communicated to posterity. Third, the reader of history could be any individual to whom a historical narrative is addressed—the elementary school student, citizen, historian, and so on. I must stress two things about this classification. First, the functions of agency often shade between categories. Second, one should think of historical understanding not as proceeding in a linear sequence but as going round and round in, basically, a "hermeneutic spiral."[79]

These three moments of mimesis can be described even more clearly by making them points on a spiral, rather than following Ricoeur's model of the circle. At the first point, $mimesis_1$, lie *doxa,* or community conventions, popular opinions, historical chronicles—basically, the raw material of which narratives are made. This would be the locus of "common values." It is also the residue of human action and experience that have not yet been given meaning by being placed within a narrative. An author or speaker begins to craft this raw material into a narrative at the stage of $mimesis_2$. As the author emplots events in a narrative, she builds the structure of the text that will later imbue meaning for a reader. In $mimesis_2$, author and text make their contribution to the "world of the work," which is the ultimate referent and source of meaning of any imaginative text. In $mimesis_3$, the reader becomes the primary agent, as he engages in the process of interpretation that accompanies the act of reading. Ricoeur's argument also suggests that, ideally, the act of reading results in a "change [of] acting."[80] By linking reading and acting, $mimesis_3$ "marks the intersection of the world of the text and the world of the hearer or reader; the intersection, therefore, of the world configured by the poem and the world wherein real action occurs and unfolds its specific temporality."[81] Action in time in turn produces more raw material for the construction of narratives, which brings the process full circle to mimesis$_1$.

Ricoeur later applied this framework to historical narrative, wherein it is also characterized by a dialectical movement between explanation and understanding. Such a spiral would look something like this: historical events occur and are recorded, historians and curators translate these events into explanatory narratives of human action, readers engage these narratives in order to understand the meaning of the past for the present, and then readers become actors and contribute again to the cycle of interpreting human action.[82] This spiral represents the ongoing process of creating public memory, in which each generation reshapes the past for its own present. Juvenile biographical narratives play a noteworthy role in this process by representing agency and inviting young readers to exercise it. Too often, said Marc Aronson, juvenile biography is "celebrated for how it can be *used,* not for what it *does,*" and the primary standard to assess texts becomes whether it is good for preparing book reports.[83] Examining biographies through the framework of the agential spiral pinpoints the moments in this rhetorical process where agency is enacted and represented, showing the work that biographies do.

While this book uses the agential spiral to read juvenile biographies, the concept can also be employed in rhetorical analyses of other practices of public memory. As outlined in previous work, I believe that the agential spiral is a valuable tool for addressing two questions raised by rhetorical studies of public memory. First, how is it that memories enable both imitation of the past and, as Hannah Arendt put it, "beginning something anew"?[84] Many rhetorical scholars studying public memory have rightly observed that memories can serve both conservative and progressive goals. The agential spiral shows how these complex dynamics occur within texts and practices. Second, how can scholars account for the equally crucial roles of individual action and collective engagement in shaping public memories? The agential spiral tracks the rhetorical influence of both individuals and groups by pinpointing moments of agency that nonetheless depend on and create relationships with other agents. As I have argued elsewhere, "To view representations of the past through the nested lenses of rhetoric, public memory, and the agential spiral is to focus on how human beings—individually and in groups—forge connections with people of other times through the medium of public agency."[85]

This book employs the agential spiral in order to illuminate how juvenile biographies represent the agency of their subjects, reflect the agency of their creators, encourage agency in their readers, and function as vehicles of public memory in the United States. Early in the book, I outline my approach to public memory as a rhetorical hermeneutic. The emergence of "memory" can be characterized as an alternative to "history," both in public and academic discourses. Specifically, significant academic and public discourses have shifted toward a more participatory, accessible kind of historical construction, signaled by the term "memory." The survey of the history of African American children's literature offered in this study attends closely to the rhetorical features of that literature such as its implied audience and political tone. As a preface to later discussion of stand-alone juvenile biographies, I also analyze biographical sketches published by, about, and for African Americans in the 1920s—an originary moment for this body of texts. Sketches about Wheatley and Truth by Jessie Fauset in *The Brownies' Book* (1920-21), Elizabeth Ross Haynes in *Unsung Heroes* (1921), and Hallie Quinn Brown in *Homespun Heroines and Other Women of Distinction* (1926) show how biography was used to correct racist history and instill public virtues in present and future "race leaders." Later discussions of stand-alone biographies investigate the ways that different agents affect the construction of public memory by applying the concept of the agential spiral to analyze biographical texts about Wheatley, Truth, and Chisholm. Creators are the "pivot" between the cultural assumptions that prefigure the stories of these women's lives and the anticipated uptake of future readers. Texts are constructed in order to invite young readers to engage and respond to agents of the past in particular ways. I examine how these biographies imply, identify, and address their young audiences in order to prepare readers to "take up" the story and thereby "refigure" it in the real world, as Ricoeur put it.

Examples from contemporary American media clearly demonstrate that interest in how the past is represented to children is ongoing and accelerating. However, this interest is also severely constrained by a widespread cultural assumption (among adults) that history can be either complex, ugly, and true *or* morally clear, pleasing, and false. In order to challenge this assumption, I also discuss how texts about Wheatley, Truth, and Chisholm published in the late 1990s and early 2000s have made a tentative turn toward encouraging a more participatory role for young readers in memory culture.

Ultimately, this book explores a broad public question: How should American children be taught to remember the past? By addressing that question, this book draws the attention of rhetorical studies to an infrequently considered audience: children and young people. Traditionally, rhetorical criticism and theory have focused on audiences constituted of adult listeners, who are typically treated by rhetors (and some critics) as fully socialized selves with determined values. Yet, as Courtney Weikle-Mills argued, young people in the United States have also long been addressed as entities capable of some form of public participation.[86] Children in the United States invariably encounter discourses about participation, publicness, and the past, whether in the classroom or in the home. These discourses not only encourage the acceptance of certain values agreed upon by the community but also communicate ideas about the past and prepare student listeners for future judgment and action.[87] Texts that circulate such discourses invite young people to become active agents in the transmission of cultural values and ideas. The psychologist Jerome Bruner argued that students learn best when they adopt an "*active* role as participants rather than as performing spectators."[88] And, as many children's literature scholars have pointed out, children enact this active role with or without the authorization of adults, as they "expertly field the co-scripts of narratives and material culture" and tweak these into new scripts.[89] I argue that by reading the texts examined here, children are invited to adopt certain values and to embody the kind of agency that may in the future become a model for others.

By providing children and young people with some of their earliest glimpses into lives lived in the past, biographical texts lay the foundation for the public memory in which these young people will someday participate, whether as children or as adults. Moreover, by representing the exercise of agency in narratives about Phillis Wheatley, Sojourner Truth, and Shirley Chisholm, these texts encourage young people to reflect on their role as public agents who make history and shape its interpretation. In order to assess these texts, I employ a critical framework that draws attention to the exercise of agency throughout the process of their construction. This framework focuses on how narratives are prefigured by the values of the context in which they were produced, configured into specific works by their creators, and prepared for refiguration by their readers. Through the agential spiral, we can better understand how these oft-overlooked biographies contribute powerfully to the creation of public memory in American public culture.

Chapter Two

Public Memory *as a* Rhetorical Hermeneutic

While sometimes appearing in an apparently simplistic package, children's biographies perform complex rhetorical functions. They inform and inspire; they ignore and empower; they commemorate and question. In performing these functions, they participate in processes of public memory. Memory, as Kirt H. Wilson explained, "is not comprised simply of facts about the past, nor is it solely myth. It is, instead, a rhetorically negotiated commingling of history and commemoration, each form dictating slightly different exigencies."[1] While adults sometimes recognize this complexity, they frequently assume that children cannot. Children, for this reason, are not typically invited to participate in the construction of memory. However, a small but visible number of children's biographies do invite child readers to reflect on the complex and constructed nature of history. Such texts, while rare, render history more accessible to young readers, who are then encouraged to see themselves as interpreters of the past, as participants in an ongoing democracy of memory.

Frances E. Ruffin's 2002 biography *Sojourner Truth,* part of the American Legends series, provides a striking example of such texts. The publisher's website promises that the books in the series will teach students about historical figures such as Johnny Appleseed, Sally Hemings, and Annie Oakley, explaining "why such exciting life stories continue to be retold and cherished today." Furthermore, young readers will not only learn about these "classic legends"; they will have the opportunity to "discover how a legend comes into being, and why not all the stories about these heroes are true."[2] The publisher of these texts clearly intends elementary-age readers to consider the construction of historical narrative, how that narrative reflects cultural values, and how fact and fiction intermingle. After briefly introducing Truth's life, the first chapter of Ruffin's text concludes with this pithy summary of Truth's status as "legend": "During her travels, Sojourner Truth became a famous spokesperson for women's rights and civil rights. A former slave, she became a legend while fighting for the freedom of others."[3] In the text of the second chapter, "What Is a Legend?," the narrator introduces readers to Truth as a legend by laying out the creators' definition of this concept. The narrator explains, "A legend can be a story from the past. Legends are handed down through the years. A legend also can be a person who becomes the center of stories. These legends are often heroes. Sojourner Truth is an example of a hero. She was known for her bravery and her wisdom."[4] A glossary entry in the back of the text further defines a legend as "a story passed down through the years that many people believe, but that might not be true."[5] This definition breaks noticeably from the idea of historical objectivity as the purported framework for biographical writing, exchanging it for an emphasis on storytelling and continuity, in which stories are "handed down through the years." The text also suggests that a person is not inherently worthy of remembrance but "becomes" the subject of legends.

Although the written text does not make clear how this process transpires or who drives it, the accompanying photograph invites readers to place themselves in this role. The color photograph on the opposite page depicts a contemporary African American girl who is seated, looking down at a desk, and appearing to read a book. Nothing in the photograph indicates clearly to readers what the girl is studying. But the accompanying caption strongly guides readers' interpretation: "It is fun to read legends, or stories that come down to us from the past. Some legends are about famous people, such as Sojourner Truth. The stories about Sojourner center on the qualities that she had as a great speaker and leader against slavery." This caption suggests that legends are "fun," that they establish continuity with the past, and that they deliberately select and highlight particular qualities about their subjects.

Although the text and caption outline the characteristics of legends, the book does not explicitly distinguish between "history" and "legend." In so doing, the narrative suggests a blurring between the traditional lines of historical accuracy and imaginative revision.[6] This implication is borne out in the remainder of the text, which proceeds like other photobiographies, reporting dates, incorporating factual information, and describing unfamiliar historical contexts and concepts. This combination of innovative framing with the conventions of nonfiction biographies suggests an attempt not just to make history more entertaining for young readers but also deliberately to draw their attention to the idea of history as *created.* Most important, Ruffin's book emphasizes publicly accessible stories, continuity between past and present, and historical construction in a way that enables young readers to begin to see themselves as interpreters of the past, as participants in a democracy of memory.

During the twentieth century, both academic and public discourse increasingly, though implicitly, emphasized the fundamentally rhetorical nature of historical work and understanding. While in rhetorical studies this way of envisioning our relationship with the past has been labeled "public memory," in other quarters it has gone by the names of public history, popular history-making, collective memory, social memory, cultural memory, and invented traditions. In the most basic sense, these terms acknowledge that humans construct their histories *together*. But envisioning the past as rhetorical also emphasizes the significance of emotional engagement with the past, the malleability of our shared stories about the past, the importance of accessibility, and the need for stories about the past that connect the individual and the collective. What invisibly unites all of these emphases is the human agent who feels that engagement, advocates for those changes, accesses the story, and uses history to situate himself within a cultural narrative.

The Democracy of History: Accessibility and Participation

In his 1931 presidential address to the American Historical Association, Carl Becker argued that the ordinary history-making of "Mr. Everyman" and the so-called science of the professional historian were not so different after all. Becker began by providing a pedestrian definition of history as "the memory of things said and done."[7] He used this definition to show, among other things, that history is never "complete or completely true," that history is not science but interpretation, that history should be useful to everyday folks, and—most significant for his audience of academic historians—that professional historians must change their practices to reflect these realities.[8] His address placed Mr. Everyman at the center of the historical enterprise and reminded the historian that she was always constrained by her present.

While Becker's argument proved both influential and controversial in reassessing the role of the historian, it did not directly engage the question of how "useful" history can avoid misuse and abuse. A few years later, in his scathing critique of Reconstruction histories, W. E. B. Du Bois argued a point similar to Becker's, though with much more attention to the ethical concerns of history-making driven by Mr. Every(white)man. Du Bois declared, "We have spoiled and misconceived the position of the historian." This spoilage and misconception, Du Bois believed, stemmed from a mixture not of fact and fiction or academic and popular but of "fact and desire." He explained, "What we have got to know, so far as possible, are the things that actually happened in the world. *Then with that much clear and open to every reader*, the philosopher and prophet has a chance to interpret these facts; but the historian has no right, posing as scientist, to conceal or distort facts."[9] Although "facts" played dramatically different roles for these two scholars, both criticized the idea that the historian was a "scientist," and both saw accessible history as part of the solution. Mary McLeod Bethune reiterated the theme of accessibility in her 1938 presidential address to the Association for the Study of Negro Life and History, in which she exhorted her members to produce accessible and useful history about African Americans. Bethune argued that philosophical concepts, political ideology, and historical information must go through a process of "translation" in order to become accessible at "the level of the child and the masses."[10] Like Du Bois and other leading black intellectuals, Bethune viewed such work as a necessary corrective to whitewashed American histories.

Intellectual leaders in the United States articulated the need for a more accessible and participatory history in the 1930s, but theorization addressing this need did not emerge until later. One eventual response appeared when Maurice Halbwachs's works on the phenomenon of "collective memory" became available in English in the 1950s.[11] While sociologists followed Halbwachs, literary scholars found inspiration in the ideas of Hayden White, who foregrounded the poetic and persuasive aspects of historical production in his 1973 book *Metahistory.*[12] For scholars in historical studies, the emergence of memory accompanied the shift from social history to cultural history.[13] As a result of this shift, scholars exchanged empirical data for qualitative resources, focused on practices rather than ideas or material conditions, and turned from the sweeping scope of the *mentalités* of the *Annales* School to the microhistories of Natalie Zemon Davis and Carlo Ginzburg.

Questions about the role of language in the representation of history drove late twentieth-century critiques of historiography and the emergence of memory as a key word. The linguistic turn has been viewed as the cause of several subsidiary changes in the discipline of history, including the move toward cultural history, the recognition of discursive objects as vital historical evidence, and an intensified concern about the concept of the agent.[14] Specifically, who or what are or ought to be the agents in history? Scholars who have put forth this critique typically challenge traditional notions of historical significance and causality. They have argued that certain subjects—people of color, women, and the poor, for instance—have been obscured from historical inquiry because they do not meet certain arbitrary standards of historical significance or because they are not believed to have caused any of the broad-scale changes that historians purport to explain. Many social and feminist historians, as well as scholars of African American history, have successfully challenged traditional forms of historical research. Joan Wallach Scott described how feminist historians have addressed this problem: she explained that their common goal has been "to make women a focus of inquiry, a subject of the story, an agent of the narrative."[15] Scholars like Scott argue that a dearth of historical evidence about the lives of certain individuals or groups, such as women, means not that these groups are historically insignificant but that the concept of historical significance is inadequate. This critique, in turn, has placed the concept of agency at the center of a debate over how history should be practiced.

The linguistic turn also brought the question of narrative back to the center of the debate among academic historians. Some historians criticized narrative as a narrow conceptualization of history that constrains historical understanding by favoring the perspective of Western elites. Others, such as Davis and Ginzburg, elevated narrative as the most accessible and persuasive form of historical representation.[16] Since the early 1980s, then, the relationship between language and history—how it is created and represented—has been a significant issue in historical studies and in the newer field of memory studies.

During this time, "memory" emerged as a powerful companion and alternative to the term "history." The historian Kerwin Lee Klein argued in 2000 that "memory," which quickly became a "key word" in historical studies during the 1980s, had replaced "old favorites" like "nature," "culture," and "language" as the term most often paired with "history."[17] This new pairing often entailed nothing less than the revision of "history" as the central term of the historical enterprise: "*History,* as with other key words, finds its meaning in large part through its counter-concepts and synonyms, and so the emergence of memory promises to rework *history's* boundaries."[18] Writing in 2007, Geoffrey Cubitt asserted that "memory has become, to all appearances, one of the central preoccupations of historical scholarship."[19] Cubitt's concerns about the concept of memory echo those of earlier scholars,[20] but he also has articulated the positive effects of memory's challenge to history. His observations led him to conclude that "in turning to memory, historians have been turning not just towards an interest in new kinds of subject matter, but towards new ways of organizing and labeling and describing their objects of study, and new ways of conceptualizing the nature of their own discipline and the knowledge it purports to produce."[21] Bearing out Klein's predictions, the turn toward memory in historical studies has both reflected and effected cultural changes in Western understanding of the meaning of the past. These changes are not limited to the specialized field of professional history but interanimate the realm of public values.[22]

The term "memory" also became a key word in public history, a field that coalesced in the 1970s as a means of reinvigorating connections between historians and the public. Public historians were particularly congenial to this new term, as it affirmed their commitment to "the many and diverse ways that history is put to work in the world."[23] Writing in 1996 about the relationship between memory and public history, David Glassberg pointed out that while memory was an enduring theme, new scholarship differed from the old in its efforts "to understand the interrelationships between different versions of history in public."[24] Like Becker before him, Glassberg emphasized the central role of ordinary individuals and groups in constructing these different narratives: "the meaning of a historical book, film, or display is not intrinsic, determined solely by the intention of the author, but changes as audiences actively reinterpret what they see and hear by placing it in alternative contexts derived from their diverse social backgrounds. To paraphrase Carl Becker, every person is his or her own historian, creating idiosyncratic versions of the past that make sense given personal situations and experiences."[25]

Glassberg concluded that, in light of this reality, the task of the public historian was to "create spaces for dialogue about history and for the collection of memories, and to insure that various voices are heard" rather than to supply a definitive narrative on the past.[26]

Public discussion and research on the significance of public participation and agency in history-making expanded during the 1990s. Articles in U.S. newspapers and periodicals increasingly used the term "memory" (or its cognates) to describe how groups, communities, and societies of the present relate meaningfully to the past.[27] The national survey of American "popular history-making" conducted by Rosenzweig and Thelen in the 1990s confirmed the surveyors' initial belief that "Americans take an active role in using and understanding the past—that they're not just passive consumers of histories constructed by others."[28] The release of the National Standards for History in 1994 provoked widespread debate among historians, educators, politicians, and the general public.[29] And James Loewen's critique of the teaching of American history in schools, *Lies My Teacher Told Me: Everything Your American History Textbook Got Wrong,* became a national bestseller.[30] Such evidence demonstrates that many members of the public questioned the versions and visions of history that they had learned as schoolchildren. Many respondents in Rosenzweig and Thelen's survey wanted history-making to become "a more democratic activity."[31] Moreover, members of the American public value story and its ability to connect them to the people and events of the past.[32] People want to tell their own story in a way that is meaningful to them but also demonstrates participation in a shared narrative about their family, ethnic group, religion, or nation.

Passionate public engagement with the past can be observed in heated debates about the representation of events such as the Vietnam War or the September 11, 2001, attacks and symbols such as the Confederate flag. Members of the public have also demonstrated their investment in debates about the lives of individual historical figures. Work on American memories of Abraham Lincoln, for example, suggests that, like any other public controversy about the interpretation of history, debates about the interpretation of an individual person's life can signify how people see themselves as part of a community, what they value, what they deem important.[33] As members of the contemporary American public present their own interpretations of an individual life, they read their own identities and values into those of persons past and thus recreate them in their own image. They also initiate or enter a process of controversy and revision that affects how these individuals are remembered by members of the American public. As the rhetorical scholar Ekaterina Haskins claimed, "Today the belief that ordinary people should be able to 'put their stamp on history' reflects the desire and ability of nonelite actors to co-produce narratives of public memory, not merely to experience them as spectators or interactive extras. What sets contemporary participatory commemorations apart from their historic predecessors is their self-conscious emphasis on inclusiveness, diversity, and access."[34] Whether in debates over events, symbols, or individuals, the agency of the "every person" has become central.

Situating Memory in Rhetorical Studies

The concept of memory has also risen to prominence in rhetorical studies since the early 1990s.[35] Because an interest in specifically public discourse animates the field, rhetorical scholars generally employ the phrase "public memory" to illuminate how members of the public have used language to engage in the construction and contestation of the past. Early case studies of controversies over public monuments or the construction of memory in public speeches illustrate Stephen Browne's claim in a 1995 book review that "public memory signifies and gets signified in multiple ways." Frankly admitting that this multiplicity of significations can be "daunting," Browne suggested that the challenge for the field of memory studies lay "not so much in showing how many different expressions public memory can take on, but in identifying a basis upon which we can speak of a discourse of public memory."[36] The accuracy of Browne's comment has been borne out in the years since his review was written. Since the initial critical interventions of scholars such as Browne and Zelizer, many works in rhetorical and communication studies have examined fascinating objects and texts that they categorize as public memory—everything from cemeteries to documentary films to Cold War oratory.[37]

Rhetorical scholars have been careful to point out that their recent turn toward memory studies is actually a *re*-turn to the ancient rhetorical practice of memory. Since the time of the ancient Greeks, memory has been a central technique in the art of public speech, whether in the service of entertainment, education, or political persuasion. In *The Art of Memory,* Frances Yates explained that many classical thinkers celebrated the legendary bard Simonides of Ceos as the founding father of the *ars memoriae,* the set of techniques whereby poets and orators committed ideas, phrases, and other parts of speech to memory by placing them within an imagined architectural structure in the mind.[38] A speaker trained in the art of memory could develop a highly organized and portable storehouse of experience, arguments, and evidence.

Yates documented how, like the art of rhetoric, the art of memory was at turns obscured and highlighted, denigrated and celebrated throughout its history, depending on the cultural beliefs, practices, and discursive structures of the period. As Ricoeur noted in his study of the phenomenology of memory, Plato and Aristotle, early theorists of memory, built upon an existing tradition that treated memory as central to public communication, especially poetry and oratory.[39] Aristotle and his contemporary Isocrates promoted memory as an educational practice, one that would make their students better speakers and citizens. Plato's Socrates, on the other hand, was famously wary of technologies of memory, especially writing. In the first century B.C.E., Cicero recounted the famous story of Simonides in *De Oratore* in order to commend the practice of memory. He also consolidated his predecessors' ideas of the practice in what became known as the five traditional canons of rhetoric: invention, arrangement, style, delivery, and memory. The third-century theologian and rhetor Augustine continued Cicero's work while specifically advancing the arts of memory in service of the life of inwardness. As pursuit of the *vita contemplativa* flowered during the medieval period, the Scholastics gave memory a principal place in their theology of virtues. The Renaissance and the early modern period later witnessed the dispersal of memory into many different realms, from the occult uses of the *ars notoria,* the artistic ends of drama, to the emerging art of letter writing. In a sense, as the fate of rhetoric has gone, so also the fate of the arts of memory.

The rhetorical tradition elaborating memory as a technique of public speech and action illuminates key features of a contemporary conception of memory. First, framing memory as a technique emphasizes its nature as a process rather than as only a product.[40] Considering public memory as a technique for evoking, interpreting, or debating representations of the past helps to distinguish it more clearly from the objects or body of knowledge typically referred to as history. Often critics select certain objects because they seem to be or have been treated by others as products of public memory. However, because products such as texts, sites, or artifacts do not usually possess inherent, substantive qualities that easily mark them as either "history" or "memory," analyses may produce little more than observations on an interesting object and some considerable confusion. Thinking of public memory both as a technique and as the thing accessed or created by that technical process can provide a fuller understanding of objects of study such as biographies, which can be treated either as history or as memory. In addition, considering memory in this way recognizes that memory—like children's biographies—engages participants through many modes, whether verbal or visual, especially in the contemporary mediated society.[41]

Thinking of memory as a rhetorical *techne* also emphasizes the capacities of memory rather than its deficiencies. The ancient rhetorical trope of the storehouse recasts memory as an inventional resource for, rather than as a hindrance to, thought, speech, and action. This idea guards against a scholarly temptation to focus primarily on public memory's potentially deleterious effects—hiding certain pasts, covering traumas, or promoting oppressive institutional agendas. Thinking of public memory as a storehouse evokes a more nuanced process whereby individuals or groups access and activate their knowledge about the past in order to accomplish something in the present. When studies of public memory incorporate the idea of the storehouse, there is greater potential to see memory as a process that can be enlisted by a variety of different people for different purposes. This perspective usefully broadens the field of inquiry about memory by reaching back to its ancient roots in the rhetorical tradition.

Notable recent research has worked to resist temptations to think of memory simplistically and instead consider it as a complex form with both positive and negative effects. Such work has demonstrated the power of public memory both to reinscribe traditional values and to challenge those values. For instance, scholars studying the ways that LGBTQ individuals and communities commemorate their past have shown how "counterpublic," "insurgent," and/or "vernacular" memories can serve to challenge hegemonic narratives. While it is expanding, this research remains in the minority. As Thomas R. Dunn stated in 2010:

> Frequently, the conservative contributions of memory in rendering the past as a constant, historical record are often the starting point for rhetorical analysis, while alternative means of understanding a memory text or site are overlooked. Although more critical and cultural studies have pushed the field away from this hegemonic bias in rhetorical criticism more widely, we need to do more to accelerate this shift within public memory work. The examination of multiple, alternative, vernacular, counterpublic memories outside of the conservative view can shift the locus of memory's rhetorical study from reactions to oppressive metanarratives to the creations of contrary tellings of the past. With memories as strategies, counterpublics find new ways of challenging conservative worldviews not through tactical critique, but through strategic production.[42]

Examining biographies follows this line of scholarship, showing how memories of individuals negotiate the past and the needs of the present through appeals to established values as well as the creation of new values.

Although approaches differ, scholarship on public memory in rhetorical studies has carved out a niche in the field of memory studies by focusing specifically on the public and persuasive aspects of memory.[43] Rhetorical studies of public memory share several common assumptions and challenges. The first and most critical assumption of rhetorical scholars about public memory pertains to their reasons for studying it as a specifically rhetorical phenomenon. As Blair, Dickinson, and Ott, Phillips, and Zelizer have pointed out, scholars agree that public memory is not ontologically fixed but is subject to revision, reinterpretation, and contestation.[44] This perception leads critics to view public memory as essentially rhetorical: that is, as symbolically and strategically constructed, continually contested, and always potentially revisable by various leaders, members of the public, or other rhetorical agents. Although not always explicit, a belief in the inherent rhetoricity of public memory grounds and justifies work in the field. For most rhetorical scholars, the rhetoricity of memory becomes meaningful primarily in the public sphere—hence the choice of the term "public memory."

Second, rhetorical scholars of public memory tend to view their objects of analysis as products of certain systems of power. Inspired by social philosophers such as Karl Marx and Michel Foucault and adapted for rhetorical analysis by scholars such as Philip Wander and Raymie McKerrow, this type of inquiry provides a powerful tool for the analysis of public memory. The work of Wander and McKerrow, referred to as "critical rhetoric," emerged in the 1980s in the wake of Edwin Black's influential essay "The Second Persona." In its most basic sense, the "ideological turn" of which their work was a part signaled an increased attention to the ways in which rhetoric and power intersect.[45] Rhetorical critics whose investigations of public speech attend to power dynamics are particularly well equipped to examine the construction and deployment of interpretations of the past.[46] Moreover, this assumption interfaces productively with other concepts that highlight the role of power in constructing history, such as Friedrich Nietzsche's "monumental history," Foucault's "counter-memory," and John Bodnar's "official history."[47]

Finally, many rhetorical scholars assume a certain relationship between memory and history, namely that the incorporation of more memory makes for better history. As Zelizer has reminded us, most scholars acknowledge that all memory—public or otherwise—is partial and involves forgetting, but few view forgetting as positive.[48] Rather, any attempts to silence, repress, marginalize, or forget are assumed to be inherently negative. Consequently, as Bradford Vivian rightly pointed out, rhetorical scholars are often deeply ambivalent about forgetting, one of memory's constitutive Others.[49] Such research seems motivated by a sense that concealing, obscuring, forgetting, ignoring, or otherwise absenting certain memories is always injurious.[50] The tendency to focus on the supposed dangers of forgetting stems in part from an imperative to correct histories that most people rightly deem false or incomplete, as in the approach to public memory as a source of subjugated knowledge. The continued effort to enlarge and diversify American understanding of the legacy of chattel slavery by incorporating oral histories and unearthing new source material is a valuable example of this approach. Here, the critic recovers new sites of memory that correct dominant versions of the past. Indeed, early African American children's biographies were published with precisely such a corrective purpose. Or, in a less productive move, the critic simply points out what has been omitted in or hidden by the dominant narrative and declares this to be an ideological strategy of the state apparatus or a nationalistic ethnic group. In an influential variation on this theme, critics read public memory as the process of dealing with—more often, "covering over"—what they understand as collective trauma. With regard to the role of trauma in memory studies, we should heed the warning of Ricoeur, who recommended an approach to memory not based on its "deficiencies" and "dysfunctions" but from the angle of its "capacities."[51] Most important, perhaps, is that neither the recovery approach nor the trauma emphasis, both of which originate with the anxiety induced by the specter of forgetting, takes full advantage of what a rhetorical perspective has to offer the field of memory studies: an analysis of the public, persuasive, and constitutive processes of memory. Scholars of rhetoric, as Blair, Dickinson, and Ott persuasively argued, should show instead how rhetoric forms the glue that makes certain memories "stick."[52]

An Outline for a Rhetorical Hermeneutic

Rather than considering memory as the opposite of history or forgetting, my approach in this book frames public memory primarily as a hermeneutic concept—as a critical tool that highlights the rhetorical aspects of historical representation in a variety of texts, including texts such as biographies for children. For instance, instead of arguing that public memory *is* rhetorical, one might say that public memory enunciates the rhetorical facets of history. The term thus becomes a conceptual lens that emphasizes certain features of public and rhetorical phenomena such as the representation of temporality, the construction of relations between agents across time (especially between historical characters and contemporary readers), the mutability of historical representation, public engagement with these representations, and the affective investment in the past that certain texts encourage. Recasting public memory as a hermeneutic concept enables critics to focus more closely on aspects of discourse about history that might otherwise be obscured or neglected.

As a hermeneutic term, "memory" draws attention to aspects of the representation of the past that differ from those highlighted by the term "history." I outlined these themes briefly in chapter 1, and I develop them further here in order to sketch critical applications for the concept of public memory. First, use of the term "memory" evokes an active, emotional engagement with the past. Memory reintroduces a greater sense that the sacred, ineffable, and immaterial affect how individuals see their relationship with the past. Individuals who speak about the past in this way frequently invoke a sense of emotional investment and liveliness that is, by implication, absent from history. For example, as Pierre Nora suggested, using the term "memory" supposedly captures something "living" that can be injected into the seemingly "dead" narratives of history.[53] Following in this vein, the metaphorical binary of "life/death" has often been used to distinguish appropriate, meaningful versions of the past from useless, arcane, or otherwise meaningless versions. Second, the concept of memory highlights the inherently malleable nature of certain practices involved in historical representation. While history is more often used to describe representations as fixed and determined solely by textuality, memory is viewed as more fluid, adaptable, and responsive to changing practices, including those based in text. Scholars thus often employ "memory" to blur the lines between practice and text. For example, Roman Catholic parishioners who partake in the practices of the Eucharist and rabbis who learn and interpret Talmudic texts could similarly see themselves as engaged in the work of memory. This perception of memory as a bridge between practice and text also helps to explain why it emerged as a critical term during the historical turns toward practice and language. Third, memory is often viewed as a popular, public, and personal form of knowledge about the past, whereas history usually denotes a more rarefied and specialized form. Memory is both shared by and theoretically accessible to all: it is inclusive and democratic, available to all regardless of education, ethnicity, or class. History delineates the fenced-in domain of the expert; memory marks the expansive territory of the layperson. Moreover, because memory *can* in some sense belong to everyone and anyone, it is often understood as a repository of power, namely the kind of power necessary to challenge and subvert hegemonic narratives about the past. Thus, a focus on memory can draw our attention to the dynamics of power at play in representations of the past. Fourth and finally, use of the term "memory" acknowledges that representations of the past become meaningful both on an individual and on a collective level. Indeed, memories gain potency precisely because they serve the needs of both individuals and large groups. The same memory can easily function on very different registers of scale. This shifty feature enables "memory" as a term to invite multiple, contesting interpretations. History, in contrast, is often viewed as singular, monolithic. Memory thus also constitutes an important point of intersection between individual and collective representations of the past. In an early articulation of this intersection, Maurice Halbwachs's influential study *On Collective Memory* joined the subjectivist philosophy of Henri Bergson and the historical work of the *Annales* School to show how social frameworks ground the ability to remember.[54]

In this book, I use the term "public memory" as a hermeneutic for reading biographical texts for young people. Employing this concept highlights how history is constructed by human language, contested in public, addressed to and constitutive of certain audiences, and contingent upon contexts of production. The concept operates as an interpretive guide, focusing critical attention on these specifically rhetorical elements of public memory and combining them with the other four emphases outlined earlier. Moreover, the concept of public memory disperses the practice of human agency throughout the process of historical production, interpretation, and representation. Guided by the concept of public memory, we can understand the rhetorical processes whereby a person "becomes the center of stories," to use Ruffin's words, and ultimately even a "legend."[55]

CHAPTER THREE

"A WORLD *of* INSPIRATION"

Biographical Sketches in Early African American Children's Literature

In August 1920, a new children's periodical produced by the National Association for the Advancement of Colored People published a letter from a young reader, Audrey Wright. A "delighted" Wright reported that the new magazine had "created quite a sensation" in her school. However, Wright continued, reading this new magazine had also led her to a sobering realization. "It is surprising to know," she reported, "how many high school girls know nothing or very little about our own Negro heroines such as Harriet Tubman, Frances Harper and Sojourner Truth." Fortunately, Wright had a suggestion for addressing this problem: "I believe if you could give us a short sketch of their lives every month or suggest certain books that we could read pertaining to them it would be greatly appreciated by those who wish to know more about their own race women."[1] Young women, according to Wright, had a void in their knowledge of "race women" that could be filled with a regular diet of brief biographies. Many years later, Mary McLeod Bethune also publicly acknowledged the need to educate children about African American history. She argued in her 1938 speech that "Negro History" could become truly relevant only by being brought "to the level of the child and the masses" and "placed in the language and story of the child." She exhorted her audience to do this work so as to "continue to give us that courage, race pride and ambition to face social and economic handicaps, to stimulate the Negro children to keep their chins up and their faces to the rising sun."[2] For Bethune, history needed to be presented in an accessible form if it was to function as a tool of racial uplift. Not coincidentally, these two pleas for more accounts of black history roughly bookend the Harlem Renaissance of the 1920s, a time period in which African American communities were engaged in intense discussions about the political and social implications of art and literature.[3]

African Americans have creatively enlisted the genre of biography in a project of public remembrance for children and young people. I find that, whereas contemporary biographies for children of all backgrounds tend to obscure their moral designs, biographical sketches and texts written by, about, and for African Americans during the 1920s convey historical information with the explicit goal of supplying young readers with politically and racially significant African American role models. In these texts, the conservative genre of biography becomes a rhetorical resource for pursuing progressive purposes such as historical recovery and racial uplift. To illustrate this claim, I examine introductory material[4] and select sketches from three texts whose publication in the 1920s marked the emergence of African American children's literature as a cohesive body of texts: the N.A.A.C.P.'s *Brownies' Book* (1920–1921), Elizabeth Ross Haynes's *Unsung Heroes* (1921), and Hallie Quinn Brown's *Homespun Heroines and Other Women of Distinction* (1926).[5] Although the three texts select a variety of men and women as subjects, I follow the path outlined earlier by focusing on Phillis Wheatley and Sojourner Truth. Wheatley and Truth are two of only three women, along with Harriet Tubman, who appear in all three texts. Restricting its focus to Wheatley and Truth enables this analysis to demonstrate the subtle ways in which biographical sketches represented lives differently; this kind of focused analysis of early biographies enables comparison with the later texts discussed in subsequent chapters. Examining only Wheatley and Truth also allows for a comparison of how these two notable rhetorical agents were represented at an important moment for African American culture generally and for black children's literature specifically. Whereas Wheatley exemplified the creative and intellectual potential of African Americans and their contributions to literary history, Truth became a model of common sense, strong conviction, and political influence. This analysis shows how the sketches emphasize each woman's individual agency and good character when describing her achievements and interactions with others, while subtly politicizing her life story by situating her within a history of African American action.

African American Children's Literature in the Twentieth Century

The 1920s constituted a watershed moment for both white and black American children's literature. Following a gradual separation from adult literature in the early decades of the twentieth century, in 1919 the largest publisher in the United States, Macmillan, became the first to create a separate department dedicated to "Books for Boys and Girls." Additional publishers and public libraries followed suit in the new decade. Gary Schmidt explained that "the unity of the publishing establishment with education and library and bookselling establishments suggests a coherency of purpose, and indeed, the members of these establishments worked together with remarkable consistency, particularly in their sense of what was both appropriate and essential for a child audience."[6] Although the "unity" described here applied primarily to the white publishing establishment, the growing concern with addressing the child audience crossed racial boundaries. Both white and black children's literature was distinguished by its "intended audience."[7] Yet the ways in which texts for black children imagined this audience differed notably from the practices for texts aimed at white children. First, works for black children were often written to be "overheard" by adults in the household. "Cross-written" texts, as children's literature scholars have described them, complicated the widespread assumptions that children's texts simply imposed adult ideas on young readers or that a clear boundary existed between child and adult readers.[8] While also read by adults, texts for African American children addressed their young readers as learners and as significant actors in their community. Dianne Johnson persuasively argued that these texts historically functioned as part of a "network of psychological protection, nurturance, and education" cultivated by black communities.[9] These texts emerged in response to unique community needs perceived by their creators, and, for this reason, they were molded powerfully by an accompanying vision of audience. A brief survey of the history of African American children's literature demonstrates how such perceived needs and attendant audiences were initially articulated and how they changed over time.

Most scholars trace the origin of African American children's literature as a cohesive, distinctive body of texts to the appearance of the *Brownies' Book* in 1920.[10] This short-lived periodical for African American children grew out of W. E. B. Du Bois's work with the *Crisis,* the magazine of the N.A.A.C.P. In particular, Du Bois had been heavily involved in publishing the "Children's Number," an annual issue of the *Crisis* that appeared every October from 1912 until 1934.[11] Du Bois announced his plans for a children's periodical in a 1919 issue of the *Crisis,* promising, "It will be a thing of Joy and Beauty, dealing in Happiness, Laughter and Emulation, and designed especially for Kiddies from Six to Sixteen."[12] Each issue of the magazine included a variety of content, such as fairy tales and African myths, question-and-answer columns ("The Judge" and "The Jury"), nature poetry, photos of black children ("Our Little Friends"), pieces written by readers, a news digest ("As the Crow Flies"), and even a "Grown-Ups Corner" to which parents could write letters. Well-known African American literary figures such as the poet Langston Hughes wrote pieces for the magazine. The novelist Jessie Fauset shared editorial responsibilities with Du Bois and also contributed regular columns, such as "The Judge."

While Fauset exerted considerable influence on the *Brownies' Book,* Du Bois's well-publicized views on the political uses of literature exerted more visible effects on African American children's literature and its developing vision of audience. Katharine Capshaw Smith described Du Bois as an "intellectual giant" who "reinvented conceptions of black childhood and instituted the genre of black children's literature."[13] Most important, Du Bois recognized the significance of integrating education and entertainment in the magazine so that it could become a vehicle for political change. This purpose depended on Du Bois's assumption that the black child should be treated as "culturally, politically, and aesthetically sophisticated."[14] The young readers of this magazine were not coddled, protected, or condescended to but rather were encouraged to think of themselves as agents of change and, in many cases, "race leaders."[15] Biographical sketches, both of exemplary contemporary black children and black historical figures such as Crispus Attucks, Frederick Douglass, and Harriet Tubman, provided an essential means of encouraging the type of "emulation" that Du Bois had outlined. Yet, as scholars such as Johnson and Smith have observed, while Du Bois may have articulated the vision, Fauset implemented it. Fauset's biographer, Carolyn Wedin Sylvander, claimed that Fauset was "always greatly interested in biographies, especially of historical Black personages, and especially as corrective models for youth."[16] For this reason, I treat Fauset as the author of the biographical sketches discussed in this chapter.

Notable biographical collections by other African Americans appeared soon after the *Brownies' Book.* In 1921, Du Bois and Augustus Dill published Elizabeth Ross Haynes's *Unsung Heroes,* which included seventeen sketches of African American men and women. Not surprisingly, Haynes's text was advertised in the *Brownies' Book.*[17] Haynes, born in rural Alabama in 1883, was a social worker and reformer who worked to improve the lives of black women. Iris Carlton-LaNey described Haynes as a "'race woman' with a womanist consciousness," an identity that shaped her writing and work.[18] Five years later, Hallie Quinn Brown published *Homespun Heroines and Other Women of Distinction,* a collection of more than fifty sketches about African American women. Like Haynes's, Brown's life work demonstrated her commitment to improving the lives of black women. Brown spent her very active life, which began in Pittsburgh around 1849 and spanned nearly one hundred years, giving public lectures, teaching elocution, and leading black women's clubs and church groups. As Bethune pronounced in a 1949 obituary, Brown was "a leader of great talents and many interests . . . an educator in the broadest sense of the word."[19]

The idea of the black child reader as a political actor persisted throughout the Harlem Renaissance and into the 1930s. After the *Brownies' Book* ceased publication in 1921 due to financial problems, several authors took up its mantle in ways that uniquely reflected the complex aesthetic and political commitments of the Harlem Renaissance. Writers like Arna Bontemps, Sadie Iola Daniels, Langston Hughes, Effie Lee Newsome, and others created fiction, nonfiction, and poetry addressed to black children. In the hands of authors such as these, Smith has explained, children's literature of the Harlem Renaissance "became a crucial component of the training of a generation of 'New Negroes,' as the ideology of uplift merged with the Renaissance's investment in community galvanization, militancy, and racial pride."[20]

Literature by, about, and for African Americans circulated more widely in American culture during the postwar period, addressing itself to both black *and* white audiences and, in many cases, the white publishing industry. Literature of the 1940s and 1950s, in particular, equipped young African Americans with a knowledge of and pride in their history that would enable them confidently to integrate white society. Bethune presaged this shift in her 1938 address: "The ideals, character and attitudes of races are born within the minds of children; most prejudices are born with youth and it is our duty to see that the great researches of Negro History are placed in the language and story of the child. Not only the Negro child but children of all races should read and know of the achievements, accomplishments and deeds of the Negro."[21] This call was answered by figures such as Bontemps, Hughes, and Carter G. Woodson and the authors of his Associated Publishers books. Bontemps won an early victory for black writers and illustrators aiming to reach white audiences when his *Story of the Negro* was named a Newbery Honor Book in 1949. Shirley Graham also published a number of popular fictionalized biographies during the 1940s and early 1950s about figures such as Paul Robeson (1946), Frederick Douglass (1947), and Phillis Wheatley (1949).

The U.S. children's publishing industry became more diverse during the 1960s and 1970s, after institutional and commercial barriers had been challenged by the civil rights movement. The publication of works by, about, and for African Americans increased during and after the 1960s and 1970s, when the emergence of Black Power discourse and the Black Arts Movement intensified the demand for children's books that accurately reflected the "black experience." In fact, as Johnson explained, "It is largely out of this movement, certainly, that 'Black children's literature' gained weight and recognition within the publishing world, to a level which it has not enjoyed since."[22] The Black Arts Movement exerted a particularly strong influence on the aesthetics and politics of black children's literature, resulting in more confrontational texts.[23] Figures like Woodson and Bontemps continued to publish nonfiction during these decades, but the work of fiction writers, such as the novelists Virginia Hamilton and Mildred Taylor, became more prominent as well. *Ebony Jr.!,* another short-lived periodical for African American young people, also appeared in May 1973.[24]

During the 1980s and 1990s, the discourse of liberal multiculturalism in education and children's publishing powerfully shaped African American children's literature. Many African American authors continued to write primarily for black children and adolescents, but increasingly their work was also read by white children and promoted by white librarians and educators. The growing market for new formats such as photobiographies provided additional opportunities for authors of all ethnic backgrounds to publish texts about African Americans and other people of color.[25] (Nonetheless, white creators had and continue to have more access to the publishing industry.)[26]

Expansion of African American children's literature throughout the twentieth century resulted not only from the work of publishers and authors but also from the consistent efforts of African American librarians and teachers, many of whom were dissatisfied with representations of black folks within American texts for children. Many of these individuals were black women. As the traditional custodians of African American memories and as the educators of the young, "African American women's collective position on the margins of the historical profession, outside the university, on the lower rungs of social power, and in the trenches of race reform gave them fresh perspective on history and memory that white women and black men did not possess."[27] Teachers, librarians, and community organizers promoted biographies and other trade books as an alternative to the more closely monitored—and often more racist and sexist—textbooks. Teachers such as Bethune and librarians such as Augusta Baker used biographical texts to bring the lessons of "race history" to African American children.[28] These writers and teachers promoted such texts not only to expand historical knowledge but also as usable forms of the past, intended for appropriation by readers.

"To you, my little friends": Addressing Purpose

While creators of biographies published later in the twentieth century did not consistently describe their intentions, all of the writers examined in this chapter did so in their introductory material. Moreover, they framed their biographical collections in ways that reveal common assumptions about their shared audience, the value of learning about the past, and the importance of reading about model agents. Through these three common themes, the biographical sketches written by Fauset, Haynes, and Brown in the 1920s address the black child reader as a current and future citizen and political actor, attempting to instill the kind of "courage, race pride, and ambition" later explicitly touted by Bethune.

First, each of the three texts clearly identifies a target audience of African American young people. For instance, in the October 1919 issue of the *Crisis,* Du Bois declared his plans for "a little magazine for children—for all children, but especially for *ours,* 'the Children of the Sun,'" aimed, as noted earlier, at "Kiddies from Six to Sixteen."[29] Du Bois thus outlined the intended audience for Fauset's subsequent sketches. Although less direct and precise than Du Bois, Haynes in her foreword to *Unsung Heroes* clearly addressed youths and children. She explained her motivations for writing the book by telling a story of how she had recently encountered in the library the narrative of Frederick Douglass, which was clearly "written for grown-ups" and "contained many pages" but nevertheless possessed a "world of inspiration" for readers. She stated that she wished to pass on such stories "to you, my little friends" who have "all of your years ahead of you." Haynes implied the racial background of her intended audience by quoting lines from Paul Laurence Dunbar's "Ode to Ethiopia," which use the first-person plural:

> Go on and up! Our souls and eyes
> Shall follow thy continuous rise;
> Our ears shall list thy story
> From bards who from thy root shall spring,
> And proudly tune their lyres to sing
> Of Ethiopia's glory.[30]

Likewise, the African American journalist Josephine Turpin Washington wrote a foreword to Brown's text indicating that "the youth of today and of other days" would "come under the influence" of the sketches collected by Brown. The book, in Washington's view, both educates and edifies: it "is a work which not only furnishes useful information, but—what is even more—inspires to finer character growth and racial development."[31] Brown's own introduction outlined her intention "to secure for this book the interest of our youth, that they may have instructive light on the struggles endured and the obstacles overcome by our pioneer women." Describing her subject in the previous line as the "pioneering women of our race," Brown used the first-person plural possessive to invite young readers to identify themselves with the African American women in the sketches, as well as with her as the author.[32]

Second, the creators of these texts have sought to fill a void in their community's historical knowledge by educating young people about notable African Americans. Creators have explained that stories about black individuals should correct inaccurate stereotypes about African Americans or counter negative feelings that black children might have about their race or, relatedly, members of other races. The most remarkable example appears in the *Crisis,* where Du Bois began his pitch for the *Brownies' Book* by telling a story about a little girl—"we remember her as red-bronze and black-curled, with dancing eyes"—who told the editors that she wanted to learn about her race, then followed her statement by declaring, "I hate the white man just as much as he hates me and probably more!" Du Bois lamented (but did not dismiss) this sentiment, primarily because, as he put it, educating children in hatred is "more disastrous to them than to the hated."[33] Therefore, he proposed a magazine that would, among other things, seek to make black children "familiar with the history and achievements of the Negro race."[34] Haynes likewise justified the publication of her text by characterizing it as a "telling of the victories in spite of the hardships and struggles of Negroes whom the world has failed to sing about."[35] Brown situated her text as a response to the lack of accounts of black history, saying that the volume "has been prepared from a settled conviction that something of the kind is needed." Her efforts in preparing the text derived not only from a "settled conviction" but also from an "anxious desire to preserve for future reference an account of these women."[36] These creators did not simply assume that a ready consumer is reason enough to publish a new text; they all firmly grounded their historical work in a perceived community need for the type of text they created.

Third, and most important for this study, these creators intended to provide young people with models of good character and right action. Each creator drew a deliberate connection between the biographical subjects and their readers, thereby communicating a belief that reading about admirable individuals enables young people to act admirably. Du Bois said that the magazine would be "a thing of Joy and Beauty, dealing in Happiness, Laughter, and *Emulation,*" clearly associating what in the twenty-first century might be called character education with pleasurable qualities such as humor rather than with the supposedly dull territory of morals.[37] Moreover, Du Bois laid out seven goals for his new magazine, three of which were specifically oriented toward producing certain kinds of attitudes and actions in young readers. These particular goals included teaching them "delicately a code of honor and action," enabling them to "turn their little hurts and resentments into emulation, ambition, and love of their own homes and companions," and inspiring them "to prepare for definite occupations and duties with a broad spirit of sacrifice."[38] Haynes used the language of inspiration, explaining that she was passing along the stories of notable African Americans because they had "so inspired" her. She concluded her foreword with the hope that her readers would be "so inspired by [these stories] that you will succeed in spite of all odds."[39] Clearly, Haynes shared these stories not merely to inspire but also to equip readers for future success. Finally, Brown very forthrightly told her young readers that the book "has been prepared with the hope that they will read it and derive fresh strength and courage from its records to stimulate and cause them to cleave more tenaciously to the truth and to battle more heroically for the right."[40] Brown envisioned a distinct cause-and-effect relationship between the reading of her text and the pursuit of right action. Whether they used the language of emulation or inspiration, these authors presented their biographical sketches as resources for enacting agency.

Among their many subjects, both male and female, all three texts feature the stories of three important women: Phillis Wheatley, Harriet Tubman, and Sojourner Truth. Because this study focuses on the stories of individuals who exemplified agency primarily through public language use, I here discuss Wheatley and Truth. Wheatley, as the first published African American, became a staple of the biographical genre in black communities and a popular exemplar of the intellectual potential of enslaved African peoples. Wheatley was also the subject of considerable debate among Harlem Renaissance leaders, many of whom dismissed her poetry while recognizing her significance to the black American literary tradition.[41] Truth, in comparison, was noted for her contributions to the woman suffrage and antislavery causes, especially as a powerful speaker. Having remained illiterate her entire life, Truth became a model of how strong principles and common sense could create powerful public speech. Truth's story would have wielded particular power in April of 1920, as Fauset pointed out in her sketch, a few months prior to the August 1920 ratification of the Nineteenth Amendment. The biographical sketches by Fauset, Haynes, and Brown shape these details into pithy narratives emphasizing each woman's individual agency, good character, and role in African American history.

Sketching Wheatley

Phillis Wheatley appears in these sketches primarily as an exemplar of black intellectual achievement. All three narrators negotiate Wheatley's agency in ways that emphasize her literary accomplishments yet acknowledge the ways in which her work was also enabled by white supporters. The sketches firmly ground Wheatley's actions and choices in her admirable character, thereby reinforcing her status as a model to be emulated by the young audience. Whereas Haynes's sketch shows Wheatley's good character by drawing attention to her loyalty and hard work, Fauset's and Brown's sketches explicitly name Wheatley's moral qualities. Finally, all three texts address in some form Wheatley's identity as a black woman poet and her significance, as such, to African American history. Within these broad themes, each text represents Wheatley's story of accomplishment differently.

Of the three sketches, Hallie Quinn Brown's version of Wheatley places the greatest emphasis on her individual agency. Brown's narrative deftly balances Wheatley's muscular intellect with softer "feminine" qualities. Striking this balance enables the sketch consistently to portray Wheatley as the central agent, even when she is merely causing others to act. For instance, readers learn that the little black girl for sale in the Boston market exerted a kind of emotional power over Mrs. Wheatley: "though she considered the sickly look of the child an objection, there was something so gentle and modest in the expression of her dark countenance and her large mournful eyes that her heart was drawn toward her and she bought her in preference to several others who looked more robust."[42] While Brown's sketch describes Mrs. Wheatley as "kind," the woman acts not merely out of her own sympathy or pity but rather in response to the "gentle and modest" quality of the child. In this telling, the child exerts power—albeit in a passive, appropriately "feminine" manner—over Mrs. Wheatley. When the story turns to Phillis's education, the text again makes Phillis the responsible party, rather than suggesting that others instigated the efforts out of kindness (or something else). Readers learn that, despite initial difficulties communicating, "Phillis soon learned to speak English."[43] No one else is active in her schooling until later. Brown's sketch sums up Wheatley's early learning by saying, "In the course of a year and a half a wonderful change took place in the little, forlorn stranger."[44] Although this statement does not attribute the change to Wheatley, it also does not attribute it to anyone else. As the narrative continues, Wheatley becomes the primary actor. She is the one who learned English, was "able to read fluently" from the Bible, located her own writing implements, and, ultimately, possessed the necessary characteristics of a learned individual: "uncommon intelligence and a great desire for knowledge." Only after Phillis's natural capacities and ambition are established does Mary Wheatley, Phillis's self-appointed tutor, make an appearance. Even then, the "astonishing quickness" of the pupil makes young Mary's job easy. Phillis's "uncommon manifestations of intelligence" are even credited as the reason that she was not assigned difficult household chores.[45] Many other, more recent biographies attribute this fact to the Wheatleys' kindness or their supposed opposition to slavery. Mrs. Wheatley exercises the most agency in the family: she "rescued" the child from the slave auction, "did everything to encourage [Phillis's] love of learning," and acted as a "motherly benefactress."[46] Nonetheless, Mrs. Wheatley's actions always work either in cooperation with Phillis's actions or as a natural response to Phillis's excellent qualities.

Notably, the narrative addresses Phillis's enslavement in a straightforward manner, while not diminishing her agency by portraying her only as a victim. Brown's Phillis is subject only to the "mournful reverse of fortune" in which the Revolutionary War overshadowed New Englanders' interest in Phillis's poetry.[47] Although the sketch portrays the Wheatleys sympathetically, it does not present them primarily as reluctant, benevolent slaveowners.[48] The text forthrightly states that Mrs. Wheatley "had several slaves" and that she went to the market with the intention of purchasing a young girl to work in the house.[49] The circumstances of Phillis's enslavement here serve as another demonstration of the power of her appealing nature. The Wheatleys' positive feelings are often construed as the reasonable response to Phillis's appealing temperament. As Brown's sketch explains, Phillis "showed such an amiable, affectionate disposition that all members of the family became much attached to her."[50]

Fauset's sketch contextualizes Phillis's agency more thoroughly in the dynamics of the Wheatley household.[51] Although the narrative clearly represents the horrors of slavery, generally, it also portrays Phillis's life with the Wheatley family rather positively. The narrative explains, "Of course the best thing that could have happened to this little child of misfortune would have been to be left with her mother in Africa. As that could not be, it is pleasant to realize that the next best lot was hers." Like Brown's narrative, Fauset's sketch uses words such as "misfortune" and "lot" to highlight the effects of chance rather than the results of human choice. Perhaps in an effort to "turn [black children's] little hurts and resentments" into positive feelings about their identity and enable them to overcome adversity, this narrative admits the difficulty of Phillis's situation. Yet it also focuses on the decency of the Wheatley family, insofar as they allowed Phillis's gifts to blossom. For instance, the family was "kind," received their new resident "gladly," and did not assign her "arduous" duties.[52] Phillis's talents drive the narrative; the Wheatleys and other white people simply respond in a reasonable and generous fashion. The following scene is representative: "This is what happened. One day Mary Wheatley came across Phillis busily engaged in making letters on the wall with a piece of charcoal. Phillis had already shown herself apt at picking up the spoken language but that she should display an interest in writing was a new idea to the Wheatleys and gave them much pleasure. From that day on Mary constituted herself Phillis' teacher. They progressed from letters to words and from words to complete sentences. And behold the keys to the treasure-houses of the world were in little Phillis' hands for she had learned to delve into books. Short of granting her her freedom, the Wheatleys could not have bestowed on her a greater gift."[53] In this passage, Phillis displays a natural curiosity about and aptitude for language. The narrative notes that Phillis's talents gave the Wheatleys "much pleasure," which objectifies Phillis as a source of enjoyment. However, it also demonstrates that they were not threatened but rather delighted by her abilities—a far cry from many white colonists of the period. Young Mary decides to become Phillis's tutor not out of a selfish intention to bend the enslaved girl to her own will but because she observes that Phillis has the desire to learn. Although "they progressed" together through the studies, it is Phillis—not Mary or the other Wheatleys—who ultimately holds "the keys to the treasure-houses of the world." The Wheatleys gave her a gift, but Phillis is portrayed as having made the most of it.

Indeed, the Phillis Wheatley of this narrative becomes the agency to her talents' agent, to put it terms of Kenneth Burke's dramatistic pentad.[54] Wheatley acts as if carried along by a muse. For instance, the narrative observes that she "seems to have been of an extraordinarily studious disposition," rather than saying that she studied tirelessly. Although she "read all kinds of books" and "mastered Latin," her eventual turn to poetry is driven by her mind rather than her will: "It is not surprising then that a mind so eager to take in should at least become desirous of giving out." And so readers observe Wheatley "passing through" rather than pursuing or engaging in "a period of study and preparation," after which she becomes "Phillis the writer." Likewise, Wheatley is not responsible when times get more difficult after her mistress Susanna's death; Phillis is said to have "fallen on" hard times.[55] This Phillis Wheatley makes the best of the situation, whether she is blessed or cursed.

Like the *Brownies' Book* sketch, Haynes's narrative focuses on Phillis Wheatley's literary achievements, though with less explicit attention to her character. The Wheatley of this sketch possesses a natural curiosity and a strong work ethic rather than the "uncommon" talents of Brown's Wheatley. The story of how Wheatley began to write illustrates this difference in emphasis. The sketch reports that, as Mary read or wrote letters, "Phillis stood looking at her in wonder." Phillis assumes that she should be able to undertake the same activities as her young mistress, so her observation soon turns to action. The narrator explains, "Miss Wheatley seemed to write with so much ease that one day Phillis went out with a piece of charcoal in her hand and began to try to write on the side of a wall." Mary takes notice and begins to tutor Phillis. Although Haynes's sketch does not draw attention to Phillis's talent, it does make palpable the young girl's excitement about learning, saying that the night she began learning to write she "scarcely wished to leave her writing to go to bed," which she finally did, "smiling and shaking with joy."[56] The rest of the narrative describing Phillis's studies focuses on how quickly she learned. For instance, "in less than a year and a half" from the time she began scrawling words on a wall with charcoal, Phillis could easily read challenging passages from the Bible. Her fame spread throughout the colonies "in four years," and she was "soon" reading Latin on her own.[57] Haynes's sketch also draws attention to the effect Phillis had on other (presumably white) people: they were said to have treated her as "a wonder" and "marveled" at her erudition.[58] Such people, especially admirers in England, are portrayed as having encouraged Phillis to publish her poetry. Although Phillis certainly functions as an agent in this story, she is presented as driven primarily by her own internal ambition. Individuals in power admire this ambition and, in turn, urge her to greater accomplishment.

Both Fauset's and Brown's narratives represent Wheatley as a virtuous young woman who exudes humility, resists flattery, and exemplifies loyalty. Brown's sketch takes particular care to ground Wheatley's action in her admirable "Christian" character. A "very religious" young person, Brown's Wheatley possesses "character and deportment" that lead others to consider her an "ornament to the church." She is said to have been unaffected by the recognition of her talents and the trans-Atlantic fame that followed her 1773 trip to England. Wheatley was "not turned by so much flattery and attention"; rather, because "seriousness and humility were natural to [Phillis] . . . she retained the same gentle, modest deportment that had won Mrs. Wheatley's heart when she first saw her in the market-place."[59] This Wheatley remained loyal and seemingly impervious to fame, forfeiting her planned meeting with King George III in order to be with Susanna Wheatley on her deathbed. While less focused on the religious character of Phillis's goodness, Fauset's narrative also claims that Phillis's fine character enabled her consistently to make the best of challenging situations. She wrote poetry expressing "fine sentiments," displayed loyalty to her mistress, maintained her humility even as she was "courted and petted to an extent which might well have turned a less well-balanced head than hers," and remained "proud" even when in an indigent state.[60] Although her life was always subject to the vicissitudes of the white world, Wheatley's steady character equipped her to weather both flattery and destitution, just as young African Americans of the early twentieth century might be called upon to do.

All three sketches use the tale of Wheatley's marriage to John Peters in order to contrast her virtuous qualities with his poor ones. While not explicitly drawing attention to Wheatley's character, Haynes's narrator describes in detail the difficulty of this period of Wheatley's life. The sketch sets up the appearance of Peters by telling readers that Wheatley, like many others of her day, lived to "taste the bitterness of Revolutionary War times." Readers learn that Wheatley encountered "hard times," during which she labored so arduously that she became "ill from overwork."[61] The sketch gives the impression of a great burden borne silently by Wheatley. Fauset's and Brown's narratives, on the other hand, deliberately highlight Wheatley's honorable conduct during these times. Like Haynes's telling, Brown's narrative emphasizes Wheatley's precarious position as a black woman following the deaths of the Wheatley family members and the onset of colonial unrest, when "the people were too anxious and troubled to think of the African poet whom they once delighted to honor."[62] Wheatley thus accepts Peters's proposal "in an evil hour," apparently having been deceived by his fine performances. The trying circumstances of war, poverty, and an ill-suited marriage foreground Wheatley's womanly character: Brown has told us that she was "patient and resigned" and "made no complaint of her unfeeling husband."[63] The narrator reports the death of Wheatley's three children and, finally, her death (though it is expressed quite euphemistically). Although the narrative emphasizes Phillis's remarkable patience as a wife, the text closes on a faintly feminist note by pointing out that she never took the name of her husband "but went by the name bestowed upon her by her benefactress and by which she will be known to all posterity the name of PHILLIS WHEATLEY."[64] These closing lines of Brown's sketch demonstrate a nuanced negotiation of Wheatley's character, racial identity, and womanhood. The passage suggests that Phillis "went by" the name Wheatley of her own volition, in an apparent effort to dissociate herself from her morally dubious husband and to strengthen her association with the matriarch of the Wheatley household, to whom she is reported to have felt gratitude. This Phillis Wheatley chooses gratitude toward the Wheatleys over bitterness toward her spouse and, in so doing, exercises an agency that evinces her virtues even from within her comparatively disempowered position in the Wheatley household.[65]

Wheatley's agency and personal character make her worthy of emulation by all, but situating her within African American history made her a role model for race leaders who came of age in the 1920s. These three sketches address Wheatley's identity and role as a black American in two ways: first, by addressing her African origins, and second, by highlighting her significance in the broader narrative of African American history. Brown's text depicts Wheatley's Africanness in her own words, so to speak, by opening the sketch with the first four lines from Wheatley's controversial poem "On Being Brought from Africa to America": "'Twas mercy brought me from my Pagan land, / Taught my benighted soul to understand / That there's a God—that there's a Savior, too, / Once I redemption neither sought nor knew." Although this poem was often criticized or dismissed during the Harlem Renaissance because of its supposed lack of race consciousness, in Brown's sketch it frames the ensuing narrative as a story of education, action, and redemption that began, significantly, in "far off Africa."[66] Brown's sketch reinforces this framing by foreshadowing Wheatley's future prominence. The narrator explains that in 1761 the young arrival "spoke only her native African dialect and a few words of broken English." Lacking any direction from the child, "Mrs. Wheatley gave her the name of Phillis Wheatley, little dreaming that it, and the little slave girl she had rescued, would become renowned in American history."[67] By collapsing the temporal distance between her first "few words of broken English" and her ultimate renown, this passage further dramatizes Wheatley's achievements.

Both Fauset's and Haynes's sketches render Wheatley's origins in greater detail, offering descriptions of her early days in and her kidnapping from western Africa. Fauset's narrative begins with an idyllic coastal scene, illustrated visually on the banner of the piece and verbally in the opening lines: "SOMEWHERE in Africa nearly 175 years ago a band of children were playing on the sea-coast." But the scene quickly grows sinister as the children are seized by "a number of white men." This sketch directly addresses the functions of race and the horrors of slavery by noting the racial difference of the slavers, emphasizing the "fear and anguish" of a child "torn away" from her home and telling readers that the solitary child was "very seasick" on the long voyage west.[68] In so doing, Fauset's narrator speaks to readers in their blackness and in their youth, as an audience that might experience the persistent threat of white power and fear its effects in their everyday lives.

Haynes's narrative also uses the story of Wheatley's origins to address readers as black children, with two key differences from Fauset's depiction: first, Haynes's narrative depicts Wheatley's life in Africa in greater detail, and second, it makes no explicit mention of slavery. While Haynes's sketch imagines a rich life in Africa for the child who would become Phillis Wheatley, it also foregrounds for readers the differences between their own experience and that of this child. The sketch begins with her birth "on the Western Coast of Africa." The narrator continues, "Her mother did not sit for long hours making beautiful little dresses and doing embroidery for her, for that is not the custom in Africa. Babies do not need many clothes in that warm country. There little children, and grown people, too, run around with just a piece of cloth tied about their waists." This sketch draws attention to the differences in climate—and, by extension, customs of dress—yet it also expressly attempts to speak to the fact that children exist equally happily in both North America and Africa. The sketch continues to describe the "religious ceremony" practiced by the child's mother, during which she "went out of her little thatched-roof house every morning and prostrated herself to pour out water before the rising sun."[69] The narrator portrays this ceremony as a source of delight for the young child but does not seem otherwise to link it meaningfully to an African heritage. Also seemingly in an effort to enliven the first part of the story and engage young readers, the narrator describes in some detail the scene of the child's capture by "strange-looking men." The ensuing sea voyage was "long" and "rough," and it often made the passengers "afraid." Readers learn of the journey's effects on the bodies of young travelers, saying, "Some of the children fell to the floor with spells of vomiting."[70] These opening paragraphs pulse with the emotion and sensation imagined to be at the forefront of children's experiences—the pleasures of playing with friends, the terror of strangers, the misery of sickness. Although marked as exotic because of their African home, the children in the story are also potentially relatable to young readers through common emotional and sensory experiences.

Haynes's narrative also differs strikingly from Fauset's in its meticulous avoidance of the words "slave" or "slavery." With the exception of a few euphemistic phrases, the sketch presents little evidence that Phillis was, in fact, enslaved in the Wheatley household. Whereas Fauset's sketch attempts to reclaim the actions of former slaves as evidence of agency and heroism, Haynes's emphasizes the "pain" of the enslaved individual, as Paula T. Connolly described it, without specifying that the pain was caused by the *institution* of slavery.[71] The deliberate erasure of slavery in Haynes's sketch is one strategy for dealing with the complex challenge of presenting the horrors of slavery to a young audience, a strategy, as Connolly points out, used by a minority of early twentieth-century writers of African American history for children.[72]

Having established Wheatley's African origins, these sketches affirm her role as a historical "first" and as an exemplar of African American literary achievement. They do so both by naming her a "first" and by featuring her written work. The subtitle of Haynes's story, for instance, notes Wheatley's position as the first published African American woman: "First Poetess of Her Race on American Soil."[73] Haynes's narrative reinforces this vision by reproducing—without additional comment—four selections of Wheatley's poetry, including "Hymn to the Morning," "Hymn to the Evening," and excerpts from "Imagination" and "To the University of Cambridge, in New England."[74] In similar fashion, Brown's sketch is accompanied by a well-known engraved portrait of Wheatley, labeled "Phillis Wheatley,

First Poet of the Negro Race."[75] The sketch also mentions Wheatley's epistolary exchange with George Washington during the fall and winter of 1776–77, quoting in full Washington's reply to Wheatley.[76]

After recounting Wheatley's early death, in 1784, the *Brownies' Book* narrative spends two full paragraphs explaining to readers Wheatley's historical significance. These paragraphs begin by reminding readers of Wheatley's "undoubted poetical ability," "fine vocabulary," and "broad grasp" of the classics. The narrator continues, "But these are hardly in themselves the reasons why colored Americans should hold Phillis Wheatley in such high esteem. There are others more striking. In the first place, she is the first Negro in America to win prestige for purely intellectual attainments. And she won it, oh so well! Secondly, her writing influenced and strengthened anti-slavery feeling. When the friends of slavery made as a reason for holding human beings in bondage the statement that Negroes were mentally inferior, the foes of slavery pointed with pride to the writings of this girl who was certainly the peer of any American poet of those days."[77] This Phillis Wheatley is not simply an exemplary human being; she is, specifically, an exemplary African American *for* other African Americans. By highlighting the "prestige" she enjoyed because of her "intellectual attainments," Fauset's sketch also presents Wheatley as a model for the type of liberal education pursued by Du Bois's "talented tenth." Furthermore, this narrative claims that the usefulness of Wheatley's example extends beyond her death into the nineteenth and twentieth centuries. The closing lines of the sketch reinforce this message by saying, "We are sensible of a deep gratitude toward this little lonely figure who came from Africa determined to give voice to her previous dower of song, even though she had to express it in a far country and in a stranger's tongue."[78] Readers are invited not simply cognitively to acknowledge Wheatley's importance but to feel a "deep gratitude" for her life and example. The influence of editors Du Bois and Fauset appears clearly in these final paragraphs, as they speak directly to future "race leaders" and emphasize Wheatley's intellectual achievements and her influence on political issues significant to black communities.

Sketching Truth

The sketches that appear about Isabella Van Wagener/Sojourner Truth in these three texts emphasize similar themes, including Truth's public agency, her unique character, and her role as a black woman in American history. However, the three authors negotiated these themes in ways that subtly reflected their particular goals. The two-page sketch in the *Brownies' Book,* titled "A Pioneer Suffragette," focuses on Truth's activist work for both woman suffrage and antislavery causes. Truth's famous 1851 speech at the Woman's Rights Convention in Akron, Ohio, becomes the centerpiece of that sketch. On the other hand, Haynes's sketch "The Suffragist," focuses on Truth's life before she became an itinerant speaker, devoting the first eleven pages of a seventeen-page biography to Isabella's life prior to her name change, in 1843. Most of Brown's four-page sketch chronicles Truth's public career, including less than two brief paragraphs about Truth's life prior to 1843.

All three texts nonetheless emphasize Truth's role as an agent in American public life by describing her involvement in the woman suffrage movement and by highlighting her interactions with prominent political figures.[79] Fauset's sketch in the *Brownies' Book* makes the most of Truth's activism on behalf of women's rights. This sketch spends the first few paragraphs contextualizing her life within the history of woman suffrage, seemingly to address the pressing question of the Nineteenth Amendment, which was ratified four months after Fauset's sketch was published. Readers are reminded of this significant issue: "Now that the right of women to vote is gradually being conceded throughout the United States, few people stop to realize for how many years women have had to work and fight and wait in order to reach this goal. Even our boys and girls remember the disrepute in which suffragettes were held in England prior to, and even at the beginning of, the World War."[80] After several more sentences describing the "shame, ridicule, and disappointment" of these "true heroines," Fauset's narrator introduces Truth as a unique figure: "To one of those early leaders of women the disfavor arising from being associated with the unpopular cause of Woman Suffrage meant nothing, for she had long since been associated with a cause far more unpopular—that of Abolition."[81] Throughout the sketch, Truth's involvement in women's rights is described in terms of her experiences fighting for abolition, thus subtly framing race and sex oppression as intertwined. For instance, the story of Truth's 1851 speech is introduced by explaining that she joined the cause of woman suffrage because her "keen" mind perceived that "the refusal of the right to vote to women, was only another form of slavery."[82] Thus, Truth's involvement in women's causes becomes an extension of her beliefs about racial equality. The sketch continues with a seven-paragraph report of the scene in Akron on that May day, reproduced nearly verbatim from the now-famous 1863 account written by Frances Dana Gage.[83] Subtly amplifying Truth's contributions, Fauset's narrator concludes that "the cause of Woman Suffrage is in her debt."[84] By focusing on Truth's contributions to both causes, the entire sketch delivers on its promise to introduce a "pioneer suffragette."

Both Haynes's and Brown's narratives describe Truth's work on behalf of woman suffrage, and both also portray the 1851 Akron speech as an exemplary moment. Whereas Haynes's sketch includes a short anecdote (much briefer than that in the *Brownies' Book*) with quotations from the speech, Brown's simply summarizes the event for readers.[85] Readers of Haynes's version learn that Truth "marched in like a queen" to the church where the meeting was being held and, after having said her piece, was enthusiastically applauded by the women present.[86] Brown's sketch spends less time describing the event and more time interpreting it as evidence of Truth's political contributions. Drawing attention to Truth's prominent connections, Brown's narrator claims that Truth was "a zealous advocate for the enfranchisement of women and claimed warm friendship with many of the noted women of that cause."[87] Although the reports differ slightly, both sketches conclude that Truth's speech in Akron had "saved the day."[88]

Having established Truth's pivotal role in the nineteenth-century women's rights movement, these authors further dramatized her agency by reporting her influence on political leaders, especially white men. For instance, both Fauset and Brown highlighted Truth's 1864 visit with President Abraham Lincoln. Perhaps because so little is known of this meeting, Fauset's text simply claims that Truth, "who had started out in life as nobody, numbered the greatest man in the country, President Lincoln, among her friends."[89] Brown's sketch magnifies the significance of Truth's "friendship" with Lincoln by describing its supposed political impact. According to this version, Truth "made several visits to the White House to request and urge President Lincoln to enlist the free colored men of the north in defense of the Union. He gave her audience and promised to consider the matter. Shortly after, Mr. Lincoln and Congress gave consent; and Negro soldiers, north and south, were fighting for their freedom."[90] Although Brown's anecdote does not specify dates or sources so that readers can verify the information, it clearly amplifies Truth's rhetorical efficacy. Haynes's narrative does not explicitly mention the meeting with Lincoln, but, like Brown's text, Haynes's notes Truth's effect on lawmakers during Lincoln's presidency. The day that Truth "walked into the marble room of the Senate Chamber," Haynes's narrator explains, was "not soon to be forgotten." The narrative continues, "Senators rose and shook her hand. They asked her to speak. As she spoke, some sat with tears in their eyes. When she had finished they shook her hand again, gave her a purse and bade her good-bye."[91] Haynes's narrative identifies neither the reason for Truth's visit nor the subject of her conversation with the legislators; it focuses exclusively on Truth's emotional impact. Most of these reports about Truth's interactions with prominent public figures portray her as a powerful, self-possessed public agent who acted in ways that were "recognized and heeded by others," to use the words of Karlyn Kohrs Campbell.[92]

These sketches also depict Truth's agency in moments of self-determination.[93] For instance, all three sketches include the story of Isabella changing her name to Sojourner Truth in 1843. The *Brownies' Book* sketch introduces Isabella's decision to change her name as an example of the many "strange and unusual things" she accomplished during her "long and remarkable career." Fauset's account presents this moment as solely the decision of Isabella/Sojourner, saying "she changed her name."[94] Haynes's sketch also emphasizes this moment of decision, though she borrows Truth's own, more detailed account of the story from her *Narrative*.[95]

Haynes's narrative reports that, having become disillusioned with urban squalor and degradation, Isabella/Sojourner "decided to leave New York City and travel east and lecture." She acted decisively, packed quickly, and announced her plans to her employer only when absolutely necessary, saying, "My name is no longer Isabella, but 'Sojourner.' I am going east. The spirit calls me there, and I must go."[96] This account underscores Isabella's choice but frames it as the *Narrative* does, as a response to a spiritual calling. Brown's narrator deliberately (albeit inaccurately) links the name change to Isabella's becoming freed from slavery, which increases both events' symbolic impact. Yet Brown's sketch also mitigates Truth's agency by introducing God as the central actor in the story: "She was called Isabella until she gained her freedom then she tells us that she asked God for a new name. She was given Sojourner because of her many wanderings and Truth because she was to preach the truth as to the iniquity of slavery, and because, as she said, 'God is my master and His name is Truth and Truth shall be my abiding name until I die.'"[97] By telling the story in this manner, the prominent African Methodist Episcopal churchwoman Brown followed Truth's own account of the event while portraying her subject as a model of piety.

Truth's strong character emerges in a variety of contexts: public speeches and interactions, private moments, efforts on behalf of the poor and oppressed, and domestic life. Whereas Fauset's and Brown's narratives attend to Truth's character as expressed in her role as speaker and activist, Haynes's observes Truth's character—particularly her devotion and single-mindedness—in her role as a mother.[98] The story of how Isabella won a lawsuit to restore her six-year-old son Peter to her after he was illegally sold to an Alabama family serves as the central example of these qualities. Haynes's sketch provides a detailed, three-page account of the year-long process. Evidence of Isabella's determination appears in the narrative when she first tells her former owners of her intentions: "She went to her former mistress and others concerned in the sale, saying, 'I'll have my child again.'"[99] In her efforts to file a suit, Isabella encounters ridicule, tangled bureaucracies, and unfamiliar practices such as swearing on a Bible. Haynes's narrator informs readers that "none of this seemed to disturb Isabella," who continued to confront the necessary officials and waited patiently until her child was finally returned to her, in 1828.[100] The next three pages advance the story of Isabella the long-suffering mother by narrating the many ways that Isabella attempted to help Peter stay out of trouble and improve his lot in life.[101] Rather than explicitly stating that Isabella's motherhood demonstrates good character, Haynes's detailed stories supply evidence of this character.

The narratives wrought by Fauset and Brown, in contrast, suggest that Truth's public activities provide the most compelling evidence of her character. For instance, Fauset's sketch distills for readers the meaning of Truth's choice to fight not only for abolition but also for women's rights: "Indeed her interest in this cause [of woman suffrage] is the surest proof that she was a sincere advocate of liberty. For though the needs of her own people were so pressing, she felt that it was also her business to help all woamnkind [*sic*]."[102] Fauset's account implies that Truth's involvement in the cause of woman suffrage demonstrates true generosity of mind, an ability to identify with the plight of others, such as white women. This Truth enacted her convictions even when it might not directly or only benefit her as an African American woman. This Truth possessed a commitment to liberty that extended beyond self-interest to embrace the fight for freedom on behalf of those who were different from her.

Brown's narrative fuses moral qualities, public agency, and rhetorical prowess in a particularly striking portrait. Her Truth was "earnest," exhibited "shrewd judgment and rare common sense," and "possessed a striking faith and simple piety." This Truth was "an orator of superior type," in the same category as Frederick Douglass. Here, Truth is described as "that type of genius who knew without learning and understood with the certainty of instinct," gave "homely renderings of the gospel," had a "spirit of eloquence and poetry," and evinced a "native nobility."[103] The sketch later attributes Truth's oratorical achievements to "her African dialect, quaint speeches and genial ways," as well as to her "keen wit and repartee."[104] In the event that readers are not convinced by this glowing assessment, Brown's narrative also supplies testimonies from Harriet Beecher Stowe and Wendell Phillips. For Brown, a longtime lecturer and teacher of public speaking and elocution, Truth's oratorical achievements likely would have provided the most compelling evidence for her moral excellence and agential power. Here, Truth the rhetor becomes a compelling model for young readers who hope to improve their own lives and uplift their race through public action.

All three sketches subtly situate Sojourner Truth's achievements, agency, and character within her racial identity and belonging. The texts draw attention to her early life as a slave as well as to her antislavery activism, note her African heritage and (fictionalized) African dialect, and strongly identify her with the African American community. One especially memorable tale told by both Fauset and Brown also illustrates Truth's dual identity as former slave and abolitionist. This story tells of a Boston antislavery meeting in which a desperate Frederick Douglass argued that freedom would need to be seized by force. Truth responded dramatically, rebuking Douglass with her signature frankness: "Frederick, is God dead?" The story, which the historian Nell Irvin Painter described as "the stuff of allegory, not history," was popularized by Harriet Beecher Stowe in her 1863 *Atlantic Monthly* piece about Truth, titled "The Libyan Sybil." According to Painter, Stowe's version of Truth appealed to later writers because it "made Truth an electrifying presence and a symbol of Christian faith and forbearance, a talisman of non-violent faith in God's ability to right the most heinous of wrongs."[105] For Fauset, the story became an example of Truth's "striking sayings" and, most important, evidence that she sought to strengthen rather than scold a "very much discouraged" Douglass.[106] Brown's rendering follows Stowe's closely, though Brown, notably, offered the story as an example of Truth's "great eloquence and poetry" rather than her belief in the goodness of white people.[107]

These sketches highlight Truth's African heritage and her identification with African American communities. For instance, the introduction of Brown's sketch declares, "There was born in the late Eighteenth Century [*sic*] one of the most singular and impressive characters of pure African blood that has appeared in modern times in the person of the slave, Isabella."[108] Brown's narrative continues to identify Truth with the black community several other times, noting that she was always "demanding justice for her down-trodden race," that she made many "exertions" to improve the lot of newly emancipated slaves, and that her old age did not prevent her from "traveling in behalf of her people."[109] Fauset's and Haynes's accounts likewise emphasize both Truth's consciousness of "the needs of her own people" and her many efforts "for the sake of the freedom of her people."[110] These sketches claim Truth for black Americans while also suggesting that all of her work—for suffrage, abolition, and social improvement—was done to enhance the fortunes of "her" race.

Although the accounts of Wheatley and Truth in these biographical sketches differ, they are united by a common goal, evident in both their introductory author commentary and throughout the narratives: to provide young African American readers with models who demonstrate good character and praiseworthy action and inspire those readers to act on behalf of their race. The authors of the sketches accomplished their goals by selecting certain stories or incidents from their subjects' lives, sometimes letting the carefully crafted narratives "speak for themselves" and at other times providing interpretive guidance to readers. The stories were selected, arranged, and shaped in order to highlight Wheatley's and Truth's agency within severely constrained circumstances. These sketches served both as public commemorations of important African American women and sources of "inspiration" for the African American children who were already learning to be leaders in their communities.

Reading these biographical sketches from the early days of African American children's literature also makes clear how biography has functioned as a unique rhetorical tool within black communities. While scholars of white children's literature might dismiss biography that functions as "a form of hagiography, a saint's life that was meant to inspire young readers to live better,"[111] scholars studying African American children's literature recognize that these criticisms do not apply to black biography in the same way. Scholars such as Johnson have spoken of a "tradition of using biography as a source of inspiration for Afro-American people as a group."[112]

This tradition indicates that biography praising individuals in oppressed groups *for* other marginalized audiences is not merely conservative but also potentially progressive—and even, perhaps, essential to community survival. Furthermore, examining biographical sketches from the 1920s shows how certain life stories can illuminate for young readers the "multitude of other selves" that they might construct, apart from oppressive discourses about what it means to be a child and what it means to be black.[113]

The stories told about Wheatley and Truth changed over the course of the twentieth century—indeed, they had already been altered before Brown, Fauset, and Haynes wrote in the 1920s. Henry Louis Gates Jr., in *The Trials of Phillis Wheatley,* and Nell Irvin Painter, in *Sojourner Truth: A Life, a Symbol,* illustrated how the legacies of these two women were transformed by the vagaries of historical documentation, the efforts of enterprising individuals, and the political goals of new generations.[114] Both Gates and Painter reviewed how perceptions of the significance and meaning of the lives of Wheatley and Truth have changed over time and across contexts. Each scholar charted the memory of his or her subject from the years immediately following her death into the present, paying particular attention to moments of change, innovation, and controversy. Gates and Painter both identified the question of authenticity as a primary impetus during periods of public ferment about the legacies of Wheatley and Truth: specifically, what constitutes "authentic" black womanhood and whether a figure of the past can be said to embody or promote such an identity.[115]

For instance, both Gates and Painter described how the Black Power movement of the 1960s and 1970s influenced the concept of blackness and, in turn, the perception of African Americans who lived in the past.[116] Notably, the effects of this period upon the public memories of the two women resulted in a stark contrast: Truth flourished, while Wheatley floundered. Painter explained that the myriad stories about Truth's lively speaking performances provided fodder to elevate an "angry" Truth required by certain social movements: in this context, she became "a nineteenth-century female Black Panther, an Elaine Brown and Kathleen Cleaver rolled up into one and projected back in time."[117] On the other hand, the same people who reinvented and valorized Truth sneered at Wheatley. According to Gates, perceptions of Wheatley were based almost solely on her poem "On Being Brought from Africa to America," which referred to Africa as a "pagan land" and seemed to express Wheatley's gratitude for being encouraged to accept the Christian God.[118] Gates said that Black Power activists—and members of the Black Arts Movement in particular—"had a field day mocking her life and her works (most of which they had not read)."[119]

A comparison of Gates's and Painter's narratives suggests that the fates of the memories of these two women during the 1960s and 1970s depended heavily on small pieces of information. These pieces were taken up, perhaps polished or repositioned, and used to construct new narratives about Wheatley and Truth, as well as about their meaning in history. The construction and re-presentation of these narratives depended upon the goals of people who constructed them and the contexts in which they were created. Beyond authorial intentions, the resulting texts often took on lives of their own, as they were taken up into the broader circulation of public memory in the United States. Thus, Gates and Painter described the process that I have called public memory. Gates and Painter focused deliberately on the mutability of historical understanding, the highly symbolic nature of historical representations, and the ways that the actions of individuals such as Thomas Jefferson or Frances Dana Gage promoted images of Wheatley and Truth that persist today, sometimes in contradiction to documented facts. These images have affected the children's biographies about these women, whether those were published as short sketches in the 1920s, as biographical novels in the 1940s and 1950s, or as photobiographies in the 1980s.

CHAPTER FOUR

PREFIGURATION

The Agent Placed in History

> If she had one wish for her life, it was probably to be remembered as a religious person and a skilled poet—which is how we remember her now.
>
> Sneed B. Collard III,
> *Phillis Wheatley: She Loved Words*

How do historical narratives about an individual from the past—even particular versions of these narratives—gain traction in a particular place and time? What causes some narratives and not others to resonate with audiences in that moment? As scholars of public memory have pointed out, texts and practices of public memory possess relevance in the present because they reflect the values of the culture in which they are formulated and circulated.[1] Public memories are forged from the raw material of the past and molded by the present. This can occur on a grand scale, as when narratives tout ideals such as freedom and liberty. Or it can occur on a small scale, as when a seemingly minute detail is sutured to a particular story through repetition.

Take, for instance, a striking theme in juvenile biographies about Phillis Wheatley. Five books published around 2000 use the contemporary monetary value of Wheatley's poetic artifacts to introduce her as a historical figure. For instance, the author Deborah Kent opened her 2004 biography by explaining: "At an auction in 1998, a rich New Yorker bought the original manuscript of a poem called 'Ocean.' The pages were wrinkled and yellowed with age, but the buyer paid a whopping $68,500 for it. The poem had great historical value. 'Ocean' was written by poet Phillis Wheatley, the first African-American writer to ever publish a book."[2] Other, slightly earlier texts use a similar but less dramatic example. Three texts, published during or after 1997, note that in 1984 an autographed copy of Wheatley's book sold at auction for $2,000.[3]

In each of these cases, the texts substitute a Wheatley artifact for the poet herself, using a contemporary price tag to represent metonymically her value to those in the present. The repeated reporting of such facts suggests that the creators of these texts believed that estimating Wheatley's resale value might help young readers to understand how people and things from the past become meaningful in the present.[4] Such details began to appear suddenly in Wheatley biographies in 1997. Why the change? If only one text had included such an example, it could be considered idiosyncratic—perhaps the result of an author who collects antiques or a consulting editor who is also a museum curator. But such information appears in five texts published after 1997—about one-quarter of the Wheatley texts published during this later period—which indicates that the texts are using some new inventional resource, made available by changing cultural norms.[5] One explanation is that the creators of these texts seized on a renewed American interest in the material artifacts of history, signaled by the advent of the popular television program *Antiques Roadshow;* this interest was so widespread that it was assumed to be intelligible to young readers.[6] Another, more insidious possibility is the rise of a neoliberal rationality in which human beings are understood only in terms of their monetary value—or, as Wendy Brown put it, human beings become "little capitals" competing with one another for maximum profit.[7] Instead of introducing Wheatley through an anecdote or achievement, these biographies portray their subject as reducible to the market value of her historical traces. These examples illustrate that neoliberalism has permeated even the most neglected corners of the Western educational realm. Even without the influence of neoliberalism, using monetary value to establish Wheatley's contemporary significance is deeply problematic because it treats her—once an enslaved woman—as a historical object to be bought and sold. Troubling though they may be, these examples demonstrate how biographies for children respond to dominant discourses in circulation at the time of their production.

In addition to reflecting contemporary cultural and political discourses, these biographies respond to more enduring commonplaces of U.S. public culture. These commonplaces "prefigure" the narratives in the texts, rendering them intelligible on a basic level to members of that culture. The life stories about Phillis Wheatley, Sojourner Truth, and Shirley Chisholm become recognizable historical narratives because they resonate with late twentieth- and early twenty-first-century American perceptions of historical action. Individuals who read these stories are not only learning about Wheatley, Truth, and Chisholm; they are also learning about the public culture in which these lives were lived and these stories told. As Paul Ricoeur explained, "To understand a story is to understand both the language of 'doing something' and the cultural tradition from which proceeds the typology of plots."[8] Twentieth-century American public values such as social progress and individual freedom combine with cultural assumptions about what it means to "do something" meaningful in history and thereby determine the possibilities for representing the agency of these women.

Mimesis$_1$: The Prefiguration of Agency in Public Memory

In *Time and Narrative,* Ricoeur aligned the first stage of the hermeneutic circle, mimesis$_1$, with the function of "prefiguration." This concept describes the way in which narratives are "emplotted" according to "a preunderstanding of the world of action."[9] Ricoeur explained that preunderstanding has three primary features that affect the composition of a plot: meaningful structures, symbolic resources, and temporal character. The "meaningful structures" to which he refers can also be understood as a "conceptual network" of actions, people, events, stories, and the like. The "symbolic resources" are the inventional ingredients publicly available for representing human action, much as nouns, verbs, and objects are the ingredients of a sentence. The "temporal character" of narratives refers to the possible formulations for embedding human action in the unfolding of time, as well as how time itself is conceived by society. Each of these elements—structures, symbols, and temporality—contributes to the prefiguration of the field of understanding wherein a narrative is emplotted.[10]

The preunderstanding of action in this phase of prefiguration is closely related to the concept of *doxa,* which is central to the rhetorical tradition. The literary and rhetorical scholar Andreea Deciu Ritivoi explained that this concept traditionally has been defined as "the domain of probable knowledge and contrasted to *episteme,* the realm of certainty." In addition to its epistemic definition, *doxa* has also been used to describe the "sets of beliefs widely espoused by particular audiences."[11] Ricoeur described *doxa* as "the sedimented universe of conventional ideas" that constitutes the "premises of rhetorical argumentation." All rhetors, he explained, build their persuasive discourses upon conventional ideas shared with their audiences. According to Ricoeur, *doxa* serves an integrating, socially conservative function.[12] Doxastic conventions can make biographies widely accessible, intelligible, and historically meaningful to children and adolescents in the twentieth- and early twenty-first-century United States. I focus here on the "sedimented," slow-to-change commonplaces that yield broad similarities rather than on contextual particularities that might enable the books to alter these commonplaces. More specifically, I ask, What are the commonsense ideas in contemporary U.S. public culture upon which narratives about individual historical agents are constructed? And how can the influence of these ideas be observed in the structure of the texts themselves?

American Agents: Individualism and Social Progress

Biographies have long been an important supplement to the history curriculum in public schools in the United States.[13] Stories of individual lives, whether incorporated into history textbooks, included in collective biographies, or narrated in individual biographies, continue to hold a prominent place in history education, despite late twentieth-century criticisms of this highly narrative form of history. Many scholars, including critics of the biographical genre, recognize the power of biography to reinforce certain cultural understandings of the human self and society. As the biographer Nigel Hamilton argued in his history of the genre, biography is "central to the Western concept of individuality and the ideals of democracy."[14] Children's biographies published in the United States, such as those examined here, are specifically prefigured by the American understanding of selfhood. Many of the texts about Wheatley, Truth, and Chisholm are explicitly identified as *American* stories; this is especially true in biographies that appear as part of a series about American figures. Biographical series for children published between 1949 and 2013 bore titles such as Childhood of Famous Americans (later changed to Young Patriots), Americans All, American Lives, and American Heroes.[15]

One prominent theme of these biographies is thoroughly grounded in American notions of agency: liberal individualism. According to Rob Wilson, the American practice of writing biography relies upon an assumption that the development of the self is a "conflicted drama of individuation."[16] Although Wilson was referring to biographies for adults, his observations also hold true for texts for young readers. In a study of all recipients of the Newbery Award for children's literature between 1922 and 1984, the political scientist Timothy Cook found that winners of the award between 1941 and 1981 demonstrated a "striking convergence on the American value of individual self-reliance."[17] Cook's conclusions suggest not only that the values of autonomy and independence pervade mid- to late twentieth-century children's literature but also that the texts that best incorporate these values are most admired.

Between 1949 and 2013, the majority of children's biographies about Wheatley, Truth, and Chisholm situated the basic facts about these three women within the individualistic framework described by Wilson and Cook. The most striking effects of this framework in structuring these narratives can be seen in the connection between the central agent and her actions. Of course, because biographies have traditionally focused on recounting the lives of human beings, such texts typically feature people, rather than systemic or natural forces, as the primary engines of action and historical causality.[18] This emphasis comes with risks. The education scholar Gary Fertig explained that, "without accompanying inquiry into the historical context and chronology of people's lives," teachers who use biography "risk instilling the misconception that historical change and continuity result from the personal intentions and interactions of individuals."[19] The narratives of children's biographies are particularly dominated by action, since action quickens the plot in ways that children are thought to appreciate. But the way in which these narratives revolve around the notable accomplishments of the historical subject suggests that the stories are also prestructured to favor an autonomous, self-determined individual who takes control of her life and takes responsibility for her actions.

In texts about Phillis Wheatley and Sojourner Truth, the potential for an individualistic rendering of their life stories appears to spring directly from the archives. In the case of Shirley Chisholm, such a perspective often is derived from conversations with the woman herself. The fact that evidence of these women's lives even exists indicates that they somehow distinguished themselves as individuals among their contemporaries or otherwise met twentieth-century standards for historical significance. These women achieved prominence during their own historical periods, despite their being black women in racist, sexist societies—and, in the cases of Wheatley and Truth, despite being enslaved. Because of these hostile environments, each woman's achievements can more easily appear as direct results of her individual personality and talents rather than the outcomes of wealth or privilege. Furthermore, these women pursued often-solitary vocations not commonly (or ever) practiced by African American women previously. After having been provided with a basic education, Wheatley became a poet who spent long, cloistered evenings writing her verse. Leaving behind most of her family and her home, Truth became an itinerant speaker who traveled many miles and mounted many stages alone. Though raised in a strong West Indian family and encouraged by many mentors, Chisholm was frequently the sole spokesperson in battles against the political establishment in which she was a striking anomaly. One book jacket's description of a 2009 Truth biography could, by omitting the word "big," easily apply to stories about any of these women: "A stirring portrait of a woman who pulled herself up by her great big bootstraps."[20] These are women who supposedly overcame adversity all through their own power. The fact that these women were selected for biographical treatment in some of the earliest collections or, in the case of Chisholm, decades before her death demonstrates their suitability for American narratives that favor action driven by the individual.

The theme of individual agency runs from the earliest texts to the latest, appearing equally in texts about all three women. Victoria Ortiz's 1974 biography, *Sojourner Truth, a Self-Made Woman* supplies an early example. Closely following the theme of the title, the introduction to this text firmly grounds Truth in the tradition of American individualism. Ortiz began:

> In a preface to Sojourner Truth's *Narrative,* her long-time friend and companion Frances Titus tells of the response of this tall, deep-voiced black woman to an allusion to Horace Greeley: "You call him a self-made man; well, I am a self-made woman." That, indeed, is what Sojourner was: from the raw material that was the slave known as Isabella, she made herself

> Sojourner Truth, a convinced and unshakable fighter for freedom. She made herself into a beloved and charismatic public speaker; she made herself into the friend and equal of great men and women; she made herself into a concerned and militant champion of the rights of her black sisters and brothers; she made herself into a warm-hearted, straight-backed, strong-willed and steady-eyed woman who would not be turned from the road she chose to travel.[21]

One could hardly find a better articulation of the ideal of individual agency in twentieth-century American public culture. In this passage, Truth's identification of herself as a "self-made woman" appears to leap straight from the pages of history into Ortiz's text, obscuring its careful selection by the author. The fact that Truth makes this observation about herself immediately presents her as self-aware and controlled. The text lists Truth's many accomplishments, each time repeating the phrase "she made herself" to reinforce her singular role in crafting an identity and executing actions. Truth appears sincerely committed: she is "convinced," "unshakable," "militant," "strong-willed," and "steady-eyed." Moreover, she trains these personal characteristics on uniquely American goals: "freedom," becoming the "equal of great men and women," and championing "rights." Throughout the remainder of the text, the narrator repeatedly traces Truth's accomplishments back to her "strength and independence of spirit" or her "stubbornness and determination."[22]

Despite significant differences between Phillis Wheatley and Sojourner Truth, their stories, as represented in many of these texts, follow a remarkably similar arc. Like Truth, Wheatley is portrayed as determined to overcome the incredible hardships of slavery in order to blaze her own trail. A 2008 picture-book biography about Wheatley effectively illustrates how the features of American individualism, while evolving over time, have remained intact. This text by Catherine Clinton, entitled *Phillis's Big Test,* portrays an individualism guided by the idea of self-esteem, which was prevalent in American culture and education at the turn of the millennium.[23] Like Truth in Ortiz's biography, the solitary Wheatley of this text is cast from the mold of self-determined individualism. As the title indicates, this telling of Wheatley's life revolves around the day in October 1772 when eighteen prominent Boston men administered a "big test" in order to determine whether Wheatley was the author of the poems she had submitted for publication. The front jacket flap tells very briefly of this moment and of Wheatley's life more generally. Then the blurb loses no time in characterizing Wheatley as confident and proactive: "Who would believe that an African girl could be the author of such poetry? Phillis did! She believed in herself, and took every opportunity she could to make her life better. She believed in the power of her words, and used her writing to prove her talent, and used the power of words to change a life."[24] In this passage, the belief most crucial for Wheatley's success is her own belief in herself, which enabled her to do everything in her power to "make her life better." She believes in herself not simply in an abstract way but as the kind of self-possessed person who could "change a life" (whose "life" her words might change is ambiguous).

The language of capitalizing on opportunities continues in the narrative. Throughout the remainder of the text, Wheatley is extremely self-sufficient—in one fictionalized scenario she even turns down a ride from her master, John Wheatley, in order to "make her own way."[25] The text uses such connections with other characters to emphasize the strength of Wheatley's individuality and determination. When she turns down Mr. Wheatley's offer, she appears to diminish his control and to increase her own. Later in the text, when no other person or group is identified as the instigator of the examination, the text strongly implies that Wheatley actively participated in organizing the event: "To prove the poems were her very own, the teenage poet consented to be cross-examined by eighteen of the most learned and powerful men of Massachusetts."[26]

In another scene, Wheatley's determination to prove herself is so strong that the author must introduce another agent, John's wife, Susanna Wheatley, in order to temper it. The narrator describes Wheatley's flashback to late-night preparations for the "big test" that lasted longer than her mistress thought prudent or necessary. During these preparations, Wheatley recalls, Susanna "had taken away the candle at midnight." Susanna tries to persuade the young poet that her "talent will speak for itself."[27] Susanna prevents Wheatley from continuing her studies, thus inhibiting her ability to act of her own accord. However, readers enter into the scene with the recognition that Wheatley already knows that her "talent will speak for itself." Her ambition to prove herself through hard work becomes even clearer as her mistress, acting in a motherly fashion, enters the scene to put a stop to Wheatley's frenzied preparations.

Texts about Shirley Chisholm also emphasize her individual agency, particularly what contemporary American culture might call "leadership qualities." Like Truth and Wheatley, Chisholm is described as "determined." Four of the seven books examined in this study use the word "determination" at least once in reference to Chisholm, to describe her persistence in excelling in school, searching for a job as a teacher, or campaigning for political office.[28] Several of these texts incorporate direct quotations from Chisholm to support this characterization. Nancy Hicks's biography, published a year before Chisholm's 1972 presidential bid, best exemplifies such an approach. The text begins by describing the rather demure, unremarkable appearance of an unnamed woman. The narrator concludes this description by upsetting reader expectations: "To look at her you might think she is a nice librarian. . . . Do not be fooled. This lady is tough."[29] Not only is this woman "tough," she is also "uncompromising" and "a champion of unpopular causes." The story supports these claims by quoting Chisholm, though without direct attribution or specific source. The text reports that Chisholm declared, "If you are a leader, you're supposed to act like one. You're not supposed to straddle. I want to be this kind of free agent until I die." Hicks used this quotation to frame the subsequent narrative, saying, "This is the story of the life of this free agent."[30] This example deftly ascribes to Chisholm qualities traditionally valued in American leaders such as toughness, commitment to principles, and the willingness to sacrifice in order to defy those in power. As the quotation from Chisholm indicates, leaders cannot just pose as leaders; they must "act like" leaders. For both Chisholm and the creator of this text, acting like a leader means acting freely, as a "free agent."

Having established the nature of her central character and storyline, Hicks returned to Chisholm's origins, reading into her subject's childhood those qualities that later made Chisholm a "free agent." This young Shirley exhibits the characteristics of a self-possessed agent even from her earliest days. The narrator tells of firstborn Shirley's arrival in the St. Hill household on November 30, 1924, saying that "from the very beginning, there was something special about the child." The narrator cites young Shirley's early achievement of milestones such as walking and talking, as well as her "assertive" nature. The passage concludes by interpreting the meaning of these childhood accomplishments in light of her later character: "Even at an extremely early age," the narrator explains, "she seemed to have the makings of a leader."[31]

As the child grew, lessons from her flinty grandmother and experiences in school reinforced her leadership capacity. The text narrates this exchange between young Shirley and her grandmother: "One day, when she and Shirley were alone on the farmhouse porch, she picked up the little girl and sat her on her lap and told her about success. It was a speech that Shirley would hear over and over again during the six years she lived with her mother's parents. 'Shirley, nothing can stop you if you are *determined* not to be distracted by the world of temptation,' her grandmother said. 'If you have strong character and *determination* and if you apply yourself, you will rise to the top.' Shirley began to apply that lesson with her sisters and cousins."[32] In this conversation, success is predicated upon determination, hard work, and character, but also upon that quintessentially American value of competition. Success, in this context, means "rising to the top," asserting one's dominance over others, arriving at a level where one will necessarily be alone.[33] The text reports that young Shirley applied these lessons in interactions with her family and others, saying that she "usually won" at sports and "almost always got what she wanted." Notably, however, the narrator explains, always coming out on top "did not make [Shirley] spoiled or soft. She was resourceful and self-sufficient. Even as a little girl she showed signs of independence. She washed her own socks and took care of her own possessions. And when it came to the principle of a thing, if she thought she was right, she would argue to the end."[34] As the narrative progresses, these qualities continue to develop and shape Chisholm's story of leadership and success. The maturing Chisholm soon learns to temper her individual ambition and cooperate with others in order to achieve broader success. Chisholm is said to have realized that she could be a "maverick" while also working with those in "established politics." Rather than upsetting the individualistic leadership qualities praised earlier in the narrative, however, this passage praises personal conviction while acknowledging the role of teamwork in success. Hicks has explained that Chisholm's decision to work with others was "part of her general philosophy of trying to work with everyone, while keeping her own integrity and determination to fight for the things she felt were important."[35] This Chisholm is an all-American leader: tough, determined, and ambitious, yet willing to work with a team.

Woven through these narratives of self-determined individuals is the persistent theme of progress. The American myth of progress finds double expression in these biographies, on both the personal and the social registers. The texts describe three agents who work continually to improve their own lives and in so doing also advance social and historical progress.[36] Phillis Wheatley, as Clinton's text explains, "Took every opportunity she could to make her life better." According to Kent's text, her poetic achievements "proved that an African could become fully educated," thereby providing fuel for antislavery reformers.[37] As the Ortiz text says, Sojourner Truth "made" a powerful, effective personality "from the raw material that was the slave known as Isabella." And, as Susan Taylor-Boyd's 1990 biography claims, Truth "set in motion" the agitation for social change that "persisted into the twentieth century with the work of civil rights activists and women's rights advocates."[38] Likewise, Shirley Chisholm led in order to improve the lives of marginalized groups, as in a passage that explains that Chisholm wanted to use her political campaigns to "help the progress of women and African Americans . . . by staying in the public spotlight."[39] Other texts depict an ascendant Chisholm reflecting on "how far black people had come" because of the work of Martin Luther King Jr., Thurgood Marshall, and the Student Nonviolent Coordinating Committee.[40] These biographies exemplify the modern, Western assumption that both our individual lives and our collective life are steadily improving. Moreover, they articulate intersections between an individual life and a broader historical trajectory, a project that Charles Taylor identified as a necessary response to the Enlightenment understanding of the human relationship to time as linear rather than cyclical.[41] In this sense, these texts fit with what Wilson described as the central objective of American biographies: "to represent another personality who can strikingly act out the liberal project of American culture as a consensual adventure toward achieving states of freedom and risk within a globally regenerative plot of self-invention."[42] Juvenile biographies built on this basic plot address themselves specifically to children by situating supposedly child-oriented themes of progress—education, physical growth, and emotional maturation, for example—within the larger framework of self-improvement and social progress.

The biographies build a narrative of social progress upon ideals fundamental to contemporary American public culture, including equality, freedom or liberation, and civil rights.[43] These ideals render the narratives of Wheatley, Truth, and Chisholm intelligible as "American" stories of "achieving states of freedom," as Wilson put it. In the cases of Wheatley and Truth, the story primarily concerns legal freedom from enslavement. Yet almost all texts also promote a definition of freedom as a psychological or spiritual state. Such texts assume that a broader definition of freedom would be more widely comprehensible and therefore accessible to readers. A reader need not fully understand the experiences of enslavement in order to appreciate the value of freedom, the texts suggest.[44] Or, conversely, spiritual freedom can be experienced even within the confines of physical enslavement.

A passage from Kathryn Kilby Borland and Helen Ross Speicher's 1968 text about Wheatley exemplifies the idea of freedom as a state of mind rather than primarily as a legal status. The narrator explains, "A few weeks before they were to set sail, the Wheatleys called Phillis into the parlor." John Wheatley gives her a paper to read, and Phillis eventually realizes that it is "a paper giving her her freedom." Speaking from an ambiguous point of view, the narrator tells readers that "it was a generous thing for the Wheatleys to do, but Phillis had always felt free." Phillis tells the Wheatleys of these feelings, and Susanna Wheatley replies, "'You will always be a part of our family, just as you are now, but we do not want you to go to England as a slave, even in name.'"[45] This passage reinforces the idea that freedom exists not only "in name" or on a "paper" but also in the way Phillis reportedly "felt" throughout her life with the Wheatley family. Phillis Wheatley, this text suggests, had an expansive yet highly personal view of freedom, one that was considered relatable to young white readers of the 1960s or even the twenty-first-century readers of the 2005 revised version.[46]

A psychologized understanding of freedom likewise structures the biographies about Sojourner Truth. In several cases, texts combine lessons about freedom with the American narrative of progress to produce a story in which Truth expands her understanding of freedom throughout the course of her life. Typically, the narratives begin with the idea of legal freedom from bondage, adding layers of meaning as the texts proceed. Freedom goes beyond manumission to include "freedom from poverty, hatred, and discrimination," "freedom to learn," "freedom of choice," freedom of movement, responsibility, the ability to work for pay, and home ownership.[47] But more than anything, narratives of Truth manifest the idea that freedom is learned. A 2009 picture book by the noted author-illustrator team of Andrea Davis Pinkney and Brian Pinkney exemplifies this underlying theme. Readers learn that after becoming legally free from slavery, Isabella "went to New

York City, where she could be truly free."[48] "Belle," as this text identifies her, improvises her own definitions of freedom. As she lived in New York, "Belle soon learned that to celebrate freedom, she had to speak her beliefs. For her, freedom meant helping others. Freedom meant putting her foot down for what she knew was right. Freedom meant she would 'travel up and down the land' to share her ideas. That's when Belle changed her name. She gave her slave name the boot, and called herself Sojourner Truth. She said the name Sojourner was just right for someone who was a traveler. And Truth—well, that was what Sojourner did best—she told it like it was."[49] In this passage, the ideal of freedom works powerfully with the two other American values mentioned earlier: individualism and progress. Here, Belle draws upon her experiences to determine her own meaning for the idea of "freedom." She needs no instruction or divine revelation but gradually learns for herself. As the narrative proceeds, Truth's understanding of freedom becomes yet more abstract: "As she traveled, she learned even more about the meaning of freedom. She found that freedom is not a place. Freedom is the fire that burns inside. And Sojourner Truth, she was full of fire."[50] This passage sets the stage for the climactic expression of Truth's freedom, which in this text is her famous 1851 Akron speech.

In Chisholm's story, freedom appears primarily in the form of civil rights for black Americans, women, and other marginalized groups. Freedom, for instance, appears in Hicks's story about how Chisholm became involved in Brooklyn politics. The narrator explains that Chisholm had learned the lessons of history, of "Reconstruction politics" and of contemporaries like Malcolm X, all of which led her personal ambition into the political realm. The narrative quotes Chisholm as explaining, "'What most fail to realize is that in Brooklyn there have been black people working toward political freedom for over twenty years. They do not realize that political groups in all the Bedford-Stuyvesants of this country have been struggling, organizing, collecting money to fight toward freedom from white political control of black communities.'"[51] Here, Chisholm herself envisions a freedom that entails the interaction of both individual and group agency. While individual leaders may seek personal freedom, efforts on behalf of civil rights operate collectively to secure shared political freedom.

The consistent presence of familiar themes such as individualism, progress, and freedom marks the life stories of these women as "American" stories meant to be accessible and intelligible even to the youngest Americans. Because these themes are so fundamental to the national narrative, they most often appear primarily as underlying structures of meaning. The understanding of Wheatley, Truth, and Chisholm as agents is built upon what Ricoeur described as a prefigured "field of action" that frequently elevates individual agency over collective action. Although certainly indebted to neoliberal emphases on individual action, these themes appear as timeless values exemplified by a variety of Americans, including these three African American women. But, one could ask, wouldn't anyone's story prefigured by such values find the traction that these women's stories have? In the case of these women, biographies are structured by underlying assumptions not only about what makes a life comprehensible and compelling but also about what makes a life historically significant.

Prefiguring Historical Significance

The values that prefigure the field of action in these narratives make them more persuasive as stories to readers in U.S. public culture. But because these books are neither fiction nor propaganda but educational texts about historical subjects, they must also depict their subjects as compelling and important agents within American history. Biographies for children are therefore prefigured by assumptions about what makes Phillis Wheatley, Sojourner Truth, and Shirley Chisholm historically significant. Out of all of the people who populate the American past, why should young readers learn about these women? Biographies about these women argue that their subjects are significant by emphasizing their role as witnesses to or participants in important moments of American history, their exceptional positions as historical "firsts," and their connections to people deemed prominent.

Assumptions about historical significance structure the biographies in a more diffuse and varied manner than do the more generalized American values of individualism, progress, and freedom. In part, the greater variation among texts is related to the discursive shift toward the accessible, popular history-making captured by the concept of memory. Tangled up in this shift were new approaches to history that challenged the assumption that "historically significant" people, events, or deeds were those that were already most prominent in the archives—military campaigns, political leaders, and the activities of powerful institutions. Professional historians and laypeople alike soon discovered that many historically significant stories and events were hidden in plain sight, obscured and suppressed by the assumption that history was made by elite white men. These historical recovery projects sought to bring figures such as Wheatley, Truth, and Chisholm from the margins back to the center of historical scholarship and education.[52] Thus, the destabilization of the "sedimented universe of ideas"[53] concerning historical meaning catalyzed an increase in the number of biographies about black women written for children and published in the late twentieth century. Even in such a context, the texts had to make claims about why the young readers (and the gatekeepers to this audience—parents, teachers, and librarians) should purchase, check out, or even just spend time reading about these women. Claims of historical significance, then, often combined the now-established assumption that a full history must include people of color and women with a persistent demand to provide children and adolescents with standards for historical knowledge and meaning.

Claims of historical significance are often predicated upon assumptions about how an individual life should be related to the larger trajectory of history. Does the individual appear separately from her historical background, as if her life existed in a timeless vacuum? Or is the individual deeply contextualized within the moment by reference to contemporary groups, events, and movements? Perhaps the individual merely supplies a vehicle for the story of a particular period or event? Biographies about Wheatley, Truth, and Chisholm exhibit each of these possibilities. Each of these approaches enacts a different notion about what constitutes historical significance for an individual life. When the individual is foregrounded at the expense of historical context, significance tends to depend upon "private" achievements and personal character. When the historical background occupies as much storyline as the life of the individual, significance assumes a certain public impact, which can be measured by the scope of influence and the eminence of contemporary associations. In this section, I characterize the narrative structure at these two poles as "history *of* a life" and "history *through* a life." Most of the texts in this study fall somewhere along a spectrum created by these two poles. I use these phrases to describe the emphasis developed in the texts, whether it is primarily upon the individual's life history or upon the history of a nation, community, or group of which this individual happened to be a part.

At first glance, biographies about Wheatley appear to fall into the first category, while those about Truth fall into the second and those about Chisholm represent both. To some extent, this appearance is a result of the differences in the recorded actions of and extant texts produced by the women. Wheatley, although she lived through a critical time in the history of the United States, was invested in what might be described as conventionally "private" pursuits, such as writing poetry, reading, and performing domestic work.[54] Little historical evidence suggests that Wheatley was directly involved in the public, political activity of the budding nation, at least in the sense that her contemporaries would have defined political engagement. Moreover, although she corresponded with many people, she was not closely associated with the smaller communities of which she could have been a part, such as the community of enslaved persons or, later, that of free blacks. Despite the considerable public circulation of Wheatley's poetry, her social isolation and the perceived privacy of the poetic endeavor lend themselves to a more privatized narrative of her life. In this way, mid- to late twentieth-century texts about Wheatley contrast with the sketches from the 1920s, which much more clearly framed her as significant for a black American public.

Sojourner Truth and Shirley Chisholm, on the other hand, utilized their talents in order to become deeply involved in the political movements of their respective times. Both women traveled widely, gave numerous speeches, and possessed charismatic public personae that made them appear to have been more intimately involved in and therefore more vital to the times in which they lived. Yet such simple classifications—both about the individual historical women and of the texts written about them—break down upon closer examination. Truth and Chisholm were not only public people, and Wheatley was not only a private person. All three women were likely concerned with both their own personal affairs and the events that occurred around them. Although the lives of these women were certainly not identical, biographies about them exhibit a striking parallelism when depicting their historical significance. How do these texts—both individually and as a group—make claims about the historical significance of their subjects by situating their life stories within broader historical trajectories? A reading of these biographies demonstrates that although the lives may have been quite different, the ways in which the lives are integrated into the scheme of history tend to follow similar patterns.

Texts that exemplify the "history *of* a life" approach focus almost exclusively on the actions of the protagonist, while excluding, minimizing, or decontextualizing the historical details that might situate the character in a meaningful past. Such texts seem intent primarily on providing an exemplar for the reader, a role model sufficiently detached from her historical setting so as to be relatable and transferable.[55] Although all the texts published between 1949 and 2013 participate in some form of modeling, texts published early in this period focus more consistently on models of good character. The "history of a life" told by these texts is structured by the notion that exemplary historical lives are characterized by certain personal qualities. In other words, good character, as manifested in moral action, defines historically meaningful agency.

Three books published in the early 1970s represent this approach: Susan Brownmiller's 1970 *Shirley Chisholm,* Margaret Fuller's 1971 *Phillis Wheatley: America's First Black Poetess,* and Helen Stone Peterson's 1972 *Sojourner Truth: Fearless Crusader.*[56] Although only Brownmiller's text can be described as expressly feminist, all three texts were written by women about women at a moment when stories about the women of history were on the rise.[57] The two later texts were published as part of a series of biographies entitled Americans All. Although the title of the series suggests an intense focus on the Americanness of these individuals (and thus the historical context of this Americanness), the stated purpose of these "fast-moving stories of real people" is to "show the way to better understanding of the ingredients necessary for personal success."[58] In other words, the creators of this series hoped that its "inspiring life stories" would serve as models for readers. To accomplish this goal, the series creators explained that the stories emphasize "specific abilities, character, and accomplishments" of these "famous people." The historical figures come from a wide range of fields, but the values emphasized in the texts remain consistent throughout the series: "the good use of ability, determination, and hard work."[59] The introduction suggests that the biographies in the series concentrate on individual lives and qualities rather than on a historical narrative about a group, community, or nation. The structures and conventions of the texts bear this out.

One way in which these texts emphasize the story of an individual over historical context is through tone. The books strike a literary, subjective tone rather than an informative, objective one, using imaginative description and figures of speech to evoke the world of the subject. For instance, the narratives rely heavily on simile to portray the physical appearance of their subjects. All three narratives make particular note of how Wheatley, Truth, and Chisholm appeared at various ages, some in ways that require the texts to move well beyond data provided by the historical record. Fuller's text explains that, at thirteen, Wheatley was "not very tall or large" but was nonetheless "healthy." As if providing evidence, the narrator offers this description: "Her brown eyes were big and bright, and her dark complexion was as smooth as a chestnut shell."[60] Peterson's text proceeds similarly, as the narrator explains that thirteen-year-old Belle "stood tall and strong." The narrator embellishes this claim with a comparison: "She stood among other girls like an oak among saplings."[61] Whereas Fuller and Peterson framed the external appearance of their subjects as a reflection of internal character, Brownmiller read Chisholm's appearance as a positive reflection on her healthy environment. The narrator details the young Chisholm's rich home life on Barbados with her grandmother, saying, "Shirley was a fat little girl. There were so many good things to eat on Barbados. No one ever went hungry."[62] Most biographers describe Chisholm as petite, if they describe her at all. In describing Shirley as "fat," Brownmiller's narrative appears to be making a point about the abundance of the island on which Chisholm was raised—and, by implication, the family in which she was reared. These three texts read robust health and physical beauty as evidence of those qualities of good character that constitute "the ingredients of personal success."

In addition to establishing a literary tone through description of physical qualities, these texts use historical events to advance the life narrative. Wheatley's story, for example, includes an anecdote about the repeal of the Stamp Act in 1766. However, this anecdote functions primarily as a means of developing the relationship between Phillis Wheatley and Mary, one of the Wheatley children, and as a way of introducing the circumstances surrounding the writing of Phillis's first poem. The scene appears in chapter 2, titled "Phillis Writes a Poem." It begins: "A little before daylight one Sunday morning in May 1766, a strange event took place in Boston." Thinking she hears bells chiming, Phillis wakes Mary in order to investigate. The "town crier" passes by on his horse, declaring that "the Stamp Act is dead!" John Wheatley, the household patriarch, echoes the crier's exclamation,

"Long live the king!" A confused Phillis asks Mary what is going on. In response to this inquiry, "Mary smiled" because "she always enjoyed explaining things to Phillis." After describing the central location of the Wheatley home, the narrator uses young Mary as the mouthpiece to explain this historical event. After Mary says that the king had repealed the Stamp Act in response to colonists' arguments, the narrator notes that "her voice rose on a note of triumph." Phillis's response: "'Isn't that wonderful,' Phillis exclaimed shyly. 'The king must be a great man.' Phillis' heart rejoiced with the people of Boston, and she wanted to express her joy too." This desire, explains the narrator, resulted in Wheatley's first poem, which praised King George III for repealing the Stamp Act.[63] Similarly, Brownmiller used minimal historical background to frame and enrich Chisholm's story, rather than the other way around. Chapter 6 of Brownmiller's text, titled "She Can Lead," begins with some brief context to set up Chisholm's entrance into Brooklyn politics: "The year 1960 was significant for black people in the United States of America. Down South the sit-ins had begun. Started by black college students, the new civil rights movement spread like fire until it reached the North. Even in Brooklyn, a new courage and militance were noticeable."[64] The narration of historical background shifts rapidly from the national to the local to the personal, and the focus remains on how Chisholm's career evolved.

On the other end of the spectrum, texts that narrate "history *through* a life" bury the protagonist deep in her historical context, providing substantial historical detail and explanation of events. Three biographies—one about each woman—effectively represent this tendency. The first is part of an extensive and popular series of biographies called Childhood of Famous Americans, which began publication in the 1940s.[65] Borland and Speicher's *Phillis Wheatley: Young Colonial Poet* (1968) describes Phillis Wheatley's world and interactions in great detail. The text attends closely to her feelings about the Revolutionary War and General George Washington, whereas it mentions her poetry only in passing. Compare the following description of Wheatley's response to the repeal of the Stamp Act to the same anecdote in the Fuller text. When Wheatley visits England, her sponsor arranges a visit with King George, to whom Phillis had written a poem of gratitude upon his repeal of the Stamp Act in 1766. The following passage describes her response to this news: "In her heart, Phillis felt that it would be bad to be presented to the king, even if she still felt the way she had when she wrote the poem. But now it would be worse, because she felt he had been wrong in his treatment of the colonists. What if her face showed how she felt about it?"[66]

Besides communicating Wheatley's trepidation at meeting the king of England, this passage suggests that she has moved away from the positive feelings that had originally inspired her poem. Like so many other "patriots" portrayed in this text, Wheatley exchanges her approval for a feeling of indignation toward King George.

Here, the narrative focuses neither on Wheatley's poem nor on the potential honor of an audience with royalty. Instead, the narrative uses Wheatley as a mouthpiece to communicate the purported feelings of American colonists during that time. This fits with the text's overall approach: to teach young readers about the colonial period through the eyes of a young person who lived through it.[67] Wheatley's personal narrative recedes into the background, while the events and personages deemed important during this historical period come to the foreground. This text reinforces the assumption that Wheatley's historical significance derives largely from the lucky fact that she lived during this period of transformation in the story of the United States.

Sojourner Truth also lived during momentous times. However, her life lasted nearly three times longer than Wheatley's. Truth's long life afforded her the opportunity to become involved in a wide variety of public causes prominent throughout the nineteenth century, such as religious reform, the antislavery movement, and women's rights. Through this involvement, Truth met several leading individuals, many of whom contributed to the development of her reputation in her own lifetime.[68] Unlike Wheatley's reputation, which was established primarily through her published poetry, Truth's reputation appears to have been more a combination of her public activity and her striking personality, upon which many contemporaries commented. Because of this reputation and the abundant traces it left in the historical record, the text that sets up this "history *through* a life" approach to Truth's story must go to greater lengths to make her historical background stand out against such an individual. Although there are fewer examples of this approach in biographies about Truth than in biographies about Wheatley, they nonetheless help us better to understand how notions of historical significance prefigure these texts.

A representative example of this approach is Edward Beecher Claflin's *Sojourner Truth and the Struggle for Freedom* (1987), which is part of a series edited by the well-known American historian Henry Steele Commager. The back of the book features a description of the series, titled Henry Steele Commager's Americans: Profiles of Americans for Young People. This description explains that the volumes are intended for readers ages ten to thirteen and that they aim to "present the lives of famous figures from American history in vivid, entertaining narratives that will appeal to young readers."[69] The text itself soon reveals its primary emphasis on teaching students about American history, its major events, its relevant periods, and the overarching political ideology of liberal individualism. Although the text continually refers back to Truth's life as the central thread, it presents the United States of the antebellum, Civil War, and Reconstruction periods as the principal character of the story.

The narrative begins with a scene that highlights the intersection between Truth's life and the life of a nation in crisis. At "seven o'clock on January 1, 1871," in

Tremont Temple in Boston, a "large crowd" gathered: "Though most of the people in the audience were white, they had come to celebrate a history-making event in black history." Most of these people were abolitionists, "well educated and wealthy, the cream of Boston's social elite."[70] Soon, a larger-than-life Truth takes the stage to testify about her early life in slavery. This scene then introduces Truth, portraying her as if she is telling her own story directly to the reader. Yet, when placed in context with the rest of the text, the scene functions as a way of introducing the historical context relevant to the text's creators (that is, New England reform movements). As the text proceeds, the narrative strongly suggests that the story of the "struggle for freedom" belongs not to Truth as an individual but to the people of the United States as a group. Familiar elements of American public memory from this period dominate the narrative: a benevolent and color-blind Abraham Lincoln, a generic history of opposition to injustices, the inevitable victory of the Union in the Civil War, and so on.[71] In this text, Truth's life functions primarily as a lens through which to view the lessons of American history.

Rather than rehearsing (white) American history, the biography about Shirley Chisholm written by the eminent African American historian and children's nonfiction author James Haskins ties her life to the fortunes of African Americans. Chisholm's history, in Haskins's hands, becomes a rendition of black history. Haskins's biography thus participates in a project similar to those of early black biographers in the 1920s. Haskins attended carefully to the racial dynamics of Chisholm's times, beginning his narrative by describing the "unprecedented prosperity" of the 1920s America into which his subject was born. The narrator does not leave readers at this generic level of historical insight but takes special note of how this prosperity affected blacks, especially those who were enticed to emigrate from the Caribbean.[72] This narrative discusses in detail the various West Indian neighborhoods in New York, explaining that immigrants like Chisholm's father, Charles St. Hill, had been attracted by opportunity and arrived in the United States "full of hope for a better life."[73] Notably, this text also discusses the social dynamics among black Americans and Afro-Caribbean immigrants, supplying a level of detail about certain prejudices that most other biographies ignore. For example, the narrator explains, "As a group, West Indians were much distrusted and disliked by American-born blacks, who called them 'pushy,' 'crafty,' 'clannish,' 'the Jews of the race.' When a West Indian 'got ten cents above a beggar,' a common American black saying ran, 'he opened a business.' Among West Indians the group regarded as most ambitious and pushy was the Barbadians. In other words, while buying a house and ensuring their children's education was the goal of all West Indians, for Barbadians it was an obsession."[74]

In addition to describing the histories of black communities, Haskins's narrative brings Chisholm into this history by providing an account of her developing race consciousness. This text explains the origins of Chisholm's own awareness of her race by describing the influence of Marcus Garvey on her father, who, the text reports, viewed Garvey as "a modern messiah who had been sacrificed to the cause of black pride and consciousness."[75] Over the next few pages, readers learn that Charles St. Hill taught Shirley and her sisters about politics and prejudice. He was said to have "instilled in them a strong racial consciousness," which Haskins's narrator is careful to point out "was a positive, not a negative consciousness."[76] Although race consciousness appears primary, this narrative also attends to Chisholm's development of a "feminist" and later a "political" consciousness through her reading about figures like Harriet Tubman and Susan B. Anthony.[77] This 1975 text presents "consciousness" as a sense of political awareness of one's individual position within a larger structure of power; as such, this concept links individual minds and lives such as Chisholm's with the movements of the day. Haskins rendered a rich picture of black life in New York City at the beginning of and throughout Chisholm's life, not merely to hold up an example of individual accomplishment but to situate that accomplishment within the trajectory of African American history.

These texts illustrate how underlying assumptions about historical significance shape biographical narratives. The variations among these texts reflect the variety of ideas circulating in American public culture about what makes an individual historically noteworthy. In texts that narrate the "history *of* a life," significance often depends upon the good moral character of an individual, which renders her a suitable exemplar. This approach also relies on a view of history as a repository of moral lessons that are to be learned and internalized by the younger generation. Texts that narrate "history *through* a life" follow a definition of historical significance that operates on a grander scale. In this telling, the lives of Wheatley, Truth, and Chisholm are not compelling merely for their own sakes but because they provide unique insight into a grander story of a nation, a particular period, or a specific group.

These texts exhibit other variations on the theme of historical significance. Many base implicit claims about historical significance on each woman's position as a historical "first." In the biographies of Wheatley, Truth, and Chisholm, these claims rely upon a combination of identity and accomplishment, which together place each woman at the germinal moment of some tradition, social change, or movement. In the case of Wheatley, texts highlight her position as the first published African American female poet. Typically, these statements focus on the publication of her collection of poetry in 1773, an accomplishment that is usually qualified by additional comments about her identity as an African American, a woman, or both. The opening statement of Clinton's *Phillis's Big Test* illustrates this common approach: "In 1773, Phillis Wheatley became the first African American to publish a book of poetry."[78] As the opening of Wheatley's story, this statement situates her within two transhistorical categories of people, African Americans and people who have published books of poetry. It does this while highlighting a specific critical moment in Wheatley's life. The arc of her life intersects with the tradition of people who have published collections of poetry, and it marks the entrance of African Americans into that category.

Judging by the texts, Truth's status as a "first" functions differently from Wheatley's position as the "mother of African-American literature."[79] Wheatley has come to be seen as the initiator of a literary tradition, but Truth occupies no such comparable position. But this fact does not prevent texts from basing claims of historical significance on Sojourner Truth's singular personality and her work as a black female public speaker. Most texts emphasize Truth's uniqueness by painting her as a kind of "force of nature."[80] Andrea Davis Pinkney and Brian Pinkney's 2009 picture book biography, *Sojourner Truth's Step-Stomp Stride,* provides a striking example of the "force of nature" characterization. The text opens by introducing a larger-than-life figure: "She was big. She was black. She was so beautiful. Her name was Sojourner. Truth be told, she was meant for great things. Meant for speaking. Meant for preaching. Meant for teaching the truth about freedom. Big. Black. Beautiful. True. That was Sojourner." The repetition of Truth's physical characteristics—all preceded by the adjective "big"—evokes the style of the tall tale, as in the story of Paul Bunyan and Babe the Blue Ox. Truth's blackness becomes an identifying characteristic that rendered her both a peculiarity during her time and an important figure in an American history traditionally dominated by the white and male. But her beauty is something not often commented upon by contemporaries. In fact, many contemporary reports—albeit tainted by racism—characterize her as a rather homely woman, even gaunt and frightening.[81] Most important, however, is the way that the texts link these characteristics to Truth's apparent destiny as a doer of great deeds. This brief introduction frames the text using the twin pillars of Truth's unique physical attributes and her historical significance.

Other texts published between 1949 and 2013 highlight Truth's unprecedented legal achievements as a means of classifying her as a "first." During her lifetime, Truth acted as plaintiff in at least three cases: one in 1828 against Solomon Gedney, who had illegally sold her son Peter to a slaveowner in Alabama; a civil case in 1835 against Ann and Benjamin Folger, who had maligned her reputation; and a final suit in the mid-1860s against a streetcar conductor who had injured her.[82] According to several texts that reference the 1828 case, that legal victory secured Truth's position as "the first African-American woman to win a lawsuit in the United States," "the first black woman in the United States to ever win a court case," and "one of the first African American women to ever win a court case."[83] Some texts amplify the historical significance of this action by drawing attention to the unequal power positions of plaintiff and defendant: one text specifies that Truth was "the first African American woman to win a court case *against a white man,*" and another calls her "one of the first black people ever to *fight a white person* in court in a country long governed by laws *favoring whites over blacks.*"[84] In each of these claims to historical preeminence, Truth's race and gender make her accomplishment particularly noteworthy. The few texts that attempt to claim the status of historical "first" for Truth on other bases rely on dubious generalizations or outright inaccuracies.[85] However, the presence of such claims, despite their contradicting the historical record, attests to the pride of place accorded to those first to mark certain achievements on behalf of their particular identity groups.

Biographies about Shirley Chisholm repeatedly highlight her role as a political "first" among black women. All of the texts examined at least mention the facts that in 1968 Chisholm became the first black woman to be elected to Congress and in 1972 became the first black woman to run a major-party campaign for president of the United States.[86] As such, these texts appear to have the most straightforward—even formulaic—case for their subject's historical significance.

In addition to linking these women's lives to pivotal events and historical changes, many of the texts emphasize their connections with other prominent figures. Connections with such individuals provide another point of intersection between each woman's personal narrative and the broader American historical narrative. More important, associations with famous individuals raise the profile of these lesser-known women and, in so doing, enhance the women's stature as historical figures. Because young readers may be less likely to know about these black women than about, say, George Washington, biographies about them must make a compelling case that their subjects are worthy of historical study. Thus, although the introduction of these women into historical education in the United States can expand young people's understanding of what qualifies as history, many of the texts must rely on children's assumed knowledge of canonical figures to establish a kind of significance by proxy.

For example, texts about the life of Phillis Wheatley feature a variety of famous people, almost all of them male.[87] Some texts highlight her connection to the English preacher George Whitefield and, through him, a connection with the Great Awakening. The elegy that Wheatley wrote for Whitefield in 1770 was said to have catapulted her to fame in the English-speaking Atlantic.[88] Several texts mention Wheatley's connection with Crispus Attucks, the only black man to die in the Boston Massacre.[89] Although these figures may be less well known than Paul Revere or Thomas Jefferson, their inclusion both bolsters Wheatley's profile and implies some degree of involvement in two movements that biographers suggest were central to her identity: religious fervor and African American patriotism.

The biographies develop the most extensive connections, however, between Phillis Wheatley and the Founding Fathers. The texts introduce these associations through two events in Wheatley's life story: her 1772 examination by eighteen of

Boston's leaders and her possible 1776 meeting with George Washington. Because the 1772 examination brought her into contact with several prominent men and paved the way for the publication of her book, many biographies highlight this event.[90] Although no record of the meeting exists, several texts describe Wheatley's performance as a rousing success.[91] Catherine Clinton and Robin Doak chose language similar to Henry Louis Gates's, saying that Wheatley passed "with flying colors."[92] Such texts interpret the event as a personal triumph over adversity, and some expand its importance as a symbol of collective triumph over ignorance. For example, Doak's narrator explains that, beyond proving Phillis's unique gifts, the statement from these prominent men "showed the people of Boston and other cities that they must rethink their ideas about blacks and their abilities."[93] As a well-known signatory to the Declaration of Independence, John Hancock is the most recognizable among this group of elite white men. Wheatley's connection to historical celebrities like Hancock both situates her within the familiar narrative of American independence and bolsters her position within that narrative. Thus, if Wheatley's literary abilities are not enough to convince readers of her historical significance, then these texts assume that the attention that she received from prominent individuals in a pivotal time will convince them. In narratives about events such as the examination, Wheatley's accomplishments are confirmed and amplified through the connections to prominent individuals like Washington and Hancock. To some extent, texts operate under the assumption that the relatively obscure, young, African American, and female Wheatley must be augmented by these associations with older, purportedly wiser, and more famous white men.

Among these supposedly superior beings was George Washington. Wheatley may have met Washington in 1776, when he was general of the colonial army, after she had composed a poem and sent it to him on the battlefield.[94] In some texts, Washington's assessment of Wheatley functions as a kind of argument from authority for her importance. For instance, a 2003 text by Rick Burke claims that when Washington finally discovered Wheatley's poem among his many papers, he read it and "loved" it. But this narrative does not stop at Washington's appreciation of Wheatley's hymn of praise; after all, what upwardly mobile military man would doubt the "great poetical talents" of a poet who had praised his valor in battle?[95] The text continues with a more definitive testimony to Wheatley's intellect: the slave-owning Washington "told others that he thought Phillis was a genius, or a very smart person."[96] Other texts highlight the particular significance of Wheatley's speculated audience with Washington, given her identity as a young black woman. In Susan Gregson's 2002 text, the narrator notes, "She was the only woman in the group of people who waited to see the general. She also was the only African American. Again, her poetry had helped her do something few people did."[97] Another narrator, citing an anonymous group of "scholars," observes that Washington's 1776 letter to Wheatley "might be the first time in [his] life that he addressed a Negro woman as 'Miss.'"[98] One text even claims that Wheatley's poem influenced Washington's military performance. The narrator of Doak's 2006 text speculates that Phillis's poem for General Washington may have "inspire[d] this great leader to victory."[99]

The majority of the texts at least mention Wheatley's meeting with Washington, and a few portray this scene as a crowning moment in Wheatley's life story.[100] Ann Malaspina's 2010 illustrated text, *Phillis Sings Out Freedom: The Story of George Washington and Phillis Wheatley,* focuses exclusively on the events surrounding Wheatley's decision to compose a poem for Washington. According to the narrator, Wheatley wrote to Washington as a way of doing her part to "help free the colonists."[101] Carol Greene's 1995 text takes a full five pages to narrate this meeting, which is described as an "important moment in Phillis Wheatley's life."[102] Also, in both the first version (1968) and the revised edition (2005) of Borland and Speicher's biography of Wheatley, the narrator emphasizes Washington's positive effect on Wheatley's emotional state during the meeting: "His smile and his voice seemed so warm that Phillis was no longer nervous. She felt at ease and talked freely, but realized that meeting this great man would be one of the most important things which would ever happen to her."[103] The surrounding narrative provides very little explanation about why this meeting carried such importance for Phillis Wheatley. What made her realize that this moment was so significant? Why did she think that Washington was so important? Wouldn't a meeting with King George III—planned during Wheatley's 1773 visit to England but later canceled—have been important as well? Shouldn't the publication of her own book be considered the most significant event? By attributing this "realization" to Wheatley rather than keeping it in the realm of the narrator, the text strongly suggests to readers that they should accept it as historical fact rather than as a judgment made by the text's creators. These creators possessed the benefit of hindsight, which enabled them to perceive and represent this meeting through centuries of American memory about the first president. In addition to bolstering Wheatley's significance through an association with Washington, an episode in which he praises the intellect of an African American woman represents the slave-owning Washington as more open-minded than he likely was.

Unlike the lesser known Wheatley, Sojourner Truth is arguably one of the two best-known African American women from the nineteenth century (the other being Harriet Tubman).[104] This position stems in part from Truth's long career of public speaking and activism, which brought her into contact with many well-known figures of her time. In fact, as several scholars note, Truth herself seemed to recognize that her associations with individuals like William Lloyd Garrison, Harriet Beecher Stowe, Frederick Douglass, and Abraham Lincoln could raise her public profile, thus increasing attendance at her speeches and enabling her to make a better living through sales of her *Narrative.* Therefore, she often acted quickly to take charge of the public knowledge of these interactions by fashioning and circulating her own versions of them.[105]

Although many biographies for children recount Truth's notorious rebuke of Douglass and some mention her meeting with Harriet Beecher Stowe, the author of *Uncle Tom's Cabin,* accounts of Truth's 1864 encounter with Lincoln best exemplify how association with famous personages functions to raise the profile of a marginal individual. Truth's meeting with Lincoln provides a particularly apt contrast with Wheatley's experience of meeting General George Washington. Wheatley's meeting—if it occurred at all—seems primarily to have been a private experience whose public implications were recognized only much later, whereas Truth's meeting with Lincoln was publicly reported by Truth herself soon after it occurred.[106] Because Wheatley's encounter with Washington cannot be verified, it must be presented as a private experience whose significance is judged either by the character Phillis Wheatley or by the creators of the biographical text.

In texts about Truth, the connection with Lincoln serves not only to justify her as a historical figure worth knowing about but also to portray her as a historical agent who possessed rhetorical power. She was not just someone who lived but someone who affected the course of history. The description of Truth's meeting with Lincoln in Peterson's 1972 biography follows this pattern. As other Truth biographers have done, Peterson devoted an entire chapter to this incident, titled "A Talk with President Lincoln," as if referring to a chat between old friends.[107] In the chapter just previous to this, readers learn that Truth's heart "overflowed with joy" when Lincoln issued the Emancipation Proclamation in 1863.[108] Peterson's narrator begins the next chapter by telling readers that, during this time, "Sojourner's thoughts turned to the problems of the newly freed black people," many of whom had settled in and around the District of Columbia. Specifically, she considered their plight and wondered if "the nation" would understand and respond to it. "The question came back to her over and over," the text explains. "One day in 1864 she made a decision. 'I'll go talk with President Lincoln.'"[109] As a black woman who had been enslaved, Truth would have likely thought of the challenges that other black people would experience upon emancipation. In this text, however, her thoughts about the problem and its solution move beyond individuals to consider structural issues. Rather than seeing the solution to the freed slaves' problems as an individual, private enterprise, Truth immediately shifts her thoughts to the public and national level. Continued consideration of the problem leads her to devise a somewhat grand solution: a "talk" with the president. This setup of the interview with Lincoln suggests that Truth thinks and acts on a historic level, transcending the spheres of influence to which she might ordinarily be confined. The account of the interview itself, which is paraphrased from Truth's own account of the meeting, suggests that she is justified in thinking such grand thoughts because her contemporaries recognize her as a person of stature and influence.[110] The narrator of this text uses certain elements of Truth's own version of the events in order to highlight her purported influence upon President Lincoln. The Peterson text exchanges the cordial banter of Truth's version for a more serious tone. For instance, after admiring the Bible presented to Lincoln by the black population of Baltimore, Truth dramatically makes an incisive observation: "she raised her eyes and looked directly at the president," then says, "'This government once sanctioned laws that would not permit my people to learn enough to enable them to read this book. And for what?' she protested. A look of sadness came over the president's face."[111] Although the dialogue follows Truth's version very closely, the verbs and descriptors in the passage turn this into a climactic scene emphasizing the efficacy of Truth's earnest persuasion. Truth's query "And for what?" becomes a "protest" that provokes the president to "sadness." He cannot change the past, but he can feel remorse for it. Although Truth's own version claims no such persuasive effect, in Peterson's story Truth becomes the kind of historically significant figure who can sway the emotions of presidents.

Because Shirley Chisholm was still living when many of these biographies were published, creators apparently needed fewer associations with famous white men to make the case for her historical significance. Four of the seven texts mention President Richard Nixon, though only one in order positively to highlight a meeting that Chisholm had with him.[112] The texts by Haskins and Scheader identify Nixon primarily as an individual who thwarted the plans of Chisholm and her congressional colleagues.[113] Gerald R. Ford, on the other hand, is assessed slightly more positively, appearing in photos with Chisholm after meeting with the Congressional Black Caucus or signing a bill to establish Women's Equality Day.[114] Whether praised or criticized, these presidents do not enter the narrative in order to render Chisholm more significant by association; they supply political background information. Most texts instead favor connections with figures like Martin Luther King Jr., Malcolm X, or black women role models such as Harriet Tubman. In these biographies, reference to such figures serves less to provide significance by proxy and more to demonstrate the importance of Chisholm's contributions to African American history. For example, Brownmiller's text cites Chisholm's efforts to pass a bill to establish King's birthday as a national holiday, a cause to which she "gladly lent her name."[115] The name "Shirley Chisholm" became well known after her 1972 presidential bid, so texts published in the 1970s would not have depended on associations with more famous individuals to make an argument for Chisholm's significance. The creators of texts published after the 1970s but before Chisholm's death in 2005, such as Scheader and Jackson, would have been able to speak with their subject directly or simply rely on reminding readers of her role as a dual historical "first."

The emphasis on associations that Phillis Wheatley and Sojourner Truth had with famous contemporaries provides an argument for the historical significance of the two women. Creators of texts about Shirley Chisholm, in contrast, emphasized her interactions with prominent individuals but relied primarily on her own active political presence or historical proximity to readers. In all three cases, stories are based on the cultural premise that biographies of the agents of the past must also be intelligible as the life stories of historically significant individuals. That is, these biographies for children often imply that we remember their subjects today because of the impression they made on (in Wheatley's case), influence they had on (in Truth's case), or proximity to (in Chisholm's case) other famous people of their time.[116] Yet most texts go beyond this by implying or directly stating why each woman is worthy of a biography and, more important, of readers' sustained attention. The ways in which the texts contextualize these women reveal that the perceived agency of an individual directly affects the formulation of public memory about that person.

As a genre, biography is built upon the assumption that stories of individual lives can humanize, enliven, and enhance historical understanding. Although this assumption has been criticized by some scholars, biographies as individual life stories remain an important tool for librarians and educators trying to teach young people about the past.[117] The robust market for biographies for children, moreover, suggests that popular enthusiasm for these texts remains high and that their underlying messages remain resonant. In part, the persistence of the public memories formulated by these texts depends upon their ability to articulate the life stories of Wheatley, Truth, and Chisholm within the larger narrative of American values and Western notions of historical significance. Different juvenile biographies about each of these three women all begin, presumably, with the same "chronicle" of facts about their subjects. These facts are derived primarily from these women's actions, which left their mark on the historical record. Prefigured by the cultural context in which they are produced, the narratives reconstruct these facts to provide a sketch of the agent who acted in history. Yet even the seemingly simple assemblage of facts requires another agent or group of agents, who by selecting, combining, and contextualizing are always also interpreting.

CHAPTER FIVE

CONFIGURATION

The Agent Writing History

> Biography . . . is not a matter of flinging all the facts onto sheets of paper. You are not a grocer tossing potatoes into a sack to make up ten pounds. One fact is not the same as all other facts. Some are more important: they weigh more, they mean more, they suggest more, they reveal more. You need to select from that mass of facts, and to place them in a certain order.
>
> Milton Meltzer,
> "Notes on Biography"

> This is the story of Sojourner Truth as I understand it.
>
> Jacqueline Bernard,
> *Journey toward Freedom: The Story of Sojourner Truth*

All texts hoping to gain traction within a particular culture must address themselves to the commonplaces shared by that culture. While teachers, librarians, parents, caretakers, and children are more likely to choose biographies that rely on familiar conventions, they may also find some manifestations of these conventions to be more compelling than others. Recognizing this fact, publishers continue to produce biographies for children as new information emerges, memories of an individual shift, contemporary concerns change, and new audiences appear. Creators of biographies therefore can become a critical point of articulation between the old and the new.

Paul Ricoeur would call these creators the "pivot" of this analysis. In *Time and Narrative* Ricoeur called mimesis$_2$ the "pivot" of the process of emplotting narratives meaningfully in time. By describing mimesis$_2$ in this way, Ricoeur emphasized its mediating function: in order for a narrative prefigured in mimesis$_1$ to be refigured by a reader in mimesis$_3$, it must undergo a kind of alchemy that recuperates the same old stories of public opinion into potentially new stories about the possibilities of future action. In order to generate such possibilities—to enter the "kingdom of the *as if*"—a narrative must be configured for optimal translation. This configuration phase features an "interplay of innovation and sedimentation" that ensures that the resulting narrative will be not simply a reproduction of the culture in which it was constructed but rather a singular work that presents resources for future action, whether literary or political.[1] If the prefiguration of mimesis$_1$ highlights the similarities among historical narratives shaped by the same cultural context and historical subject, then the configuration of mimesis$_2$ highlights the remarkable variety within this same body of texts. Or, to focus on the significant agent, mimesis$_1$ prefigures the field of action in which the historical agent exists, whereas mimesis$_2$ features the configuring choices, self-conscious and otherwise, of the agent who writes history.

The moment of configuration occurs uniquely within each individual work, as guided by the interpretive capacities and productive imagination of an individual agent or group of agents who become the creators of the text. In this chapter, I examine the variety of ways in which the agent(s) writing history configure the agency, relationships, and temporality of their historical subjects within the confines of the text. Some creators explicitly draw attention to these choices in their texts. Some simply execute their conscious choices in ways that leave implicit marks on the texts. Still others may not be fully aware of their interpretive role, yet their texts nonetheless also bear the marks of rhetorical selection and arrangement.[2]

In constructing a text about Phillis Wheatley, Sojourner Truth, or Shirley Chisholm, creators begin with a series of facts about the life of the historical figure. These facts anchor the narrative, yet they also allow for an inventional range that in turn produces many different versions of the same life story. Creators thus participate in a fundamentally rhetorical process of invention, in which they use old ideas or facts in new ways. This invention is neither simple fabrication nor basic rearrangement. As Debra Hawhee aptly described it, such invention is "an action that happens in the thick of things." "This mode of invention," she continued, "is not a beginning, as the first canon [of rhetoric] is often articulated, but a middle, an in-between, a simultaneously interruptive and connective hooking-in to circulating discourses."[3] Creators work between commonplaces and contemporary circumstances in order to configure their texts. I focus here on how creators act upon these stories by selecting, interpreting, combining, and arranging information about the lives of their subjects into cohesive narratives. The choices of these creators, in turn, configure Wheatley, Truth, and Chisholm as intelligible, compelling agents. Moreover, an examination of the unique configuration of agency in each individual text, layered upon the field of action as prefigured by *doxa,* shows how these texts function not only to reinforce existing values but also to provide resources for future agents to take new, innovative action.

Ricoeur's description of mimesis$_2$ highlights the "mediating function" of configuration. Ricoeur identified three ways in which this mediating function operates in the configuration of narratives. First, configuration mediates between the individual event and the story as a whole, by assigning an event a place of significance in the unfolding of a plot. Second, it joins and relates disparate aspects of the story, including various agents, actions, motivations, and outcomes. Third, it links the temporality of the story to deeper understandings of time as linear, periodic, cyclic, and so forth. This temporal mediation affects the potential interpretations of the narrative, and it has the capacity to change those deeper understandings of time as well.

Reflections on Interpretive Agency

How do creators perceive their own contributions to the process of configuration? Do authors, illustrators, or editors draw attention to these contributions so that young readers will perceive an interpretive agency at work in the text? In this section, I concentrate on how the creators of biographies about Wheatley, Truth, and Chisholm address their own role as agents who configure data from the past into narratives. While some creators draw explicit attention to their role in this process and others simply communicate the uncertainty of historical understanding, texts that foreground the choices and intentions of those people who have shaped the history being passed to young readers subtly suggest that these readers too may someday become a part of this process. If children and young people see the construction of the past as less mysterious, less the sole territory of adults, it is possible that they may envision a world in which they could someday become the interpreters and shapers of their own history. What Sara L. Schwebel concluded about historical fiction is also true of biography: "When students are empowered to understand historical fiction—like all history—as narrative construction, they can engage in debate about how the past has been represented."[4]

Among those creators who reflected upon their own inventional process, most did so by explaining their reasons for choosing these women as biographical subjects. These reasons, in turn, are connected to specific decisions to emphasize certain characteristics, achievements, or experiences of each woman. Creators articulated different purposes for crafting their texts, but all grounded those purposes in the appeal of the life of the individual woman. Creators discussed either the appeal they believe that their subject holds as a model for young readers or the personal attraction their subject holds for them as an author. Such commentary differs subtly from that provided by the creators of biographical sketches in the 1920s. Whereas creators such as Hallie Quinn Brown, W. E. B. Du Bois, Jessie Fauset, and Elizabeth Ross Haynes specifically identified black children as their audience for biographical sketches, creators of texts of the mid-twentieth through the early twenty-first centuries attempted to appeal to readers from a variety of racial and ethnic backgrounds. Texts published after the 1950s typically explain their focus on certain characteristics by framing their subjects as models for action. Other creators represented their choices as individual responses to the inherently compelling story of Wheatley, Truth, or Chisholm.[5] Most comments about textual choices appear as peritext—an author's note, a preface, or a blurb describing the individual book or the series of which it is a part.

Fictionalized biographies by Ida Bellegarde (1983), Jacqueline Bernard (1967), and Shirley Graham (1949) frame their texts by describing their subjects as models or sources of inspiration. Notably, the authors of these biographies had commitments either to African American communities or to racial justice more generally. Bernard's *Journey toward Freedom* provides an example of a text that loosely connects Truth's personal character to the civil rights movement of the 1950s and 1960s. In her preface, Bernard described her own discovery of Sojourner Truth in the archives. Her discovery was soon followed by a realization of her desire to tell Truth's story in a book for young people, in order "to make sure that they had a chance to hear something about this kind of American woman."[6] According to Bernard, "this kind of American woman" is stubborn, courageous, and strong. She struggles not only to "teach herself" but also to "help free others."[7] After describing Truth and her life of noble struggle, Bernard shifted her focus to the present, observing, "Today, many young and old Americans are waging a similar personal struggle—and continuing her journey toward freedom for all Americans." Although Bernard did not spell out her purpose, these comments frame the subsequent text in a way that reveals it: to provide a model or inspiration for those in the present who are in the midst of a struggle. Thus, by dwelling upon particular characteristics of Truth in this preface, Bernard framed the remaining text as a story of one historical agent's struggle and perseverance.[8]

Commentary framing books published as part of a series in the 1990s and 2000s tends to emphasize common public virtues selected by publishers or editors.[9] For instance, the description of the series People Who Have Helped the World, which appears on the back cover of each of its texts, serves as a statement of purpose for Susan Taylor-Boyd's 1990 biography of Truth. According to this description, the books in this series tell the stories of "the lives of extraordinary people who often had the most ordinary beginnings." The description continues: "Living or dead, they all have something in common—each has held strong beliefs and each has acted on these beliefs with courage and commitment. By example, biographies promote both self-confidence and expectations for one's own life. Each book serves these two important purposes, giving special emphasis to the person's early years, to events that molded the person's character, and to the person behind the headlines and history books."[10] This commentary characterizes the subject and the objective of these books and draws attention to interpretive choices that enable each book to achieve its goal. First of all, the subjects of these texts have been carefully selected according to certain characteristics such as "strong beliefs" and action marked by "courage and commitment." Furthermore, the creators of these texts chose to focus on the purportedly formative early years of each individual's life, selecting certain events as catalysts for the development of character. Consonant with these themes, Taylor-Boyd's book marks many events of Truth's early life, including her being sold away from the Hardenberghs and her own family, as an anticipation of her later courage and commitment.[11]

Likewise, the texts in the Americans All series select "highlights" from each individual's story, which are chosen to demonstrate his or her "contributions" to a "special field."[12] To better illustrate determination and hard work, "specific abilities, character, and accomplishments are emphasized" within each story. All of these choices, the editors explained, work together to provide a "better understanding of the ingredients necessary for personal success." This description indicates that the creators of the *Americans All* biographies envisioned their books as providing what they imagined to be widely accessible models for young readers.[13]

Other books, such as two texts about Shirley Chisholm, work to negotiate between the subject's enactment of "American" values and her commitments to improving the lives of more specific groups of people. The biographies written by James Haskins and Garnet Nelson Jackson highlight Chisholm's notable work on behalf of African Americans, women, and the working class while also situating such effort in the discourse of "American" values such as fairness, self-respect, integrity, and courage.[14] Haskins began his 1975 text by acknowledging Chisholm's generosity in providing information for the biography. He continued, "Shirley Chisholm cares not only about racial minorities and women and the disillusioned and the poor in America, but also about America's young people."[15] This articulation reinforces the publisher's claim on the book blurb that Chisholm "fills a unique role as a spokesperson for the cause of Blacks, women, and the poor and powerless everywhere."[16] In a similar fashion, Jackson opened her text with a letter to her early readers about her hopes for this book about a "great American." Jackson explained that Chisholm was taught lessons of self-respect as a young child, so that "when she grew up, she spoke out against unfairness, so that all African Americans and women, children, and the poor of all races could also have self-respect."[17] In outlining their purposes, both Haskins and Jackson carefully negotiated between characteristics that might make Chisholm widely appealing and her unique contributions to the welfare of specific groups. Because they were not beholden to the constraints of "series thinking," these creators had greater freedom to frame their narratives in a complex fashion. The careful negotiation of mainstream values and more particular commitments could also be attributed to the role of the authors, both African Americans who are also established biographers and authors for children.[18]

Other creators have explained their choice of subject through personal narrative. For instance, the author and the illustrator of the 2003 *A Voice of Her Own: The Story of Phillis Wheatley, Slave Poet,* told readers that they found the story of Phillis Wheatley appealing on a personal level. Author Kathryn Lasky explained in her author's note at the end of the book that she was "drawn to the story of Phillis Wheatley because I felt it was not simply the story of an illiterate slave girl who became a poet, but rather a story about voice and the relationship between voice, identity, and freedom."[19] Lasky's author's note highlights voice as the guiding metaphor for Wheatley's agency. This metaphor, as Eric King Watts has argued, "localizes" rhetorical agency in the individual speaker, who possesses agency as a capacity to express identity.[20] Lasky's narrative constructs attempts to communicate the author's initial attraction to the story by highlighting Wheatley's search for her own voice through education and the writing of poetry. Likewise, illustrator Paul Lee declared that he was "inspired by the story of Phillis Wheatley because it is a story of America." Why is this "a story of America"? Because its central character "overcame" incredible hardships, challenged established norms, and, most important, "proved to everyone around her that all things are possible if you work for them, and that with freedom, any goal can be accomplished." The rationales both Lasky and Lee provide for choosing Wheatley begin with their emotional connection with her. They attempt to generalize the connection within "American" values such as freedom and hard work rather than emphasizing any particular aspects of Wheatley's identity. This is particularly evident in Lasky's note, which expressly draws parallels between slavery and "every other form of oppression" and states that oppression diminishes all human beings "not simply as a race but as members of a species."[21] While the particularities of Wheatley's identity are not completely ignored, they are downplayed in favor of commonalities. Notes such as these suggest that creators of texts published around 2000 were more likely than earlier authors to explain their choice of subject and, occasionally, interpretive decisions by describing their having been inspired or moved by an individual's story. Another possible explanation is that, because the authors who engaged in this practice were not African Americans, they were more likely either to think individualistically about their connection to the past or to feel somehow compelled to make these black women's stories "relatable" to young readers who were made in the author's image.[22]

Let's Begin at the Very Beginning: Configuring Event and Story

These comments suggest that some texts include a degree of self-conscious agency by the creators of juvenile biographies. However, whether explicitly reflexive or not, the creators of these texts are part of the "mediating function" that Ricoeur ascribes to mimesis$_2$.[23] The first part of this function involves mediation between "individual events or incidents and a story taken as a whole."[24] In constructing its narrative from a series of events in the life of Wheatley, Truth, or Chisholm, each biographical text highlights certain events as significant to public memory and constitutive of its subject's agency.

The majority of these biographies, regardless of the period in which they were published, follow a basic chronological structure, bounded by the beginning and ending of a person's physical life—birth, childhood, growth, lifework, and death. In this sense, the narratives follow what William H. Epstein called the "natural attitude" toward the life as a text.[25] Although nearly all texts follow this "natural" order through the central sections of the narrative, several texts deviate from this chronological structure in order to initiate the story of Wheatley, Truth, or Chisholm. These texts use a vivid opening scene from another period in the subject's life, establishing a dramatic and powerful context through which to draw readers into the story. And although these choices may be driven by certain assumptions about the young audience—say, that children crave action and excitement—they nonetheless also possess the potential to frame that audience's perception of the subsequent narrative. This textual choice frames the subject and her story by placing a particular event in a new relationship with the narrative, thereby guiding interpretation of the subsequent narrative. While the selection of the opening scene is not the only configurational choice that links events and narrative, it serves as a powerful framing device that exemplifies the mediating function of mimesis$_2$.

Because the details of Phillis Wheatley's birth and childhood in West Africa are largely unknown, most biographies begin with her arrival and sale at the Boston slave market in July 1761.[26] This event, of course, commences the historically available story of Wheatley's life. Yet it also introduces the narrative as one primarily about slavery and freedom, about Wheatley's overcoming her initial hardships upon her arrival in the American colonies. Many of these opening scenes provide detailed descriptions of Wheatley's appearance in the market. When the young African girl arrived in the Boston slave market, her only clothing was said to have been a small piece of carpet, which the biographies often describe as "dirty."[27] This seemingly insignificant detail is by far the most common element of the narratives offered in the juvenile biographies. The opening event, brought into focus by the detail of the dirty scrap of carpet, shapes Wheatley's character and thereby configures the remainder of the narrative: she is a foreigner who uses rugs improperly, she is a child in need of care, she is a modest person who takes care to cover herself when necessary. This instance illustrates how the selection of even the most minor piece of evidence can affect the unfolding of a text.

A number of texts about Wheatley begin their narratives with the journey across the Middle Passage. Some creators used historical evidence to help their readers understand the journey, and others simply imagined what her experience might have been like.[28] This choice of opening event can shape the narrative in a variety of ways, depending on how the text describes Wheatley's experience. For instance, texts by Carol Greene and Kathryn Lasky use the sea voyage as a backdrop for the young girl's own memories of her mother in Africa. Greene's text begins with a vivid imagined description of Wheatley's journey. After the first two paragraphs, the narrative shifts into a more general description of the Middle Passage. Then the narrator turns back to Wheatley: "The little girl could not remember what happened before she came to the ship. Only one picture of her old life still lived in her mind." The narrator then fashions an image of the girl's mother, who is figuratively associated with the morning sun. The "golden picture" of her mother is said to sustain the young girl through the "awful darkness" of her journey.[29] Wheatley's recollection of her mother pouring a gourd of water under the morning sun is the only memory of her life in Africa that left its traces on the archives. Therefore, biographers must draw on this memory if they intend to use the historical record to describe Wheatley's life before enslavement. Sparse though it is, this detail enables creators to gesture toward their subject's African origins and to emphasize the injustice of taking a child from her mother.

A smaller number of texts—most published after 2000—select an opening event based on one of Wheatley's accomplishments, such as her 1772 examination by eighteen Boston men or her 1773 trip to England.[30] Creators used these events to frame the subsequent narrative as a story of achievement and distinction. A subtle difference exists between these opening scenes and those that recount an event central to Wheatley's experience as a slave. The latter texts attempt to paint Wheatley primarily as a survivor of slavery who, although powerfully constrained by her enslavement, overcame great hardship. Many of the texts featuring an opening scene linked to Wheatley's enslavement even imply that those experiences refined her character in ways that prepared her for greatness. The former approach, in contrast, makes Wheatley's enslavement part of the background that may have shaped her as an individual but was not the dominant force in her life. These texts focus primarily on Wheatley's poetic talents as the ultimate manifestation of her agency and the representative element of her life story.

Biographies of Sojourner Truth manifest similar choices. The most common selection for the opening of these narratives is Isabella's birth around 1797. However, as in the biographies of Wheatley, several creators chose an event that highlighted Isabella's beginnings in slavery: her first sale, at the age of about nine, away from her family and the household of her birth.[31] Julian May's 1973 biography, for example, highlights the lack of control that Belle and her parents had over their lives as enslaved people. The death of their master, Charles Hardenbergh, leads to the division of his property, which includes Belle's family. Despite Belle's pleading, her parents cannot prevent her being sold away to John Neely. At their parting, her parents offer this advice to Belle as a substitute for their continued presence: "Remember to obey and work hard" and "pray to God."[32] Like the texts that feature Wheatley's arrival at the Boston slave market, these biographies of Truth frame a story of slavery, freedom, and the overcoming of hardship and premature separation from one's family.

Several stories about Truth also begin with an event that exemplified her personal achievements later in life. Some, for instance, describe a well-known speech such as the 1851 Akron address or an 1871 address at Tremont Temple in Boston. Biographies such as those by Edward Beecher Claflin and Katherine Krohn frame Truth's life as a story characterized and punctuated by memorable public performances that demonstrated her speaking power and her potential to catalyze social change.[33] The creators narrated these events as if from within the perspective of Truth's contemporaries, yet their descriptions also exploit the benefits of hindsight, as they introduce their subject as being "like a queen" or as "the famous woman who had fought slavery and battled for constitutional equality and women's rights."[34] Indeed, in Claflin's book, the crowd at Tremont Temple already apparently perceived Truth's eventual impact on history, as they are said to have come "to celebrate a history-making event in black history."[35] Narrators claim to see the effects of Truth's speech upon her audience, who were clearly "moved."[36]

Other texts select a different incident to celebrate Truth's lifelong activism: her experiences riding on Washington, D.C., streetcars. Both Jennifer Blizin Gillis and Susan Taylor-Boyd began with anecdotes in which Truth defied conductors and fellow riders who did not want racial mixing on public transit.[37] As Gillis's narrator tells it through Truth's words, this is a story about how Truth knew her own "rights."[38] Taylor-Boyd's narrator adds interpretive commentary to the anecdote of resistance, saying, "The conductors often refused to stop for African-Americans. But this black woman, Sojourner Truth, had been demanding all her life to ride with the rest of humanity. She called for blacks to be freed from slavery, she demanded that all women be considered equal to men, she expected everyone in the nation to have all the rights of citizenship. Now this streetcar refused to stop because she was black. She'd have none of that."[39] This framework organizes the remainder of Taylor-Boyd's biography, which persistently reads Truth's life through the history of civil rights, in the United States and beyond.

Opening scenes in biographies about Chisholm exhibit similar variety, with the most common story being Chisholm's early years in Barbados. Unlike the stories of Wheatley and Truth, however, many authors had direct access either to the memories of Chisholm herself or to the extensive archival information about her life. While such resources provide more material for the narratives, they also limit the possibilities for what can be reasonably invented about Chisholm's life. Three texts begin by describing Chisholm's years on her grandmother's farm in Barbados as a time of educational opportunity and character development for young Shirley.[40] Although the texts acknowledge Shirley's feelings when she was leaving her parents in New York, they depict her as having a positive perspective on her island home. The entire first chapter of Brownmiller's 1970 biography, for instance, focuses on Barbados. The text begins by telling readers how its subject felt about her home: "Shirley loved her grandmother, and she loved the farm. She couldn't imagine any other kind of life."[41] Jackson's 1994 text notes that, while the boat trip made four-year-old Shirley "seasick," she "was happy when they finally reached the farm."[42] Opposite a photo of a lush green landscape, Pollack's 1994 text begins, "Barbados, a small, rocky island in the Caribbean, was a place of love and learning for Shirley St. Hill during her years on her grandmother's farm."[43] These texts note the affection Shirley had for this place, the education she obtained from the island schools, and the caring discipline she received from her grandmother. Significantly, all three texts explain that Shirley's time in Barbados was the result of her parents' decision to give their daughters a better life by working to save for their education or by giving them a childhood home with "room to run and play."[44] Here, Shirley's childhood home becomes the idyllic incubator of her own leadership qualities, as well as evidence of the self-sacrificing character of her parents and extended family. As opening anecdotes, such depictions frame the subsequent narratives as stories about the development of these qualities in Shirley Chisholm.

The most striking biographies begin with an event that structures the subsequent life narrative. These events shape the general approach and basic intelligibility of the narrative, as Ricoeur explained in *Time and Narrative.* Because the events feature the actions of the central character, they also have the potential to shape the perception of that character's agency. Texts about Wheatley and Truth depict these women as the young, often helpless victims of chattel slavery, whose lives are controlled by capricious owners and economic pressures. The experience of being sold as a slave acquaints each woman intimately with this reality and, by some tellings, prepares her for the future growth that will enable her to do Great Things. Although not subjected to the horrors of slavery, young Shirley experienced the effects of race prejudice, which made it difficult for black people like her parents to find jobs. Such challenges led to Shirley's separation from her parents for the first several years of her life—an event that young readers are invited to see as a hardship.[45] Texts orient readers toward stories of resistance to oppression, of overcoming adversity through determination, persistence, and talent. In other texts, events exemplifying notable accomplishments or historical interventions configure the narratives. Opening with Wheatley's "test" or her trip to London, Truth's most famous speech or her protests of segregation, or a description of a self-possessed adult Chisholm introduces characters at the height of their agency and gives the impression that these women were already great agents even before their stories began.

Configuring Agents and Actions

In addition to configuring certain events within the arc of the story, mimesis$_2$ mediates between prefiguration and refiguration by bringing together other factors "as heterogeneous as agents, goals, means, interactions, circumstances, unexpected results."[46] Each text takes the data of the archive, which are in large part prefigured by certain cultural assumptions about agency and the makings of public memory, and combines them in ways that have the potential subtly to alter those assumptions. The biographies configure specific individuals, actions, and outcomes in ways that influence the representation of Wheatley, Truth, and Chisholm as historical agents. These biographies configure a prominent series of events in each woman's life. These representative events are typically deemed significant, if not pivotal, to each woman's story, and they feature the actions of other important characters that often appear to block, enhance, or somehow modify the agency attributed to Wheatley, Truth, or Chisholm.

In the story of Wheatley, I examine the various accounts of how her collection of poetry came to be published in England in 1773. In the tale of Truth, I consider the anecdote of how Isabella became Sojourner Truth in 1843. Because the historical record offers only meager details of these episodes, the creators of these biographies must bring to bear more of their interpretive powers. In the story of Chisholm, I explore reports of how she became the first African American woman elected to the United States Congress in 1968. The creators began with documented and verifiable outcomes: Wheatley's text was published, Truth's name was changed, and Chisholm was elected. But the texts provide widely varying explanations for these key events. Was each woman the self-conscious, self-possessed originator of the action that resulted in the documented outcome? Or were these results achieved almost in spite of the central characters' actions? Who else is said to have been involved in these incidents, and how is their involvement represented?

The story of how Phillis Wheatley came to be the first published African American poet is central to her biography; it is her gateway to historical significance. The historical record confirms several facts about how this book of poetry came to be: it was published by the London printer Archibald Bell in 1773; dedicated to Selina Hastings, Countess of Huntingdon; and prefaced by an "affidavit" in which eighteen Boston men expressed their opinion that Phillis Wheatley had authored its poems. The original printing of the collection then circulated across the English-speaking Atlantic. Wheatley wrote the poems, but several other individuals from the American colonies and from England contributed to their ultimate publication.[47]

Biographies about Wheatley link individual agents to their own actions, to one another, and to the outcomes in ways that influence the representation of Wheatley's agency. Some texts barely mention the publication of Wheatley's book, while others spin a complex tale of how Wheatley's individual poetic achievements combined with the desires of others to produce a confluence of circumstances that led to publication.[48] For the most part, these accounts do not represent the exercise of agency as a zero-sum game where the power of Wheatley's white owners or the male-dominated publishing business simply cancels the poet's own capacity to act. Rather, many accounts exhibit an intricate combination of historical context, the individual talent of Wheatley, and the exploitation of privilege, usually that of the Wheatley family or members of the British aristocracy. These texts thus balance, in varying degrees, the agency of the individual and the collective, the action and its context.[49] Even in those texts that almost completely separate Wheatley's own desires and actions from the relevant outcome—the publication of her book—the narrative choices serve to develop her character. These texts exchange an emphasis on individual, self-determined action by Wheatley for an emphasis on the modesty, obedience, and selflessness that the creators seem to consider the marks of a humble genius such as Phillis Wheatley.

For instance, in several texts published before the mid-1970s, Phillis Wheatley is "surprised" by another character who has taken it upon herself to compile and print the collection of poetry.[50] Texts by Lucille Arcola Chambers, Margaret Fuller, and Shirley Graham describe Mary Lathrop (née Wheatley) as the feisty instigator of a secret plan to publish Wheatley's poetry. The narrator of the Chambers text, which appears to have been adapted from Graham's 1949 book, describes the scene: "One day Mrs. Lathrop surprised Phillis. She took a big roll of papers from her purse. She told Phillis that she had written enough poems for a book. 'For a book!' shouted Phillis. 'Women do not write books!' Mrs. Lathrop laughed. She said, 'I am taking them to a publisher who knows our family.'"[51] Mary Lathrop then brings the poems to the publisher, who assumes that she wrote them. When she corrects his mistake, the publisher thinks she is joking and becomes angry at her for wasting his time. Mary Lathrop leaves the publisher's office in a huff, determined to prove him wrong by completing the project. In this version, the narrator paints Mary Lathrop as the agent who has the privilege and determination, even arrogance, necessary to accomplish this unlikely task. Wheatley, meanwhile, remains a "proper," passive, modest black woman who makes no assumptions about her own importance and has few aspirations for her work. Although Wheatley forfeits what twenty-first-century readers might consider agency, she gains qualities of character that, in certain contexts, may have won her more power over her own life.

In other texts that feature the agency of another character over Wheatley's, the actions seem arranged not to preserve Wheatley's modesty but to clarify the possible motivations of those other characters. Several texts, for instance, cite Susanna Wheatley's determination to have Phillis's poems published in a book. The narrators explain Susanna's motivation by saying that she was "pleased with the popularity of Phillis's poems" or that she generously "wanted more than just the people of Boston to experience Phillis's poetry."[52] The poet complies with the desires of the Wheatley family and the Countess of Huntingdon, as she proves her poetic capabilities to learned men or attends garden parties in her honor. In many cases, Phillis Wheatley seems carried along by the actions of others, neither protesting nor consenting.

Many texts, most published around or after 2000, favor a more complex narrative, which incorporates the actions of several characters, including Phillis Wheatley, Susanna and John Wheatley and their children, the publisher Archibald Bell, the eighteen examiners, and the Countess of Huntingdon. Each of these characters plays a role in the drama of publication, which unfolds against the backdrop of late eighteenth-century Boston and London. Often, Phillis Wheatley's elegy for the famous British preacher George Whitefield becomes the catalyst for the ensuing activities. Carol Greene's narrator explains that Wheatley's poem about Whitefield made her "one of the best poets in America." It is at this point that "Mrs. Wheatley put some of Phillis's poems together."[53] Not all narratives identify a particular starting point for the process of publication. Some, such as Deborah Kent's 2004 text, simply suggest publication as the logical next step in Wheatley's poetic career: once she had written "enough poems to fill a small book . . . the Wheatleys thought her work should be published."[54] As the process unfolds, other agents become involved, including the people of Boston, who are said to have "argued" about whether the poet was an "imposter" or "a highly talented young woman with a splendid education."[55] Susanna and John Wheatley look for printing houses but are denied because the publishers "simply didn't believe that a slave girl could write such fine poems" or because "Boston was not yet ready to accept a black female poet."[56] The Wheatleys are obliged to assemble influential friends, in the colonies and across the Atlantic.[57] And in some cases, Phillis takes up her own case by sending her Whitefield elegy to the Countess of Huntingdon.[58] In such interpretations, the story becomes a tale about the struggle of conflicting desires and ideas that emerged around the figure of Wheatley and her book of poetry. These texts configure the "agents, actions, and outcomes" as a kind of network, whose power is activated at several "nodes," the most significant of which is Phillis Wheatley herself.

At least three texts published after 2000 configure these elements in a way that represents Wheatley's agency as the exercise of her expressive voice.[59] In *Phillis's Big Test,* for example, Clinton's narrative puts Phillis Wheatley at the center of her own story. According to the narrator, Wheatley "did not know why she had been brought from Africa to Boston," yet she acts decisively in the present. "She knew that she must now make the most of her opportunities," the narrator declares. "She must make her voice heard." For Wheatley, the narrator explains, this means having a book published: "She wanted her own book because books would not last just a lifetime; they would be there for her children and her children's children."[60] This Phillis Wheatley knows what she wants, and she knows how to achieve it. Likewise, Kathryn Lasky's Phillis Wheatley was "no ordinary young girl." Rather, she was a great talent with "an intense desire to learn." The Wheatley family, recognizing this talent, "encouraged her in this passion." But the poet herself sparks the engine that drives her toward the resulting achievements: "She became a poet, and had a book of verse published. With the publication of this book, Phillis Wheatley established herself as the first black woman poet America had ever known. She also found what had been taken away from her and from slaves everywhere: a voice of her own."[61] Although equipped and encouraged by the Wheatley family, Phillis used her own voice to move the process. Similarly, in Ann Malaspina's 2010 biography, Wheatley's poetry becomes the primary expression of agency, particularly when Wheatley is faced with her growing desire to "help free the colonists." Noting that "all she had was her pen," this narrative explains that Wheatley contributed to the colonists' cause by writing a poem for General George Washington. The text concludes by celebrating the Continental Army's first victory in Boston in 1776, then wraps up Wheatley's role in the story: "And with her poems, Phillis Wheatley sang out freedom—for herself and a new nation."[62] These three texts—all written by white women who were either established children's writers or academic historians or both, none published in a series—portray agency as voice, a common contemporary trope for agency. By figuring agency as voice, these texts link Wheatley's action back to her individual identity and focus on her use of speech rather than its effects on others, which becomes an advantage for creators who must establish the influence of their subjects without sufficient historical evidence. More problematically, as Jodi Melamed's work has shown, the trope of voice represents Wheatley's agency as a possession or skill that she used to express her identity and pursue recognition from the dominant society. Or, as Melamed has explained, the voice trope functions as one of the "permissible narratives of difference" within "race-liberal orders," representing racial difference in ways that are intelligible to readers raised in a white liberal society.[63] For this reason, it seems not to be a coincidence that these three texts were created by white women acting within the kind of liberal order Melamed described.

Scholars agree that the 1773 publication of Phillis Wheatley's first and only collection of verse constituted her dramatic entrance into American literary history.[64] Although she achieved fame through her poetry prior to 1773, this event marked her as the first African American to publish a book of verse. Without the publication of her book, it is possible that Wheatley would have receded from American public memory even more than she has. Likewise, without her memorable name, the woman who became Sojourner Truth might not have had as much staying power in public memory. In this sense, the name itself also operates as a site of memory, as a *lieu de mémoire*.[65] Isabella's choice to change her name went hand in hand with her decision to travel as an itinerant speaker, the role for which she is most famous. Having been "called by the Spirit," Isabella departed from New York City in 1843 with a new name: Sojourner Truth. She traveled east on a religious mission to exhort the people "to embrace Jesus, and refrain from sin."[66] Despite its rather brief appearance in the *Narrative,* the story of Truth's name change is one of the most consistently told and reinterpreted narratives about her life, which makes the historical event an important site of memory production.[67]

Few other human characters participate in this event, but Truth includes a divine agent in her *Narrative.* Because the *Narrative* functions as the primary source for this story, the creators of the juvenile biographies must choose how to represent her being "called" to speak, her choice of name, and the outcome of this turning point. Several of these texts remove the divine agency in order to make room for Truth's own actions. However, a select few maintain and even expand this spiritual aspect of the story. Jacqueline Bernard's 1967 *Journey toward Freedom* provides a fine example of a Truth character who asks for and receives guidance from a higher power. For weeks before her ultimate departure from New York City, she had reflected on her life: "Her past mistakes lay like patches of burned forest in her mind. But sometimes, underneath, she could feel a new growth pushing up, a growth she knew in her heart would be far more beautiful than the old. More and more she began to wonder what lay ahead for her. And more and more this woman came to believe that the Lord had been preparing her for a great mission, and soon would direct her feet into that new way." The narrator explains that she did not yet know what this "new way" might be. So Isabella asked God what to do. "And it seemed to her that he answered, 'Go out of the city.'"[68] Her employer, Mrs. Whiting, thought she was "crazy," but that did not stop "the spirit that was no longer Isabelle." She acted on God's instructions, departing the city on June 1, 1843, for Connecticut. Eventually, she received a new name: "Firmly she plodded on, past fields of corn and potatoes and tidy homes. She expected at any moment to receive her new name from the Lord. The old name, given in slavery, would not do for God's pilgrim. And then, just as she had known it would, the new name came—quietly, like an old friend. She recognized it immediately: Sojourner."[69] In this telling, Isabella does not actively seek this particular vocation, yet she is open to following new directions from God. The calling that Isabella receives from "the Lord" enabled her to strike out on her own in ways that were unusual in her day, even "crazy." While this representation makes her appear almost passive, it also gives her license actively to create her own persona and pursue her own goals. Moreover, the appearance of the name, as if out of the blue, downplays the performative strategies Truth used to craft such a memorable persona around such a memorable name.

Texts published in the 1990s and 2000s place Truth firmly in charge of the name change, rather than following Bernard's depiction of dual divine-human agency. Narrators of such texts employ the language of decision and self-definition to describe Truth's choice to adopt a new name.[70] In Jane Shumate's 1991 text, the narrator tells readers that "before setting out, Isabella changed her name. She decided that it was not right for a preacher to have the name of a slave. . . . She decided to call herself 'Sojourner,' which means traveler, and 'Truth,' because she was going to preach the Gospel."[71] By framing the choice as a reflection of a shift in identity, this narrator marks the new name as a profound outward sign of an inward decision to become a new person. Laura Spinale's version emphasizes the change of name and work as a reflection of Truth's own desires or "wants." Spinale's narrator explains that many years after gaining her freedom, "Isabella decided to travel the country and speak out against slavery. She took only the clothes on her back, 25 cents, and a new name: Sojourner Truth. A 'sojourner' is one who travels. Sojourner wanted to travel, and she wanted to tell the truth. This is Sojourner's truth: All people, regardless of their color or their gender, deserve equal rights."[72]

One of the most powerful renderings of the naming narrative appears in Anne Rockwell's *Only Passing Through: The Story of Sojourner Truth*. Rockwell's narrator charts a more circuitous route of decision and self-definition, through Truth's own dreams and ruminations. The story occupies a full page of text, opposite an evocative landscape illustration, presumably of the Hudson River, by the illustrator R. Gregory Christie. Because of the highly spiritual language on the previous page, a young reader familiar with Christian scripture could easily connect this image with other biblically significant bodies of water such as the Jordan River and the Red Sea. The narrator begins, "In 1843, Isabella woke from a vivid dream. A voice had told her she must leave New York. It said she was meant to travel around the country telling of her time in bondage—telling people what it meant to be a slave. She had to be a voice for all the silent slaves still in bondage."[73] Here, the calling of "a voice" comes to Isabella in a "dream." In this telling, it is not necessarily "the Spirit" but her own subconscious that instructs her to go. The new name comes to her gradually on her journey northeast: "As she walked, memories of her life found words, and many were those she'd first heard in the Bible. One was 'sojourner.' Isabella knew it meant someone who was only passing through—staying awhile, then moving on to another place. She now believed that she was meant to be a sojourner, always moving on to spread her message. And she knew she'd never serve any master but the truth. Isabella became a new woman that day. It was as though the life she'd known up till then belonged to someone else. A new one was beginning. The old life had become a tale to tell, a story to bring freedom to others. Her old name belonged to her old life. From that day on, she was never called Isabella again. Her name was Sojourner Truth."[74] This passage characterizes the moment as the definitive turning point in her life. Her days are divided into those "in bondage" and those marked by her new identity. Moreover, through this process, Truth's "old life" is transformed from a simple collection of experiences into "a story to bring freedom to others."[75] The original version from the *Narrative* projects no outcomes beyond Truth's general notions about preaching, teaching, and sharing her story. But Rockwell's narrator reads the story of Truth's name through the backward glance of the historian, as Hannah Arendt put it, in order to insert the perceived outcome of Truth's decision: bringing freedom to others.[76]

Shirley Chisholm's election to the U.S. House of Representatives in 1968 secured her position as a historical "first" and provided biographers with an important plot point to advance her life story. This event provided an opportunity to display the agential qualities attributed to Chisholm in other parts of the narrative. Because several parties were involved in this event, it also serves as a useful example for exploring how texts variously depict the dynamics of agency within the same event. The House of Representatives official biography of Chisholm features the following groups and individuals: the court that ordered the creation of a new district in Bedford-Stuyvesant; Stanley Steingut and the "Democratic political machine"; her three African American Democratic primary opponents, Thomas R. Jones, Dolly Robinson, and William C. Thompson; her Republican challenger, James Farmer; "the people"; Puerto Rican immigrants; and, of course, Chisholm herself.[77]

The most basic account of the event can be found in Garnet Nelson Jackson's 1994 early-reader biography. This episode functions as the climax of the narrative, as the text omits Chisholm's 1972 presidential bid and supplies only a short summary of her career after 1968. The narrator of this text puts Chisholm at the helm, beginning the story by stating that, four years after being elected to the New York State Assembly, "Shirley decided to run for the United States Congress." Although, as the narrator explains, it would be an uphill battle to be elected as an African American woman, Chisholm "believed in herself." She acted on this belief, going "door to door asking people for their votes."[78] The narration of this episode concludes: "Shirley won that election, too. She became the first African American woman to serve in the United States Congress."[79] While the people whose votes she sought also wield some control over the situation, Chisholm is the primary agent. Chisholm decided; Chisholm believed; Chisholm won. In this twenty-seven-page photobiography the need for verbal economy combines with an action-based narrative to render Chisholm as a deliberate, self-possessed agent.

More than Wheatley with her book publication and Truth with her name change, Shirley Chisholm is represented in these biographies as an agent who skillfully leverages the power of others to become the first black congresswoman. These texts feature Chisholm as a "nodal" agent, astutely articulating and activating the agency around her.[80] This approach enables creators to focus on Chisholm as the subject while also acknowledging the contributions of others to her success. Several of these biographies repeat anecdotes that illustrate this approach. For instance, five of these texts trace Chisholm's aspirations to political office to the encouragement she received as a college student from Louis Warsoff, one of her white professors at Brooklyn College. These narrators recount a conversation between the two, after Warsoff had heard Chisholm exhibit her speaking skills in the debate club.[81] All of these accounts share the same basic elements: the professor hears Shirley speak, they talk about her future plans, Warsoff urges her to consider going into politics, and an astonished Chisholm reminds him that she is "black and a woman." Brownmiller's 1970 text provides a vivid example, one that makes an explicit connection to Chisholm's later run for Congress. After being encouraged by the professor to consider politics as a career, Shirley responds with skepticism: "'Professor Warsoff,' Shirley began formally, 'I'm black and a woman. How many black women do you know of in politics? How many black women are there in the United States Congress?' 'None,' the professor answered, lighting his pipe. 'But there's got to be a first sometime, don't you think? And if there's got to be a first, I think you'd be the right person. Frankly, I think you're the sort of person who wouldn't settle for anything else.'"[82] As the conversation continues, Warsoff urges his student to think about participating not in "corrupt politics" but rather in "politics that brings about change." Shirley connects this vision of politics back to her reading about figures like Susan B. Anthony and Harriet Tubman and realizes that her teacher is talking not about the past but "the future, and her role in it." According to the narrator, this conversation alters her perspective: "Shirley left the professor's office with her head spinning. Politics! Would she ever dare?"[83] Louis Warsoff becomes the first person besides young Shirley's father to encourage her interest in and apparent talent for political work. In most biographies, this moment shifts Shirley's viewpoint in such a way as to prepare her eventually to run for and be elected to Congress.

These texts represent a variety of forces, groups and individuals as contributing to Chisholm's eventual election. Some mention the 1964 *Wesberry v. Sanders* Supreme Court decision that led to the realignment of New York's 12th Congressional District, which created an opportunity for Chisholm to run.[84] Several highlight the support of Chisholm's first husband, Conrad, and her former mentor Wesley "Mac" Holder, both in helping her decide to run and in managing her campaign.[85] These texts note the many individuals and groups, including the white Brooklyn political machine and black men (represented by her Republican opponent, James Farmer), who also opposed Chisholm, both mitigating her actions and providing obstacles that emphasize her persistence.

Men were not the only ones helping Chisholm, however. Notably, these texts also identify women as a key symbolic source of Chisholm's agency. While all of the texts acknowledge this support, the three biographies from the 1970s relate a particularly poignant story in order to illustrate it. Texts by Brownmiller (1970), Hicks (1971), and Haskins (1975) tell the story of how Chisholm received a financial contribution of $9 that had been collected from a number of women in her community, which solidified her resolve to win a seat in Congress.[86] These three books have several similarities that help to explain why the authors might have focused on this episode. First, they were all published soon after the event, when the episode loomed larger in Chisholm's recent victories. Second, these books were published as stand-alone biographies rather than as part of a series that might dictate which events to include and how to represent them. Third, these books were written by authors whose writing for children was only part of a guiding commitment to antiracist and/or feminist work. Brownmiller, a noted journalist and white feminist whose work grew out of her involvement in civil rights, went on to write the influential *Against Our Will: Men, Women, and Rape* (1975). A pioneering journalist, Hicks was the first black woman to become a reporter for the *New York Times.* Hicks and her husband, Robert C. Maynard, also established the Maynard Institute for Journalism Education, which has trained minority journalists for decades.[87] And Haskins was a longtime black educator and author who used his historical work to recover black voices and correct negative images of African Americans.

While Haskins's account notes that the contribution from neighborhood women caused Chisholm to work "doubly hard," the accounts of Hicks and Brownmiller represent Chisholm's receipt of this gift as a turning point in her political career.[88] The narrator in Hicks's biography tells readers that, in the winter of 1967, Chisholm was "weighing her own political future," deciding whether to run for the 12th District seat. While considering her options, she asks herself whether she could be "certain" about the people's support.[89] As if following Chisholm's imagined question, the narrator immediately shifts to this story as an explanation of how Chisholm eventually made her decision: "On one of her nights home in Brooklyn she was sitting and reading when the doorbell rang. At the door she found a delegation of women from the community. They were there to tell her to run for Congress." The narrator reports that these women—"all mothers of families on welfare"—had voted to decide that they wanted Chisholm as "their candidate." As a demonstration of their commitment, they had "taken up a collection," which amounted to $9.62. The narrator provides further detail, both about the encounter and its impact: "They had placed the money in a crumpled paper bag and brought it right over. That was the moment when Shirley Chisholm decided to run."[90] Brownmiller's account likewise depicts this as a turning point for Chisholm, though in a more dramatic fashion. The narrator of this text tells readers that the "Negro woman" who appeared at her door that night handed Chisholm an envelope. In it, she "found $9.62—all in coins," evidence of the small contributions eked out by many. Chisholm's response is emotional and compassionate:

"With tears streaming down her face, she hugged the lady tightly. 'I know what this money means to you,' she whispered. 'We'll make it together—you and I.'"[91] This episode prompts a serious conversation between Shirley and Conrad about running for Congress. Although this decision does not arrive quite as swiftly as in the Hicks text, it functions in the same manner. In these cases, aside from being a well-timed and compelling example of sacrifice, this anecdote renders Chisholm a consummate agent while situating her actions firmly within the context of her community. This Chisholm ran for Congress not because she was ambitious or power-hungry but because the people—especially the poor, overlooked women of Bedford-Stuyvesant—wanted her as "their candidate." Concern for marginalized others and their wishes motivates this woman.

Whether in conversations with Professor Warsoff, deliberations with her husband, or encounters with potential constituents, the Shirley Chisholm of these biographies functions as a determined, self-possessed agent who activates several sources of agency. The biographies tell her story, but they also situate that story in a network of relationships that, for the most part, enhance rather than detract from Chisholm's individual agency. These biographies represent Chisholm in ways that exemplify Karlyn Kohrs Campbell's claim that agency is simultaneously "communal, social, cooperative, and participatory" and activated from within unique subject positions, such as Shirley Chisholm's.[92]

Configuring Time

In the process of configuration, creators constructed texts that mediated between what they deemed to be significant events and the life stories of Wheatley, Truth, and Chisholm. This phase of the agential spiral also involves emplotting a variety of elements—"agents, goals, means, interactions, circumstances, unexpected results," and the like—within the narrative as a whole.[93] Finally, the configuration of these biographical texts mediates between our general understanding of narrative temporality and the many episodes that make up the chronicle of the life of a historical individual. In order for a story to be "followable," its creators must assemble and arrange the episodes selected for inclusion in the narrative. Then, the assemblage of events must be transformed into a complete story—or, as Ricoeur put it, "the unity of one temporal whole."[94] What does it mean for a reader to "follow" a story? According to Ricoeur, "to follow a story is to move forward in the midst of contingencies and peripeteia under the guidance of an expectation that finds its fulfillment in the 'conclusion' of the story." The conclusion, he explained, "is not logically implied by some previous premises" but perceived through a reading of the story in its entirety. The conclusion "gives the story an 'end point,' which, in turn furnishes the point of view from which the story can be perceived as forming a whole. To understand the story is to understand how and why the successive episodes led to this conclusion, which, far from being foreseeable, must finally be acceptable, as congruent with the episodes brought together by the story."[95] Depending on how episodes are brought together by a plot that moves toward a particular end, the reader's understanding of the story may be directed in different ways. The way that a story ends, Ricoeur argued, communicates not only something about the meaning of that story but also something about time in general. Thus, different endings contain the potential to communicate different understandings of temporality.

Earlier in this chapter, I discussed how the opening scenes of these biographical texts have the potential to frame powerfully the relationship between event and story and thus the possible meanings of the story as a whole. Although the concluding sections of these texts differ, many share in common one critical theme: temporal continuity. The children's literature commentator Penelope Lively argued in 1973 that child readers need a sense of continuity with the past, which supposedly fosters feelings of security.[96] Although Lively's claim about what children need can reasonably be challenged, the effects of such an assumption can be observed in several of the biographies in this study. Texts published as early as 1967 and as late as 2008 present the ends of their stories not only as the conclusion of a life but as a continuation of that life's work. This continuity specifically appears in the form of remembrance, both through commemorative practices and through ongoing action.

Bernard's 1967 biography of Sojourner Truth provides an example of texts published early in this period. After reporting Truth's death, in 1883, Bernard's narrator imagines how Truth herself would have considered the end of her life: as the potential beginning of the work of others. The narrator imagines Truth's thoughts: "The work she had set out to do that day still lay around her, unfinished. The work of the Lord was never done. In fact, it must have seemed to the old fighter, as she lay dying on her couch at 10 College Street, that the work of the Lord was being rapidly *un*done—that the world, even as she lay there, was moving backward."[97] Bernard's narrator not only emphasizes how much work was left to do when Truth died but even suggests that some of Truth's gains were being rolled back, making it even more critical for agents of the future to continue "the work of the Lord." Other, more recent texts sound a note similar to Bernard's. Suzanne Slade's 2008 picture book also supplies an image of continuity by giving the impression that Truth's activities went on even in spite of her physical death. After stating the date of Truth's death, Slade's narrator explains that "she never stopped working to help others."[98] Although the narrator has just reported Truth's death, the placement and ambiguous wording of this phrase suggests to readers that her work lives on. Texts such as Bernard's and Slade's illustrate the significance of creating a sense of temporal continuity in these texts despite the distinct beginning and ending of the lives of their biographical subjects.

Several other twenty-first-century texts close with a deliberate orientation to the future that projects Truth's lifework forward through the practices of remembrance and the actions of those who succeed her. Kathleen Kudlinski's 2003 biography, for instance, concludes by describing Truth's funeral, by drawing attention to the various memorial artifacts peddled "so we don't forget this powerful woman," and by mentioning NASA's 1997 *Sojourner* project.[99] A 2002 text by Peter Roop and Connie Roop concludes with a more symbolic orientation toward the future, rather than a direct address to the audience. In the final chapter, titled "Sojourner Truth Remembered," this text describes Truth's death and funeral, the work of friends to preserve her public memory, and a few commemorative acts. The chapter concludes with a description of the statue that today stands in Battle Creek, near the highway that bears her name: "Today a larger-than-life statue of Sojourner Truth stands in Battle Creek. She gazes into the distance, toward the day when no one is enslaved, and everyone enjoys the same rights."[100] These sentences deftly weave the past into a present that is always looking toward the future. Although readers are not directly addressed, they are subtly called to use the statue to consider their own place in the continuation of Truth's story. Language choices emphasize the ongoing and outreaching nature of Truth's influence: in Battle Creek, her "memory continues," scholarships "are given" in her name each year, and her memory has "gone beyond Earth" in the form of the space probe.[101] But these concrete commemorative acts do not have the last word, as even the inert statue seems poised for activity, waiting for the day when readers inspired by Truth's story will continue her work by becoming historical agents in their own right. Whether noting the ongoing efforts to commemorate these women, describing the more controversial points of their public memory, or simply presenting their life's work as an ongoing project, juvenile biographies configure time as continuous rather than discontinuous.[102]

While emphasizing continuity, each work proposes a slightly different end to the story. Some speak of Sojourner Truth as a continuing "inspiration for supporters of equal rights," although others simply observe that she "inspired many people" during her own day.[103] Some texts recognize Phillis Wheatley's poetic ability to help people "see the good things in their lives," whereas others note her position in an unfolding discourse on race.[104] Some biographies conclude by describing Shirley Chisholm's ongoing political work, while others share her articulated desire to be remembered not as a first but as a "catalyst for change."[105] While still operating within the larger framework of public memory, the conclusions of each of these texts afford slightly different possibilities for understanding the impact of Wheatley, Truth, and Chisholm, the connection between their lives and the course of history, and the comprehension of time in general.

Using Paul Ricoeur's theorization of mimesis$_2$ illuminates how biographies about Phillis Wheatley, Sojourner Truth, and Shirley Chisholm undertake subtle innovations upon the narrative prefigured by *doxa.* Creators took the historical evidence about these women's lives—rendered intelligible by basic Western assumptions about agency and historical significance—and arranged the information in ways that both reinforced those assumptions and offered possible innovations to them. Although I have discussed some authorial and editorial reflection on the construction of these texts, I have focused primarily on the configuration evident in the texts themselves. These texts exhibit their own mediating function between cultural assumptions and the projected uptake of readers in their configuration of events within a story; their unique combinations of agents, actions, and outcomes; and their synthesis of the elements of the story within a temporal frame. Focusing on the second phase of mimesis foregrounds the agency of the creators of these texts—their self-conscious role as interpreters of history and shapers of young minds, as well as their nonconscious or unarticulated role as the purveyors of values and promoters of public memory. But the focus here also highlights the agency of the texts themselves as fulcrums of cultural values, historical contexts, individual voices, sites at which all of these elements combine to create new possibilities for the reader, who will interpret and appropriate the texts.

CHAPTER SIX

REFIGURATION *and* APPROPRIATION

The Agent Reading History

> "Don't you think that your life story will encourage the young people who are growing up now?" Conrad asked. Shirley didn't answer. She didn't have to. Her smile said it all. She was very, very happy.
>
> Susan Brownmiller, *Shirley Chisholm*

> It is the reader who completes the work.
>
> Paul Ricoeur, *Time and Narrative*

The agent writing history may have intentions toward her young audience, which may or may not be acknowledged and expressed. She may configure the text in a way that seems engaging and easy to follow. But, as with any persuasive text or act, these intentions may come to nothing beyond being represented in the text. No matter how creators of such texts may try, child and adolescent readers reject, reinterpret, or simply misunderstand the meanings that adults have constructed for them. Young readers may use their developing interpretive capacities to discover unintended meanings in a text. Young readers therefore appropriate and respond to texts in diverse and unpredictable ways.[1]

Although the study of reader response to texts is an important research pursuit, it is not my central concern here. Rather, by performing a rhetorical analysis, I aim to demonstrate how biographies of Phillis Wheatley, Sojourner Truth, and Shirley Chisholm are constructed in order to engage readers and to elicit responses within a certain range of possibilities. Such analysis provides an important background for scholars who later analyze the responses of actual children and adolescents. The texts function as invitations to young readers to perceive the stories of agents of the past as resources for future action. This type of engagement goes beyond a reader's ability simply to understand a given text to include his potential ability to incorporate that text into his life. This process is not simple imitation or emulation but inventive appropriation. "To appropriate," as Ricoeur explained, "is to make what was alien one's own."[2] Biographical texts, as sites of public memory, operate in ways that explicitly and deliberately invite appropriation by readers. The texts are strongly oriented toward a moment of refiguration, wherein the meaning of the narrative is "restored to the time of action and of suffering in mimesis$_3$" through the participation of young readers.[3] These texts operate as "a set of instructions that the individual reader or the reading public executes in a passive or a creative way."[4] Biographies of Wheatley, Truth, and Chisholm exhibit their hybrid role as texts for children and as texts of public memory by addressing themselves to imagined audiences who are in turn invited to use the narratives of the past as resources for action in the future.

Refiguration: Text Becomes Resource

In *Time and Narrative,* Ricoeur specified "refiguration" as the action of mimesis$_3$. This moment, he explained, corresponds with the stage of the interpretive process that Hans-Georg Gadamer called "application."[5] The reader is the focal agent at this phase of the agential spiral, and her primary action is to "refigure" the work by reading it and translating it back into the world in which she exists. In this sense, "the act of reading is . . . the operator that joins mimesis$_3$ to mimesis$_2$."[6] Adapting Aristotle's work, Ricoeur explained that mimesis$_3$ creates a crucial space for translating the imagined world of the work into the actual world of the reader.[7] Texts invite readers to envision a possible world that, in part or in full, can be actualized in the material world through their action (though not always in predictable or easily traceable ways). Biographical texts invite young readers to envision such a world through the lens of the past, in this case a lens specifically focused on the experiences of Wheatley, Truth, or Chisholm. By recapturing the vision of a world that is superimposed on—or made to appear organically derived from—the events and emotions of these women's lives, young readers can become almost an extension of these women's lifework, part of a common historical trajectory, and active interpreters of the public memory through which such stories are sustained.

Ricoeur's conceptualization of refiguration is significant to a rhetorical analysis because it insists that texts affect the world beyond language. His work does not merely present a critique of poststructuralist visions of the text but also offers an insightful and sensible alternative to such ideas by rejecting the false choice between full, conscious authorial intention and the completely closed world of the text.[8] Rather, his approach treats authorship as one textual influence among many. Ricoeur's formulation of refiguration, he explained, "is part of a hermeneutics that aims less at restoring the author's intention behind the text than at making explicit the movement by which the text unfolds, as it were, a world in front of itself."[9] Like Ricoeur and Karlyn Kohrs Campbell, I acknowledge authorial or "creatorial" intention as an important aspect of reading these biographical texts, yet I also place this intention within the larger context of textual production and addressivity. Surely "texts have agency," as Campbell stated, and the intentions of creators leave indelible marks on those texts. But both textual and authorial agency are "linked to audiences" and begin with "the signals that guide the process of 'uptake' for readers or listeners enabling them to categorize, to understand how a symbolic act is to be framed."[10] Serving as audience guides for this process of uptake, biographies for children construct public memories of Wheatley, Truth, and Chisholm that resonate with and serve as resources for young readers.

"For the Youth Who Are Drifting": Identifying and Addressing the Audience

In many texts written for children, authors are very explicit, even overbearing, about their intentions. Contrast this scenario with popular history and biography for adults. In adult literature, such intentions are buried more deeply, because adult readers are supposedly better equipped to read between the lines and to infer intentions. Texts for children, in contrast, tend to be exactly the opposite: they are judged primarily on their ability to produce effects on their audiences. Scholars such as Perry Nodelman have argued that even the placement of a book in the category of children's literature is "not so much about the text itself as about its intended audience."[11] Texts for children often clearly exhibit their addressivity through rhetorical markers intended for imagined readers.

Rhetorical scholars have developed a rich vocabulary for describing the features of addressivity in texts, including concepts such as the implied audience, the universal audience, and the second persona. As Chaim Perelman and Lucie Olbrechts-Tyteca suggested, rhetorical speakers craft their performances by imagining "an ensemble" of people they wish "to influence by . . . argumentation."[12] Biographical texts for young readers may not be linguistically marked as arguments in the traditional sense, but they do persuade. They aim, albeit in a diffuse manner, to portray historical understanding and agency in ways that their readers can and should adopt. These texts also promote certain interpretations of the lives of Wheatley, Truth, and Chisholm. But, in order to do so, they must first develop a sense of the readers that they hope to address and thereby persuade. Edwin Black dubbed this implied auditor the "second persona," an imagined person or group of people addressed by a discourse as well as a person or group of people the discourse seeks to create and persuade.[13] This imagined audience can be general, insofar as it is related primarily to the category of the biographies for children. Or the audience can be more specific, varied according to authorial purposes or other markers within the text. Beyond intending a text for children, an author may write for smaller subgroups of children defined by specifics of age, gender, and ethnicity, as in the biographical sketches written by Hallie Quinn Brown, Jessie Fauset, and Elizabeth Ross Haynes in the 1920s. Some creators address such differences directly, but others take a more indirect approach. For instance, many authors and illustrators use tone, a simple form of address, or images in order to address an audience of young children or early readers.[14]

The relationship between the producers of discourse and its receivers is fraught with inequality and misunderstanding, regardless of the rhetorical situation. But the case of texts written for children can be particularly problematic, in large part because, as Beverly Lyon Clark observed, "We tend to assume that what it means to be a child, what it means for an adult to understand a child—never mind what it means to write from or for a child's perspective—is unproblematic."[15] Authors, illustrators, and the adult reading public often operate under the assumption that everyone who has experienced childhood can understand it and write accurately about it, despite the fact that every adult has become removed from it. Because of the wide gap between child and adult, the imagined audience in children's literature is, in a sense, doubly removed from the actual audience.

Adult conceptions of childhood strongly influence how texts address young readers. Discussing elements that constitute children's literature, Nodelman pinpointed a seemingly obvious yet vital quality that such texts share: they "address young readers in terms that make their youth a matter of significance."[16] In a basic sense, making youth "a matter of significance" means crafting a text that children can understand and enjoy. But making youth "a matter of significance" also means using narrative to highlight the identity and social roles of children and adolescents. Conventions about the identity and role of children, of course, are by no means universal or fixed, especially in the United States. Surveying research about these changes, Karen Sánchez-Eppler concluded, "The histories that we do have of American childhood tell of the gradual and uneven transformation of cultural attitudes toward children, which increasingly cast children as distinct from adults, their specialness valued in emotional rather than economic terms."[17] The practice of defining childhood primarily by its distinctness from adulthood has powerfully shaped children's literature. Although societies and scholars have debated which characteristics constitute this distinction (and whether there is a distinction at all), most recognize childhood as a time marked by change. Nodelman has observed that, because of this common perspective, children's texts "assume not only that children can change but that they must—that the ability and inevitability of change is part of what defines them as children." Such texts assume that children should and will mature, and they communicate to readers that this is desirable.[18]

Biographical texts about Wheatley, Truth, and Chisholm generally imply an imagined audience rather than address the group outright. However, there are two significant exceptions to this generalization. First, a small number of authors and editors explicitly named their intended audience in a preface or author's note. These creators expressed designs upon a specific subset of young readers. Second, several texts directly address the reader from within the context of the narrative. In these instances, the narrator breaks from the story in order to explicitly provoke psychological engagement from readers.

Most children's literature authors avoid making specific comments about audience, as this can exclude potential consumers and readers. The more vague the audience characteristics, the more accessible the text is thought to be. James Haskins's *Fighting Shirley Chisholm,* for instance, simply identifies its audience as "America's young people."[19] In an instructive counterexample, the author and editor Ida Bellegarde deliberately identified the target audience for her four-book biographical series Black Heroes and Heroines.[20] Bellegarde wrote several books over the course of her lifetime, including a 1939 collection of poetry titled *Lisping Leaves* and several books about speaking and etiquette, such as *Little Stepping Stones to Correct Speech* (1973) and *Understanding Cultural Values* (1980). Like Shirley Graham before her, Bellegarde was a highly educated black woman who turned to writing books for children.[21] Her reasons for writing this short series of biographies remain unknown, but one might speculate that Bellegarde saw these stories as a corrective to the statistics that led one scholar in the 1980s to declare "black youth in crisis."[22]

Bellegarde explained that her series of biographies was "dedicated to the black youth who will be inspired to follow in the footsteps of those intrepid black leaders who achieved eminence in spite of almost unsurmountable [*sic*] odds."[23] Like Brown, Fauset, and Haynes before her, Bellegarde explicitly named the racial identity of her audience. In the subsequent foreword, Bellegarde clarified her purpose and further specified her intended audience as those "black youth" who appear to her to be in need of direction: "This book is written because of a concern for the welfare of persons who are falling prey to a pernicious sickness plaguing our country today—the loss of goals—and for the youth who are drifting into lives of meaningless and purposeless existence. It is the hope that the chronicling of the lives of these heroic men and women will inspire today's youth to discover goals, or at least to point the way, and that within these pages the young reader will find someone worthy of emulation."[24] Bellegarde's "black youth" are in crisis, poised on the edge of danger and in dire need of guidance. Equipped with the tales of African Americans of yesteryear, Bellegarde has set herself up as the guide to positive role models and healthy living. Like Du Bois and Fauset, Bellegarde has provided models she hoped would be "worthy of emulation." Unlike the earlier writers, Bellegarde implied that the dangers threatening young readers come from within themselves rather than from their white supremacist environment.

Throughout the text, Bellegarde's narrator interprets particular moments in Phillis Wheatley's life story in ways that reflect an adult's stern perspective on the poor choices and actions of dissolute youth. The narrator constructs the story of Wheatley's life as one of childhood listlessness and kindly adult guidance, as this passage from early in the narrative demonstrates: "Phillis was fortunate to have had the concern and care of a kind mistress. Since childhood she was ambitious to achieve something, but not knowing what to work for or what goals to work toward. Being in the Wheatley home provided the direction she finally took."[25] The narrator uses Wheatley as a proxy for the youth "not knowing what to work for or what goals to work toward." This revealing passage ascribes a specific kind of agency to Phillis Wheatley by characterizing her as an inherently ambitious individual who allowed herself—intelligently, the narrator implies—to be guided by the good "fortune" of landing in an environment where her ambition could flourish.[26] Here, the text uses Wheatley's life to acknowledge the importance of environment to agency and personal success while maintaining an emphasis on the importance of aspiring to "something."

As if providing a counterpoint to this admission, the narrator seizes on the character of John Peters, Phillis Wheatley's husband, as a warning to those who would allow their environment to dictate their own self-image. Although first introduced as "the debonair, articulate and very caring person of her own race, a free man," Peters comes under fire as the narrator acknowledges the "different opinions" about him. The narrator explains that "some observer said that John Peters' problem was that he let his goals he had set for himself, even though they became unattainable, control his whole life." According to the narrator's interpretation of this anonymous observer, this led Peters to become "embittered."[27] Folded within the story of Wheatley's marriage and subsequent pregnancy is another cautionary tale against becoming "pregnant too soon."[28] Throughout this text, the narrator capitalizes upon every opportunity offered by Wheatley's life story to speak to the youth whom she sees as being in need of "goals," in danger of becoming "embittered," and prone to becoming "pregnant too soon." The narrative moves in lockstep with Bellegarde's prefatory material by communicating that readers should set "appropriate" goals, yet not become frustrated when they fail to meet those goals. Bellegarde's narrator accomplishes this through subtle commentary on the facts of Wheatley's life, which appears as reportage rather than editorial. The commentary works enthymematically to urge readers to consider how they might be judged if they, too, make the unfortunate choices of Wheatley or Peters.[29]

A second way in which an implied audience enters explicitly into a narrative is through direct address by the author or narrator. Such address occurs in authorial commentary that appears separate from the biographical narrative, as well as within the narrative itself.[30] The form of these examples varies from a simple colloquial address such as "child" to regular invitations to "imagine" a particular experience of the text's main character.[31] Generally speaking, these direct invocations invite the audience actively to engage the narrative by relating emotionally to the experiences of Wheatley, Truth, or Chisholm. The texts that utilize direct address do not explicitly ask readers to pass judgment on the *historical interpretation* of these women's lives. Rather, the texts ask readers to imagine how they themselves would have acted or felt in certain moments had they been Wheatley and Truth. Here, readers are explicitly instructed to enter the text as the doorway to the "kingdom of the *as if.*"[32]

Four texts provide the most notable examples of direct address of the reader: Bruce Fish and Becky Durost Fish's *Phillis Wheatley* (2006), Garnet Nelson Jackson's *Phillis Wheatley, Poet* (1992) and her *Shirley Chisholm: Congresswoman* (1994), and Edward Beecher Claflin's *Sojourner Truth and the Struggle for Freedom* (1987).[33] These texts cover a wide range of time as well as readership, from Jackson's text for early readers to Claflin's biography for the middle grades. In the Fish and Fish text, the authors have addressed readers through an author's note, which appears early in the book, after a historical timeline and a brief paragraph summarizing and introducing Wheatley's life story. The note is fashioned as a letter to the reader, typeset in italics and "signed" in script by "Bruce + Becky." It begins: "Imagine what it would have been like to be taken from your family by strangers when you were seven or eight years old. That's what happened to Phillis Wheatley." In these opening sentences, the authors are speaking to readers as children, tapping into a supposed childhood fear and urging them to imagine their own responses to such an experience. The next sentence immediately directs the thought experiment of the previous passage, as the authors explain: "We admire Phillis for surviving such a terrible experience and having the courage to go on with her life." The note continues by describing Wheatley's confidence, determination, and achievements. This Phillis Wheatley did not let people prevent her from "trying to reach her goals," and she "didn't back down" from her tasks.

Although the note begins by appealing to the emotions, it concludes by appealing to the capacity of judgment. The authors have explained that Wheatley went to England to get her book published. The final paragraph says, "Some people think Phillis would have lived longer and had more influence if she had stayed in England. The laws in England allowed slaves who stepped on English soil to become free, so Phillis didn't have to return to Boston and care for Mrs. Wheatley. As you read this book, decide whether you think Phillis should have stayed in England or continued to help the Wheatleys." In this short author's note, readers have been taken on a condensed journey from victim to responsible agent. The note begins by encouraging emotional identification with Wheatley's "terrible experience" and ends by inviting reasoned judgment about one of Wheatley's major decisions. The overarching strategy of this author's note appears to be to use dramatic moments in Wheatley's life to engage readers in her story and with her as a character. Both moments emphasize Wheatley's agency as enacted through choice, whether to respond to tragedy with "courage" or to sacrifice possible freedom.[34]

Jackson also used a "dear readers" note to orient children to the stories in her early-reader books. Although these notes are much briefer than the one written by Fish and Fish, they both feature directives for children based on the lessons they might learn from Wheatley's and Chisholm's life stories. In the biography of Wheatley, Jackson explained that writing helped young Phillis "feel wonderful" despite a situation that made her "sad." The author then recommended writing to her readers as a way of working out their own feelings. Thus, Wheatley quite explicitly becomes a model for how children might act when faced with adversity.[35] Summarizing Chisholm's life in the reader's note, Jackson explained that her subject was "taught early in life to respect herself and her abilities. When she grew up, she spoke out against unfairness, so that all African Americans and women, children, and the poor of all races could also have self-respect." The author then related these lessons directly to her readers, exhorting them, "Let's remember what Shirley believed—that we should fight for the happiness and peace of all."[36] Encapsulating the lessons of each woman's life in a few sentences, Jackson then used those lessons to direct readers to action, whether writing or fighting.

Claflin's text uses a different convention to send a similar message about audience engagement. Rather than addressing the reader through a distinct author's note, Claflin's text scatters moments of direct address throughout the body of the narrative. In this text, the narrator breaks from the flow of Truth's story in order to invite readers to reflect upon it in some way. Some passages suggest a primarily emotional engagement. For example, in a passage near the beginning, the narrator relates the story of how two of Isabella's siblings were sold to another farm, unbeknownst to Isabella's parents. The two children were lured by the promise of a sleigh ride, only to be tricked into being taken away from their family. After telling this story, the narrator directs the reader, "But imagine what it would be like if your brother or sister could disappear anytime. You might never know what became of him or her. No one would tell you. . . . Worst of all, each time the master called, it might signal your turn to be sold. It could happen anytime."[37] This moment closely parallels the opening sentences of the author's note in the Fish and Fish text by appealing to what is presumed to be the universal childhood emotion of fear, especially fear of separation from one's family. Yet Claflin's commentary exhibits much greater detail than Jackson's, which uses simple emotional descriptors such as "happy" and "sad."[38]

As the text proceeds, the narrator occasionally suspends the narrative to invite a response from readers. The most memorable instance of direct address occurs during one of the more unforgettable moments of Truth's life: her decision to leave

New York City to embark on a speaking career. After trying to recount how Truth herself came to this decision, the narrator asks the reader: "Have you ever faced a decision like this? You know there is something that you want to do very strongly, but you cannot say exactly why? Sometimes your impulses are not logical. They can't be explained. A plan gradually forms in your mind. It becomes stronger and stronger every day. Finally, one morning you wake up with the certainty that you must go ahead with your plan, no matter what happens."[39] In this passage, the narrator attempts to use the reader's own supposed experience in order to help explain an action that seems inexplicable. Although focused on "impulses" that may not be "logical," the passage's central concern is a pivotal decision, an action that forever changed Truth's life and her influence on history. Readers are here invited to engage Truth as a historical agent by imagining how they might someday respond to their own call to action.

As if providing bookends to the text, the narrator concludes the narrative with a final address to the reader. "If you visit Battle Creek today," the narrator explains, "you will find Sojourner Truth's tall marble gravestone flanked by boxwood hedges. . . . Stand in front of that peaceful monument and you may find it hard to imagine how she stirred thousands of people during her lifetime. We have no recordings of that great, rolling voice—and of course no one can duplicate the power of her presence. Sojourner spoke from the heart, and each word carried the force of her personal wisdom and experience. But we can recognize her challenge." Readers are addressed at three separate points in this passage. In the first, the narrator uses the old Aristotelian rhetorical strategy of "bringing before the eyes," wherein a listener is invited to picture something in his mind.[40] Readers are urged to envision the "tall marble gravestone flanked by boxwood hedges" so that they can in turn envision the woman for whom that "peaceful monument" was constructed. The narrator speaks to young readers as if certain that this stone would not be enough to evoke an appropriate response. A more immediate, palpable experience is needed. But since there are "no recordings of that great, rolling voice," and "no one can duplicate the power of her presence," the narrator returns once again to the power of Truth's life story. Then, in the final sentence, the narrator shifts into the first-person plural, saying to the audience that although it is impossible to know this woman of the past, "we can recognize her challenge." According to this narrator, Truth "challenges" readers to recognize the need to "exercise their greatest freedom, the right to speak."[41]

These four texts directly address the audience in order to further engage readers with certain salient moments or lessons from these women's lives. The first step of engagement in these examples involves diminishing the psychological distance that exists between each of these women and twentieth- or twenty-first-century children. By encouraging readers to imagine themselves having the experiences of these women, the texts urge readers to eliminate barriers of time, emotion, culture, and age, all in one swift motion. In these texts, imagining the lives of the past becomes a critical means of acquiring knowledge about the past. In the authorial commentary about audience and the narrators' direct addresses to the audience, the texts imply that, for children, narratives about the past must be imaginatively engaged in order to be learned. Creators of biographical texts for children may have some degree of influence over how readers take up this invitation to engage the story, but once the narrative is in their hands and minds, there is no telling where it might end up. This is the source of the power of these biographies as texts of public memory: they are addressed to an audience that, whether directly or indirectly, is empowered to take up the text and thereby refigure it.

Inventing Inner Lives

Texts that directly identify, address, and construct audiences provide useful counterexamples to the majority of biographies, which take an indirect approach. It is far more common for juvenile biographies to encourage reader engagement by providing access to particular aspects of the psychological and emotional lives of their subjects, as Shirley Graham and Ann Rinaldi do in their biographical novels about Phyllis Wheatley.[42] Many texts thus supply characters with whom young readers can identify and who can serve as models of development and maturation. As Maria Nikolajeva explained, most texts for children operate under the assumption that characters ought to "think, behave, and speak the way the implied readers are assumed to think, behave, and speak."[43] Nodelman has likewise observed that a common characteristic of texts for children is their "childlike protagonists," combined with the tendency to "focalize the events through the responses of those characters."[44] By encouraging young readers to consider the identity and status of a fictional or historical character, creators of such texts encourage readers to reflect on their own belonging to such a category and to anticipate their inevitable departure from that category.

Biographical texts about historical figures present a challenge in this regard. Fictional texts for children can invent child protagonists, which makes it easier for authors to make youth a "matter of significance."[45] Child readers are supposed to identify naturally with protagonists that are represented as peers. In fiction, narrators can also provide readers access to the thoughts and motivations of these characters, which are often designed to make emulating the characters' actions and choices more straightforward.[46] But texts that are allegedly based on historical characters cannot simply invent a childhood for their protagonists; they must shape a narrative that appears compelling and authentic from within the parameters of the historical record, which often provides little insight into historical childhood experience. The available information about these three women's childhoods varies greatly in volume and quality. As might be expected, the least is known about Wheatley's childhood and the most about Chisholm's. Truth provided an account in her *Narrative,* but the material in that text also deviates from historical fact, as some scholars have discussed.[47] Biographies employ a variety of narrative techniques in order to make up for this deficit in plausibility.

Creators of biographical texts thus face a difficult task: to render the historical subject "childlike" and emotionally resonant while maintaining a sense of faithfulness to the historical record.[48] In order to meet these requirements, texts frequently employ a third-person omniscient narrator to establish a seemingly direct perspective on the internal workings of an otherwise opaque historical character. By making the central character more transparent, such a narrator allows the narrative to be "focalized" through that historical figure.[49] That is, creators of these texts intended to draw readers into the narrative by providing seemingly direct access to its primary actions and experiences, those of the biographical subject. The convention of the third-person omniscient narrator enables the texts to oscillate between an objectifying historical perspective and a highly personal perspective, which yields two distinct but related results. First, it circumvents the historical problem of attributing unknowable feelings, thoughts, and mental states to persons such as Wheatley, Truth, and Chisholm, who were either long dead or well past childhood at the time the biographies were published. Instead of relying solely or primarily on the strategy of inventing direct dialogue or internal monologue (which, of course, also occasionally occurs), most texts make the source of knowledge of inner states ambiguous by ascribing that knowledge to the narrator. Second, by introducing this perspective on the main character, the convention of the third-person narrator encourages identification with that character.

I noted earlier the purported power of evoking childhood fears as a means of compelling reader interest. Although few texts directly instruct readers to imagine themselves in the midst of these women's challenging childhood experiences, most texts about Wheatley and Truth appeal to readers' emotions by using terminology that suggests vulnerability and fear. For instance, texts from throughout the period that begin Wheatley's life narrative with her arrival in the Boston slave market describe her variously and repeatedly as "weak," "little," "small," "frail," "frightened," "thin," "terribly afraid and helpless," "fearful," a "small frightened waif," "illiterate," a "thin, sickly looking child," a "skinny little African girl with . . . sad eyes," and, of course, "young."[50] Likewise, biographies of Truth emphasize her fearful emotional state during the first years of her life, describing her as a "frightened, lonely slave child," "lost in private fears," "worried," "trembling," "scared," and feeling "great agony."[51] In several instances, these feelings appear seemingly in spite of young Isabella's unusually tall stature and her physical strength.

Two texts from the early 1970s demonstrate how these themes of fear, weakness, and lack of control emerge as characteristics of childhood in the context of the biographical narrative. In a text by Margaret Fuller on Phillis Wheatley and one by Helen Stone Peterson on Sojourner Truth, the narrators introduce the main characters as children caught in frightening situations.[52] The opening scene of Fuller's narrative describes a slave market in eighteenth-century Boston, where the harsh sounds of an auctioneer's voice fill the air. There, a "thin child stood on a big block of wood." The narrator tells readers that "heavy chains were on her ankles, and for clothing, she wore only a piece of carpet tied at the waist."[53] As if this strange scene were not enough, the narrator explains directly to readers that this young girl looked so "terribly afraid and helpless" that John Wheatley feels compelled to outbid all of the other potential buyers at the market that day. He wins the bid and demands that the auctioneer remove the girl's chains. As she looks up into the face of her new owner, explains the narrator, she appears as a "frail, fearful child." John Wheatley brings her to his home, where her encounter with the rest of the Wheatley family leaves her "wide-eyed with fear."

But, like the young audience to whom her story is being told, Fuller's Wheatley is eager to be comforted. Soon after entering the Wheatley home, the young girl finds comfort in the other black slaves living in the household—first in the porter, Black Prince, and then in the kitchen maid, Aunt Sukey. Phillis Wheatley's first interaction with the latter in particular provides an opportunity for the narrator to characterize the girl's feelings directly: when Phillis is brought to Aunt Sukey, the older slave "held her close for a minute," and Phillis "put her arms tightly around her and felt secure in her embrace."[54] The text here is accompanied by an illustration of the two embracing, with Aunt Sukey wearing an expression almost of rapture, as the cook, Lima, looks on. These first few pages of the text introduce Phillis Wheatley as a frightened child in a strange situation who finds comfort in trustworthy black adults rather than in the white members of the Wheatley family. Through this introduction, the text's creators attempted to draw readers into Wheatley's story by providing them access to her emotional experiences. In addition, the creators' invention of the interaction between Sukey and the young girl seems intended to appeal to the readers' own supposed experiences of childhood fear and adult protection.[55]

Likewise, when readers of Peterson's text meet Belle Hardenbergh (Peterson's name for Isabella), she is asking her father why her mother is working so late. Readers quickly learn that the slaves of the Hardenbergh household work hard and live in poor conditions, "in the damp cellar under his big house."[56] The narrator shares a few details about the main character—she speaks only Dutch, her full name is Isabella, and she is "tall for a nine-year-old"—before establishing an atmosphere of uncertainty and fear, much like that evoked in the Fuller text. Belle's mother returns from work with news of the master's worsening illness: "Mau-Mau Bett sobbed bitterly. 'When the master dies we'll all be sold.'" Then Belle's mother explains that the two children will also likely be sold away. "Belle was terror-stricken. She flung her arms around her mother. 'Mama, don't let it happen!' she begged. Belle felt that without her parents she could not go on." After a strangely pessimistic interjection by her husband, Belle's mother reminds the children that "the only way we can go on is by trusting God." According to the narrator, "this evening her words had new importance for the frightened girl." She "begged" to know where God was, and her mother responded by "singing African songs her mother had passed down to her." These songs evoke various strong feelings for the young girl: "Belle did not understand the words, but she knew some of the songs had happy sounds. Others seemed filled with sorrow. Leaning close against her mother, Belle wept."[57] In the opening scene, Belle is a child character full of "childlike" emotions, such as a desperate fear of the unknown and of abandonment. Despite her own sorrow about the impending separation from her children, Mau-Mau Bett manages to exude a protective, comforting presence through her assurances and songs.

Both the Fuller and the Peterson texts immediately begin to develop emotional lives for their main characters. Both employ narration from a third-person perspective that frames the direct dialogue ("Mau-Mau, I'm so afraid of being taken away!"). Moreover, both introduce their characters in unmistakable states of fear. By attributing feelings of fear to the two girls at the outset of their narratives, the creators of the texts mark their protagonists as *children* and thereby structure the subsequent stories of their lives. The particular use of fear as a framing device reflects adult assumptions about childhood and its attendant emotions. This assumption that fear is a "childish" emotion seems first of all intended to appeal to child readers, who are assumed to have had a similar experience of fear, albeit in different situations. The creators likely believed that the readers of these biographies would identify with the feelings of young Phillis and Belle, thus overcoming the apparent strangeness of these girls' historical situations. The representation of fear also seems intended to structure the relationship between the child protagonists and the adults around them. Although forced into frightening and uncertain scenarios by white adults, Phillis and Belle are swiftly comforted by black adults. These scenes emphasize the fear inherent in the institution of slavery, even while they portray empathy among enslaved people. The texts' creators supposed that positive relationships with adults were also part of their readers' experiences and thus could provide further basis for identification. At the same time, relying on fear as the dominant emotion frames each protagonist as vulnerable (that is, subject to the control of adults and/or whites) and sets the stage for a narrative of personal growth that entails increasing courage and control over one's life. The use of emotion in this way makes the story centrally about the evolution of an individual rather than about the events of history.

Biographies about Chisholm do not feature fear as the emblematic emotion of their subject's early life. However, they do address the ways in which the choices of adults shaped her girlhood, and they imagine for readers the emotional implications of those choices. These textual strategies are most obvious in the stories of young Shirley St. Hill's moves between Barbados and Brooklyn during her early years. Creators have used these accounts as an opportunity to provide readers a glimpse into Shirley's most formative childhood experiences, often by sharing information about their subject's inner world. Although not all texts depict the same emotions, most emphasize the poignant nature of this time in Shirley's life.

Some texts describe the difficulty that Shirley experienced in leaving her parents in Brooklyn to live with her grandmother and sisters in Barbados. Garnet Nelson Jackson's biography begins by describing the sea journey from Brooklyn, contrasting the beauty of the scenery with the negative experiences of young Shirley: "A ship sailed across miles of blue water. Waves sparkled in the sunlight. But four-year-old Shirley did not like the trip. Traveling on a ship made her seasick."[58] This opening description seems intended to engage the imaginations of young readers through simple, vivid description. But the narrator also incorporates insight into Shirley's experiences, particularly the emotional and physical impact of the voyage. Several texts use Shirley's and her sisters' perspectives to highlight the common childhood experience of encountering a new place. Texts tell readers that, upon their arrival in Barbados, "the girls realized that their new home was a lot different from Brooklyn," so much so that even the "night sounds" seemed "strange."[59] Such an experience may be familiar, though not always negative, to young readers. However, most children would have significant difficulty leaving their parents for several years, and some texts invite readers to imagine this challenge by conveying the St. Hill children's feelings when their mother left them on the island and returned to Brooklyn. Both Raatma (2011) and Scheader (1990) related this moment closely to childhood by explaining that the girls were "too young" or "too small to understand" the reasons for this separation.[60] Both texts also describe the negative emotions associated with this moment, describing the "tearful goodbye" and explaining the children's "lost and lonely" feeling.[61] Scheader's text provides further detail, letting readers into the emotional life of her subject: "Shirley, knowing she was the oldest, tried to be brave in front of her sisters. But she ended up crying just as hard as they did."[62] In highlighting feelings of sadness or vulnerability, these representations bear considerable similarity to those in biographies about Wheatley and Truth. However, many more biographies about Chisholm also emphasize young Shirley's positive feelings, particularly her strong attachment to her home in Barbados. The narrator of Brownmiller's text, for instance, opens by telling readers that "Shirley loved her grandmother, and she loved the farm."[63] Other texts also describe young Shirley's feelings of happiness in her life and in her experiences on the farm.[64] Like Wheatley and Truth, Shirley Chisholm endured separation from her parents as a young child that left her vulnerable and, likely, sad. But unlike Wheatley and Truth, young Shirley St. Hill was not enslaved. She remained surrounded by family in an idyllic setting where she received both love and education. Despite these differences, texts about Chisholm similarly utilize these early stories to invite readers into the emotional life of their child subject.

As the stories of Wheatley, Truth, and Chisholm proceed beyond vulnerable beginnings, most texts maintain reader access to the inner lives of their subjects. For instance, all three women eventually perform notable deeds, which the texts frequently render more poignant by describing their *personal* meaning for Wheatley, Truth, and Chisholm. The texts reflect to readers that these women led meaningful lives because of their personal qualities—determination, belief in themselves, intelligence, independent spirit, and so on. Such personal qualities are exemplified both in the emotions and thoughts ascribed to the women and in the narrator's reflections upon them.

Some texts, such as Bellegarde's 1983 biography, overtly identify these qualities. But in most cases, biographies use inner monologue and self-reflection to highlight and valorize certain qualities over the course of the life story. Readers are supposed to identify more easily with Wheatley, Truth, and Chisholm because they have access to their feelings, thoughts, and motivations. Through such devices, the texts are also able subtly to suggest the ways in which readers ought to respond to these life stories. The narrative representation of these women's inner lives constitutes a kind of subtext, or what Nodelman called a "shadow text."[65] That is, the text invites a reader to consider this formulation of the narrative: adults in my life might tell me that Phillis Wheatley was important for her fancy poetry and other things that adults like, but we kids know that she was important just because of who she was. Not only does this shadow text act as a secret communiqué to child readers; it also subtly instructs readers that they should relate to figures of the past as potential peers. The texts move—sometimes adeptly and other times awkwardly—between official historical report and intimate insights into the main character's thoughts and feelings. This emphasis on "getting into the head" of the protagonist implicitly claims that the most authentic, basic way of relating to anyone from the past is through identification. Although biographies for adult audiences frequently offer richly intimate details of a figure's private life to readers, authors rarely presume to assign thoughts or emotions to the protagonist without then drawing attention to the fact that they have done so. The style of these biographies for children indicates a belief that any history for children must "come alive" more so than those for adults and that children should not be burdened with the challenges involved in historical representation.

Growing into Agency

By and large, these biographies structure Wheatley's, Truth's, and Chisholm's lives as narratives of physical, ethical, and psychological growth. This structure neatly combines a convention of life narratives (a chronological movement from birth to death) with the assumption that childhood is a time of change and that the child, as Anna Mae Duane has argued, is a "model for progress."[66] A narrative that foregrounds the development of a historical character therefore appeals to the child reader's supposed experience of being in a constant state of flux. Yet it also reinforces the broader cultural notion that moving from childhood to adulthood means moving from immaturity, innocence, and lack of agency to maturity, knowledge, self-control, and agency. By appealing to imagined reader experiences and relying on cultural assumptions about children, the growth narrative both addresses and constitutes its audience of child readers. Through stories of growth and development, readers are invited to perceive similarities between themselves and these historical women. They are also invited to envision their own lives in the way that the texts' creators describe the lives of these women: as journeys of learning and agential growth.

As growth stories, these biographical texts exhibit marked similarities. Several themes of development are woven throughout the texts, working together to move narrative and reader from "childhood" to "adulthood." The subject journeys from one state of mind or status to another: from legal slavery to emancipation, from ignorance to knowledge or wisdom, from passivity to self-control, from victimhood to agency, from dependence to responsibility. Each one of these changes plays metaphorically upon the others in a given text, as all of them refer back to the underlying trope of growth. In these stories about black women, such changes are also complicated by the fact that racist narratives in the United States have figured even adult African Americans as "children."[67] Through these story lines of personal progress, young readers are invited to view themselves, first, as beings who are in the process of changing into adults and, second, as individuals who should become agents. The biographies often conflate the process of becoming an "adult" and becoming an "agent," yet the two also appear distinct within certain narratives.

The historical facts about each woman's life guide the emphases of the growth narratives. In the cases of Wheatley, Truth, and Chisholm, these facts lend themselves to contrasting adaptations in themes of childhood, education, and personal development. Wheatley's story seems tailor-made for children's biography, because her most noted accomplishments occurred during her youth. Moreover, her life can easily be narrated as a long series of remarkable educational achievements, which typically culminate in the 1772 examination or the 1773 publication of her poetry collection. In this way, Wheatley's journey from child to adult is framed primarily in terms of academic mastery. Truth, in contrast, made most of her public impact after the age of thirty. Unlike Wheatley, Truth was accustomed to hard, physical labor. Truth claimed to have learned most of her life lessons through this work. Moreover, Truth repeatedly avowed her lack of interest in the kind of intellectual pursuits that contemporaries such as Frederick Douglass valued deeply.[68] Truth's journey to adulthood is thus communicated in terms of gaining worldly wisdom. Most biographies of Chisholm possess the advantage of direct access to their historical subject: Chisholm was still living when six of the seven texts in this study were published. Creators could therefore use firsthand accounts from Chisholm in order to create rich portraits of her entire life rather than merely focusing on the period with the most verifiable evidence. While Chisholm did not ascend to public prominence until middle age, these texts treat even her childhood as a formative period. Like Wheatley's narrative, Chisholm's story revolves around education, a familiar mode of growth and progress for young American readers.

Coming-of-age stories of Phillis Wheatley focus on her intellectual progress as she moved from a place of seeming ignorance to one of knowledge. Texts layer other aspects of growth upon this principal theme, the most common of which are the movement from dependence to responsibility and the change from child to adult. Within these basic confines, there is some variation in how certain signs of growth or impending adulthood interact with others. For example, one text continually contrasts Wheatley's mature intellect with her undeveloped domestic skills.[69] An anomaly in this time period, Bellegarde's text tells a tale of misdirected growth, wherein Wheatley—while gaining the education respected by American colonists—loses knowledge of and respect for her African roots and eventually dies in poverty after a period of depression and poor choices.[70] Most texts, however, describe Phillis Wheatley as growing from a frail, frightened, and illiterate child into a confident, independent, responsible, and highly learned young woman. Another critical element in all of these texts, of course, is Wheatley's manumission from slavery when she was around the age of twenty.

A pair of anecdotes illustrates how texts emphasize Wheatley's humble beginnings in order to frame a growth narrative. Cynthia Salisbury's 2001 text begins with a scene in May 1773, when Wheatley is boarding a ship bound for England. The narrator notes that Boston Harbor "was the exact place where only twelve years before she had arrived—a frightened, illiterate African child who had been kidnapped from her home and family by slave traders." The narrator continues with a comparison of the two sea voyages: "This journey, however, would be different. Instead of traveling in the dark hold of a ship, chained with other slaves and sold to the highest bidder, Wheatley would travel as a first-class passenger." The narrator then describes Wheatley's education, taking special care to showcase her apparently innate talent. As in other texts, this marine voyage is contrasted with the trip that originally brought her to Boston. But making this anecdote the opening scene directs readers to use the two Atlantic voyages to frame the protagonist's life narrative. Phillis Wheatley's transformation from cargo to "first-class passenger" exemplifies her progress, and her education explains it.[71]

In Shirley Graham's 1949 biography, the narrator uses a secondary character to highlight the child's apparent lack of knowledge upon her arrival in Boston. After Susanna Wheatley takes possession of her human chattel, she asks the seller whether the young girl can talk: "The clerk snorted. 'Talk! Lady, she just been picked off a tree! She don't know *nothing*!'"[72] The clerk's snort and disdainful tone signal his ignorance and prejudice toward enslaved Africans. Readers are thereby invited to judge this man so unlike themselves. Yet at the same time, his low expectations for Wheatley stand in for those of the broader society. Having been reminded of the expectations for a young enslaved girl, readers are prepared to be even more surprised by young Phillis's ability to achieve. The phrase "just . . . picked off a tree" has an additional valence: it connects the child with unspoiled nature in a way that highlights and links her apparent ignorance and innocence. The text continues to develop this theme of Wheatley as a child of nature—comforted by green things and soil, primitive, and preverbal.[73]

Word choices and narratives such as these, as they appear in the beginning of the texts, invite child readers to recognize and identify with the markings of childhood upon the protagonist (for example, innocence, lack of knowledge, fear, helplessness) and to acknowledge and take pleasure in the adult judgments upon childhood, as given by the narrator. Most biographies do promote the message that growth is and should be the desired end of all healthy children. The texts argue that "growing up" means gaining control over one's life and influence over others. However, not all of these texts equate "growth" with "adulthood," instead acknowledging that, as Marah Gubar has argued, "growth is actually a messy continuum, an ongoing process that involves losses as well as gains."[74] While growth is valorized across texts, the specific ideals toward which the protagonist grows vary. The texts variously link growth to abstract but widely accessible public values, such as individual responsibility and bravery in the face of adversity. The complex relationship between "agent" and "adult" becomes particularly apparent in the biographies of Sojourner Truth.

Isabella/Sojourner Truth's coming-of-age tale features a woman who grows in worldly wisdom as she breaks free from her own apparently benighted notions about slavery and increasingly recognizes the problems with the world around her. Many texts also set this journey alongside Sojourner Truth's physical growth. Unlike the Wheatley biographies, which emphasize their protagonist's small stature and apparent frailty, most of the Truth biographies make special note of her legendary height, remarkable even when she was a child.[75] In many texts, her early physical height and strength foreshadow her later psychological and spiritual strength. Such textual choices imply that Isabella grew into her physical body by developing her inner self. Thus, young readers hear a common but nonetheless powerful message about the path to adulthood: it is the inner maturity that counts. "Growing up" is (ostensibly) not about how big you are or how old you get. It is about who you are and how you act. Although such a narrative clearly valorizes maturity, it also illustrates that "development is a messy and variable process affected by cultural and social—as well as by biological and physiological—factors."[76]

Julian May's 1973 text, for example, fashions a story in which growth has nothing to do with age. "Belle," as the protagonist is called here, grows up as she learns from experiences that one must be free, independent, and self-controlled. The text first mentions her physical growth during her time with the Schryvers, her third owners. The narrator says that thirteen-year-old Belle "had plenty to eat," grew "six feet tall," and even had to wear men's shoes because her feet were so big. Yet during this time, Belle also "almost forgot how to pray." The narrator invites readers to contrast her physical growth with religious regression. After Belle claims her freedom in 1826, the theme of growth reappears: "In the weeks that followed, Belle worked for the Van Wageners and slowly began to 'grow up.' She was nearly 30 years old. But for most of her life she had been treated like a child. It took time for her to learn to know her own mind—realize what freedom really meant."[77] This passage links enslavement with the lack of self-knowledge and in turn equates this state with a kind of artificial childhood. Here, "growing up" involves coming to "know her own mind" and realizing "what freedom really meant." Even though she was "treated like a child," presumably through no fault of her own, she still had to deal with the ramifications of a "childhood" enforced by bondage. This construction invites child readers to see Isabella, despite her "adulthood," as not so different from themselves. She too was on a journey toward wisdom, independence, and self-knowledge. Portraying Belle as an adult still learning also suggests the potential for the cross-reading long practiced in African American communities.[78]

Later in the text, readers are urged to develop further the connections among these various attributes, as the narrator frankly discusses the drawbacks of legal freedom. The narrator explains, "Freedom for a slave brought many problems." In addition to feeling isolated from fellow African Americans, Belle "began to forget the bad parts of slavery and remember only the secure feeling of being taken care of—of not having to think for herself." As icing on the proverbial cake, she even "missed her kind master, Dumont." The narrator identifies three significant drawbacks of manumission: loss of black community, loss of care (specifically from Dumont), and the demands of independent thought. If readers happen to miss the point, the narrator concludes the passage by declaring, "Belle still had not grown up."[79] In this story, the narrator both provides readers with knowledge and withholds it. Readers may recognize that Belle is not yet "grown up," yet they do not have access to the narrator's perspective on what might finally constitute Belle's arrival at adulthood. Of course, child readers can and likely will fill in their own ideas about what it means to "grow up." Eventually, the text provides this information as well. Belle later moves to New York City to work. During this time, the text reports, she learns the Bible, engages in social reform, begins preaching, and starts using her physical strength to protect others. The narrator situates this period of development firmly within the growth narrative: "She was growing up fast now, and her excellent mind was making up for the empty slave years." This growth also includes her discovery of rhetorical agency, the ability to persuade: "She was amazed that her words were able to stir the hearts of others."[80] Here, the narrator augments the concept of growth by adding characteristics such as responsibility and voice. May's text invites child readers to "grow up" along with Truth and makes it clear that such a journey, though worthwhile, is neither easy nor inevitable.

In a longer text published nearly twenty years after May's, Edward Beecher Claflin also spun a story of growth, though this time with a stated political goal: freedom. The concept of freedom expounded in Claflin's book demonstrates characteristics that fit closely with the Enlightenment ideal of agency that Charles Taylor described in *Sources of the Self*.[81] In addition to getting older, Truth grows into the kind of ideal agent valued by Western, democratic societies. She comes to value formal education (seemingly in spite of her own refusal to accept it for herself), she learns to desire choice and self-possession, she adopts a public persona with a powerful voice, she recognizes people worthy of emulation, and she joins political movements.[82] The story of Truth's development comes full circle when Truth herself takes on the responsibility of teaching others to reach for this ideal. When discussing Truth's work with the Freedmen's Bureau in Washington, D.C., the narrator explains to readers that "slavery left permanent scars" on the individuals whom Truth was serving. The narrator further reminds readers that before emancipation "all the basic necessities had been provided by someone else." In other words, dependence and lack of agency inflicted these "permanent scars."[83] Truth gradually realizes that "the emancipated slaves had to learn everything—everything!" According to the narrator, they had to learn how to take care of themselves after having been "born again" into a new life of freedom. In Truth's purported words: "They have to learn to be free."[84] The emphasis on learning—the desire, capacity, and opportunity to learn—underscores an Enlightenment narrative of the path to agency as a journey toward fuller and clearer vision.[85]

But the focus on *learning* to enact freedom also speaks specifically to the youthful audience of Claflin's text. The narrator urges readers to connect the learning within the text to the learning outside the text, in which they themselves are engaged while reading. By continually describing Truth and other formerly enslaved people as in the process of learning, recognition, and realization, the text clearly articulates the value of individual progress toward maturity. Yet, to portray enslaved persons like Truth, who had been infantilized by the institution of racial slavery, as growing out of the role of "child" (in the worst rather than the best senses of that word) also calls attention to the fact that reaching legal adulthood is not synonymous with "growing up." For Truth and other enslaved persons, becoming an "adult" did not often result in increased self-determination or agency. These texts, therefore, promote *agency* rather than adulthood as the ideal, which leaves open the possibility for children to enact agency in ways that might become historically significant.

Shirley St. Hill Chisholm's growth story revolves around education and the development of those leadership qualities that many accounts say she possessed at a young age. Several biographies remark on her bright mind, her quick mouth, and her ability to command the respect of others.[86] The Shirley who appears in these biographies begins as "precocious" and grows into her strong personality and intellectual capacities. Chisholm's coming-of-age story also exhibits a feature not common in those of Wheatley and Truth: the development of race consciousness. All of the biographies at least mention young Shirley's reading of African American history, and several of them describe in some detail her path to consciousness. In biographies by Haskins and Scheader, this story begins at home, with young Shirley learning from her father, who had been heavily influenced by the views of W. E. B. Du Bois and Marcus Garvey.[87] Haskins's narrator explains that Charles St. Hill "frequently spoke of prejudice," often citing the many ways in which black Americans had to work harder than white Americans to accomplish the same goals. The narrative then shifts its attention to the younger St. Hill, explaining that "Shirley believed her father when he said there was racial prejudice, but she herself had not experienced any real prejudice in Brooklyn."[88] Having lived her entire young life in Barbados and the diverse borough of Brooklyn, this child had yet to learn her father's lessons for herself.

One way in which young Shirley grew was by reading about important historical figures. Texts by Brownmiller (1970) and Haskins (1975) provide the greatest detail about this aspect of Shirley's development. Brownmiller, for instance, devoted an entire chapter to describing the "Three Heroines" that Shirley discovered in her reading: Harriet Tubman, Susan B. Anthony, and Mary McLeod Bethune.[89] Significantly, this account represents young Shirley as not only learning about these women but also learning *through* them to consider new possibilities for her life. Following a dismissive encounter with a white male classmate, Shirley questions why no black man and no woman of any race had been elected president. The narrator then imagines the young girl's connection with and reflections upon her first two heroines: "There was much in the lives of Susan B. Anthony and Harriet

Tubman that the young Shirley could identify with. It made her dizzy to think of such powerful, independent women who by organization, speeches, and courageous action overcame fearful odds and helped to change the course of events of the nation. If Susan and Harriet could do it, why couldn't she? Anything was possible, wasn't it?"[90] The questioning continues as Shirley considers Mary McLeod Bethune and imagines whether that eminent woman's future could become her own: "Shirley wondered if she would ever be photographed with the President of the United States."[91] Haskins's biography likewise describes Shirley's admiration for heroes, though this text focuses most on Harriet Tubman. This text introduces Tubman in the context of Shirley's reading about African American history, explaining, "Shirley read many books on important blacks, and from this reading she became especially interested in one of them. Not surprisingly, this person was a woman. A child identifies most strongly with people whom he or she can realistically aspire to be like. Harriet Tubman was both black and female."[92] Like Brownmiller's text, Haskins's assumes that Shirley identified with Tubman because she was "both black and female." Yet Haskins also explicitly articulated these assumptions, thereby drawing readers' attention to the role that figures from the past can play in encouraging youth to "aspire" to greater achievements. These two texts also teach us something about Shirley and her coming of age. This child does not simply read to gain information about women of the past or present; she reads to appropriate lessons for her own life. She reads to imagine new possibilities for being and acting in the world.

Most biographies pick up the thread of education and growth when Shirley enters Brooklyn College in the fall of 1942. Although Shirley had previously "followed the example of her parents and older cousins" who had accepted their racially segregated worlds, Scheader's narrator claims that Shirley "began to see the society in which she lived from a totally different perspective" once she was at Brooklyn College.[93] These biographies follow Chisholm's account in her autobiography, *Unbought and Unbossed,* in which Chisholm declares, "Brooklyn College changed my life."[94] As an African American woman at Brooklyn College in the 1940s, Shirley St. Hill became a minority for one of the first times in her life. She then sought the company and conversation of other black students, which she eventually found in the Harriet Tubman Society. In this "very political and very race conscious club," students joined together for mutual support, to learn about black history and literature, and to discuss "the effect of political events on black people."[95] Several texts point to the effect of this club on Shirley's growing race consciousness, often connecting this development to the days she had spent listening to her father. A passage from Scheader's biography is representative. The narrator explains that in her discussions with the Harriet Tubman Society members, "Shirley again heard the names of people whom she had learned about when her father's friends gathered in the St. Hill kitchen. They were names that she had never learned in high school. High-school history courses covered all the important white Americans but they ignored all but a few prominent blacks." Shirley's relationships with these new friends expanded her knowledge of key figures in black history such as Du Bois, Garvey, and Douglass.[96]

As Shirley learned from these friends, excelled in classes, and honed her speaking skills in the debate club, she continued to develop those qualities that her caretakers—and these biographers—identified as early signs of later leadership. The narrator of Haskins's text concludes, "Knowing where Shirley Chisholm is now [in 1975], it is easy to see how her years at Brooklyn College were preparing her to become involved in politics."[97] Shirley St. Hill graduated from Brooklyn College in 1946, after which point her education in leadership continued as she searched in vain for a teaching position and became involved in local politics. But, in these biographical renderings, no subsequent period of her life proves as pivotal in the development of her leadership qualities and race consciousness as her childhood, adolescence, and college years.

The theme of personal growth in biographical texts for children is underscored by the American myth of progress and Enlightenment ideals of autonomy. The growth narrative that structures the life stories of Phillis Wheatley, Sojourner Truth, and Shirley Chisholm deftly combines these public values with the assumption that childhood always anticipates maturity, in its many senses. In part, biographies for children make the readers' youth "a matter of significance" by speaking to the child's presumed idea of "growing up." These texts attempt to speak to children *as children* but also as children who are growing into new forms of agency. Or, as Emma Uprichard phrased it, these young audiences are often treated as both "being" and "becoming." "'Looking forward' to what a child 'becomes' is arguably an important part of 'being' a child," Uprichard claimed. "By ignoring the future, we are prevented from exploring the ways in which this may itself shape experiences of being children."[98] These texts thus narrate the past to children in the present and urge readers to look toward the future. In this sense, while the narratives may take some conservative forms, they are also inviting young readers into this unfolding of history by enabling identification with agents who have gone before.

These biographies also exemplify meanings of "growing up" that are filtered through these women's particular stories. In the stories about Wheatley and Truth, growth can mean attaining both legal freedom from bondage and psychological freedom from the damaging effects of enslavement. In the stories about Chisholm, growth can mean achieving consciousness about both the constraints and the opportunities that emanate from her position as a black woman. Depending on how and when the lives are rendered and who is doing the rendering, "growing up" can mean gaining independence of spirit, making choices, the opportunity for self-determination, and responsibility for oneself and others. Yet, in most of the stories about these women, "growing up" at some point has a distinctly public resonance. By "growing up," one realizes one's ability to influence other people and, in so doing, make the world better. These women "grow up" to write poems, give speeches, and debate policy, thereby exercising a rhetorical agency that is commended to young readers as a worthy goal. Readers are invited to view themselves as travelers along this path toward public action. They, too, can someday become the subjects of biographies for children. The possibility of becoming an inspiration or example to future generations, however, requires the reader to embark on a journey similar to those that these women took in their day.

Although these stories valorize growth into "mature" agency, they also diminish what is left behind. Clark has observed how the valorization of maturity operates in juvenile fiction. By building their storylines upon the so-called stage theory of development, such fiction, she argued, encourages children to think about development in ways that inherently devalue youth.[99] Youth becomes the opposite of the ideal. This does not simply marginalize children; it also produces certain symbolic consequences whenever an ideal of maturity is invoked in literature and public discourse. According to Clark, "One of the attractions—but also dangers—of using metaphors of maturity is that, like stage theory, they image youth as something one grows out of."[100] Thus, in addition to orienting young readers toward the future, growth narratives in these biographies subtly encourage readers to associate the past in general with their individual past. History as a story of the past can thus be associated with childhood, immaturity, and lack of knowledge and freedom. History as a temporal process, however, is represented as something that happened and cannot be changed but also as a progressive journey of learning and improvement that is continually oriented toward the present and the future. Like childhood, history is caught up in temporality and, like children, is not only "being" but also "becoming."

None of these audience outcomes is controlled solely by the creators or the texts themselves. Rather, readers ultimately determine how these biographical texts will be refigured and appropriated. Regardless of creators' attempts to make stories about the past accessible, intelligible, compelling, and engaging, young readers may ignore or resist the invitation of the text. Wheatley, Truth, and Chisholm may remain locked in the past. History may still seem dry and boring. And yet, young readers may instead be struck by what Ricoeur aptly described as "the shock of the possible," which the texts present through their reinterpretations of these life stories.[101] Just as young Shirley St. Hill experienced when reading about Harriet Tubman, readers of these biographies may see something potentially new in the resources of the old. If such possibilities do appear to readers, they are facilitated by many of the features of the biographical texts that I have examined here. These texts present themselves as ripe for refiguration by young readers. Some texts explicitly outline their audience or directly address them, so that the implied audience might more easily become actualized. Many texts establish access to the inner lives of the protagonists, so that readers can see themselves in and understand the actions of these historical women. Texts structure the life stories of Phillis Wheatley, Sojourner Truth, and Shirley Chisholm as tales of growth, so that the audience can see how the stories resonate with their own journey from childhood to adulthood. Each of these features prepares the texts to be taken up and made useful for a readership in the present. Indeed, taken together, these features suggest that stories about people from the past, as products of public memory, are primarily meant to be taken up by reader-agents who will refigure these narratives as resources for action. These resources may be specific or general. Either way, they can persist throughout a child's education, as he or she moves into adolescence and finally into adulthood. In this way, biographies of these women become crucial sites whereby young people enter into the realm of popular history-making and public memory. Public memory, in turn, is an essential source of the background knowledge that shapes future public action and speech. These stories supply the materials for the "repertories" of public actors, which ultimately enable them to make the history that will someday inspire new biographies.[102]

Chapter Seven

"SANITIZE *and* SIMPLIFY"

Beyond Contemporary Cynicism about Children's Biography

To commemorate Presidents' Day 2010, the online magazine *Slate* ran a piece titled, "All Presidents Are Above Average," which featured a slideshow that compared presidential biographies for adults with those for children.[1] The brief introduction by Cate Plys and Robert Leighton begins, "Adults, accustomed to the harsh truths about our presidents revealed in newspaper accounts and best-selling biographies, can no longer perceive the glory of George W. Bush's Vietnam military service or admire the 'marriage' of Bill and Hillary Clinton. But children labor under no such disillusions." Unlike jaded yet knowledgeable adult readers, children who stick to reading "the thin books with the fat type" can avoid "harmful references" to prepresidential problems that may potentially complicate their understanding of these great men.

In this feature, each slide compares the biographical representations with a particular event from a president's life. For example, one slide, focusing on Richard Nixon, is captioned, "As children, future presidents are wise beyond their years, not disturbingly anti-social." The children's text quotes Nixon's mother, who calls her son "serious" and "mature" for his age, whereas the adult text characterizes the young Nixon as "fastidious" and strangely aloof. As this example is intended to illustrate, the children's texts, according to the framing of the article's introduction, represent presidents as "role models even as youngsters." The stories for children are "much more inspiring" than the same stories told to adults.

Of course, the comparisons are striking, sometimes ridiculous, and always entertaining. But the cultural assumptions supporting the piece deserve attention. First, the article resonates with the general public's dissatisfaction with contemporary U.S. history education. At least since the culture wars of the 1980s, public school history textbooks have been the subject of significant criticism and debate.[2] These debates have expanded and continued into the twenty-first century.[3] The controversy rests on the question, How should American children be taught to remember the past? Second, the *Slate* piece relies on the commonplace assumption that "harsh truths" represent reality better than other kinds of truths. And as Plys and Leighton have implied, the ability to accept such truths indicates one's maturity. Adults can supposedly handle the truth. Third, the ironic use of phrases such as "role models" or descriptors like "inspiring" depends upon a generalized disdain for moral language in popular culture. Sarcastic phrases suggest that because role models are fashioned through fibs and fiction, anyone who emulates such models has built their own sense of self on lies.

The piece and its assumptions reveal a persistent and pervasive unease with how we as Americans teach young people to remember, accompanied by an inability to provide solutions. The piece sets up a binary between harsh, ugly truths and cleaned-up, false versions of history. The adult version of history supposedly tells us what really happened, and the child's version tells us what we wish had happened. This binary presents several problems: it assumes that there are simply true and false versions of history, it jettisons moral goals as childish, it mischaracterizes nonfiction for children, and it treats children in unrealistic and disrespectful ways. Even popular articulations that exhibit greater respect for children lead with headlines like "To Lure Young Readers, Nonfiction Writers Sanitize and Simplify."[4] Biographies for children in fact exemplify much more complex and varied approaches to both understanding history and representing agency. Although some of these texts invite young readers to engage with historical subjects and events in ways that are different from those used by adults, they do share the assumption that children are in some sense agents who should learn about the past in order to participate in our culture of remembrance.

I have used public memory as a hermeneutic term to highlight the rhetorical processes of constructing history as well as the products that represent it. Public memory—as a term both for public discourse and for academic discussion—provides a meaningful way of conceptualizing the rhetorical functions of historical interpretation and representation. Public memory is "public" because it is a communal process of interpreting history that a public shares in common. Public memory is a form of "memory" because it is an alternative or supplement to professional history and, as such, does not always conform to the standards of professional history. And public memory is "rhetorical" because it attempts to both persuade and constitute particular audiences.

The *Slate* article also points to an assumption that accurate history, made up of harsh truths, cannot provide models for potential emulation. In that piece, "role models" are sanitized figures whose purpose is to edify young people by exemplifying positive thinking and personal success. Although some biographies written for children do engage in such simplification, many twentieth- and twenty-first-century biographies present a more complex portrait of the "people behind the headlines and history books" and expose children to the primary texts that help us to understand those people.[5] And, despite criticisms of the genre, biographies for children have remained an important textual source for role models and for public memory. Part of the staying power of biographies, as this study has shown, has been the result of their apparent appeal as stories about emotionally accessible human beings who act in ways that affect the world around them. Biographies will remain a staple of historical education and children's publishing, at least until the concept of the Lacanian split subject can be successfully translated into a thirty-two-page photobiographical format.

This study has presented a means for critically assessing biographies and their subjects not merely as true or false but as persuasive in particular ways. As Ekaterina Haskins has said, "I am less interested in the question 'Is this experience authentic and unmediated?' than in 'What modes of civic engagement does this participatory experience promote?'"[6] Once they venture beyond the reportage of historical data, biographical texts for children leave the land of the certain and enter the realm of the probable—that is, the realm of rhetoric. Phillis Wheatley published a book of poetry in 1773; Sojourner Truth spoke in Akron, Ohio, in 1851; and Shirley Chisholm was elected to Congress in 1968—these facts can be verified historically. But the question of how these women arrived at these moments of accomplishment, how they felt about their achievements, and what their lives should mean today can be answered only by a combination of interpretation and imagination. In this sense, biographical texts for children invent compelling narratives that aspire to be intelligible to young readers. It is these traces of invention—left by the exercise of interpretive agency throughout the process of creating public memories—that can be detected and illuminated through a rhetorical analysis that uses the concept of the agential spiral. Tracking these traces also enables us to see how biographies for children, while limited by a traditional form, possess the capacity for progressive innovation. This capacity for introducing new values becomes especially apparent when we examine accounts of the lives of these three black women. A biographer of George Washington does not need to work very hard to represent his agency; his place in history and his supposed effects upon its trajectory are widely assumed (if at times magnified or misunderstood). A biographer of Phillis Wheatley, Sojourner Truth, or Shirley Chisholm must make sense of historical significance outside the "great man" approach to history and must represent agency in ways that account for the complexity of race and gender oppression and even enslavement. Moreover, because of the ways that African Americans and women—and especially the intersectional realities of black women—have been erased from history, the representation of these women as agents can become a matter of immediate social utility. As Mary McLeod Bethune rightly claimed, black children need black role models and all children need to see the important role that African Americans have played in American history. This study has brought together the concepts of agency and memory to show that the representation of the past is about not just information but also action.

Inviting Children into a Participatory Memory Culture

The question I have encountered most while working on this book has been "What makes for a 'good' children's biography?" I have settled on this response: children's biographies should help young people understand how history is constructed, teach them that the past can be a resource for moral public action, and invite them to participate in the practices of remembering. Most significant, creators of biographies must recognize that child readers are *already* rhetorical agents and savvy consumers of media, and creators must address them as such. As David Oswell has asserted, "Children are not simply beings, they are more significantly doings. They are actors, authors, authorities and agents."[7] As my analysis has demonstrated, not all biographies engage children in this way. Yet, I have also observed that a significant minority of mainstream children's biographies published during the late 1990s and 2000s have shifted from an approach emphasizing singular, objective, authoritative, professional, stable "history" to one emphasizing pluralistic, practical, democratic, and fluid "memory." Several of the emphases of public memory, as described earlier, began to reappear in texts published after the mid-1990s, becoming even more frequent, although certainly not yet universal, after 2000. These emphases combine in fascinating ways with sometimes contradictory ideas from the old regime of historical interpretation and understanding. In other words, children's biographies have begun to reflect a shift toward what Haskins called "participatory memory practices."[8]

Textual conventions and rhetorical features rather than explicit declarations provide evidence of this shift. These texts strongly encourage child audiences to view the past as fluid, continuous, and useful. Even so, the same texts often communicate a certain level of reverence for the past and a degree of respect for the authorities who construct it and instruct young people about it. The coexistence of reflexivity and fixity in these texts results in a mixed message indicative of the transitional period in which the books were produced. During this period, a new type of text appeared that drew greater attention to the processual, mutable nature of historical understanding and representation. Texts as early as the *Brownies' Book* included discussions about the "legacy" of their subjects in order to stabilize the meaning of their lives and implied obligations on the parts of readers to carry on this legacy.[9] Creators continued to use the concept of legacy, but some later texts added treatments of two key *topoi:* first, texts addressed the changing meanings of these women's lives over time; second, the creators emphasized official commemorations as evidence of an enduring public memory. Read together, such commentaries suggest the growing prominence of the idea that the best historical narratives consist not only in reporting the deeds of an individual but also in considering how individuals and groups understand and reinterpret those deeds. In addition to emphasizing the individual's legacy—or, as Henry Louis Gates Jr. called it, the "afterlife"—a few texts published after the late 1990s challenge the idea that our understanding of historical figures ought to be stabilized and secured by professional historians.[10] This is something that does not appear in earlier texts. The most remarkable examples of this move toward historical reflexivity are Ruffin's 2002 and Mary G. Butler's 2003 books on Truth.[11] By emphasizing reflexivity about historical narratives and demonstrating the agential engagement of contemporary readers, the biographies mark a tentative shift toward a more accessible public memory.

Many of the texts published after 2000 provide a discussion of the shifting remembrances, legacies, and commemorations of Wheatley, Truth, and Chisholm.[12] Woven throughout these texts is the idea that the reader can and should take an active role not only in learning about history but also in interpreting and remaking it. Although these elements are occasionally present in texts published prior to the late 1990s, they are rare. Overall, what can be detected in these texts is a recognition that our interpretation of the past is mutable and perspectival—that it is rhetorical. Creators appear to have struggled to translate this recognition in a way that is meaningful to young readers.

Only one of the Shirley Chisholm biographies was published after its subject's death in 2005: Lucia Raatma's 2011 *Shirley Chisholm.* Like other biographies published after 2000, this text features a concluding chapter about "Chisholm's Legacy," which details the congresswoman's activities and experiences after losing her 1972 presidential bid up until her death.[13] This text exemplifies the shift from history to memory primarily in its attempts to provide a "complete" portrait of Chisholm during these years, its emphasis on continuity, and its concluding efforts to urge readers to consider how Chisholm should be remembered. The chapter begins with a clear attempt to perform a "warts and all" approach to biography: "In the years to come, Chisholm faced a number of challenges. There were still programs she wanted to create and laws she wanted to help pass. But many of her goals were not so easy to attain."[14] Readers then learn about an investigation into Chisholm's use of campaign funds (which ultimately revealed no wrongdoing), as well as her "disappointments" in Congress and "personal conflicts" such as her divorce from Conrad Chisholm.[15]

The chapter goes on to describe her departure from Congress in 1982, her professorship at Mount Holyoke College during the 1980s, and her connections with other black American leaders. In describing these aspects of Chisholm's later life, this chapter also places her in an ongoing narrative of political action and change, subtly emphasizing the temporal continuity typically associated with public memory. Both her post at Mount Holyoke and her support of politicians such as Jesse Jackson connect her to the work of the future. For instance, the narrator paraphrases Chisholm upon her departure from Congress in order to create such continuity: "She assured the people of the United States that she would continue her work—fighting for women's rights and civil rights—but she would do it in a new role." This Chisholm clearly saw her teaching role as a continuation of her political position. The narrative clarifies this by quoting Chisholm directly as she spoke of her students: "I want to make my students think. I want them to participate, to ask questions. They can disagree with me on anything, but I warn them to back up their arguments."[16] Raatma's text here emphasizes that Chisholm intended to do for her students what she had previously been accomplishing in Congress: urging people to become engaged to change the status quo.

In addition to presenting the good and bad of Chisholm's later years and emphasizing continuity, Raatma's concluding chapter draws attention to the recognition that Chisholm earned and how she herself wanted to be remembered. The narrative relates how Chisholm's achievements had been recognized during her life, as she was inducted into the National Women's Hall of Fame in 1993 and won a Trumpet Award in 2001 in honor of her accomplishments as an African American. Readers likewise learn that, at her funeral, in 2005, "hundreds of people crowded the First AME Church," in Ormand Beach, Florida, where they had come to celebrate "the contribution Chisholm made to this world."[17] These details reinforce the idea that Chisholm's lifework should be remembered by readers, because in fact it had already been recognized by many others. However, the concluding passage of this text most clearly acknowledges that memories can be shaped by individual agents. In this section, the narrator links Chisholm's "groundbreaking campaign" for president to the 2008 election of Barack Obama.[18] The narrator reminds readers that "some people thought that a black person would never be elected president of the United States." The narrator points out that Shirley Chisholm, contradicting such naysayers in her usual fashion, "always knew that it was possible" and in fact "paved the way for more people to try." The text then concludes with Chisholm's own words, which both lend authenticity to the narrative and highlight the malleability of memory: "Chisholm once said, 'I do not want to be remembered as the first black woman to be elected to the United States Congress, even though I am. I do not want to be remembered as the first woman who happened to be black to make a serious bid for the presidency. I'd like to be known as a catalyst for change.'"[19] By ending with this quotation, the text presents Chisholm as a savvy thinker who understands the power of cultural assumptions about history, such as the historical "first." Yet this quotation also presents Chisholm as embodying the belief that her opinions about the past should also matter; she wants to be remembered as a catalyst for change, and she can exhort young people to think of her in this way. Just as young readers have been invited to follow Chisholm in other actions, this concluding quotation invites them to follow her in interpreting history for themselves.

Several texts about Phillis Wheatley incorporate concluding sections that likewise describe her legacy. These sections "open the doors" to the future that began after her death, describe "the gifts of Phillis Wheatley," and announce her "place in history." These texts focus primarily on how different people at different times have remembered Wheatley differently, with special focus on what this might mean for those instructed to emulate her example (that is, young readers of biographies). In these texts, readers learn that Wheatley's reputation improved during periods such as the Civil War and disintegrated during others.[20] The creators of these texts appear to have struggled with how to represent the political controversy over Wheatley's works and actions, which other scholars have detailed so clearly. Writing in 1997, the author Maryann Weidt included an afterword in which the narrator describes the publication and use of Wheatley's poetry after her death. For instance, readers learn that "during the 1800s, Phillis and her poetry were frequently mentioned by people who sought to abolish slavery."[21] Weidt maintained a positive focus, having chosen to explain the ways that Wheatley's poetry was used to change ideas about race rather than to chart the bitter debates sparked by Black Power advocates' harsh criticisms of Wheatley's poetry.

Cynthia Salisbury's 2001 biography devotes a ten-page chapter to the vagaries of public memory and historical judgment. But, like the Weidt text, Salisbury's narrative focuses on the positive interpretations and the "popularity" of Wheatley's poetry. The narrator begins the chapter with this characterization of Wheatley's "legacy": "With a career of less than twenty years, Phillis Wheatley left a rich legacy as the first African-American woman poet. She conquered enormous obstacles and became a writer in a time when neither women nor blacks were usually respected, educated, or free."[22] Although Salisbury's narrator provides a strong interpretive guide for readers at the outset, what follows is an attempt to portray historical interpretation as somewhat variable over time, within certain parameters. The chapter section titled "The Mother of Black Literature in America" addresses the varying assessments of Wheatley's literary contributions: "During the more than two hundred years since the publication of her first collection of poetry, many critiques of Phillis Wheatley's writing have expressed different views. Most agree that the body of work she produced in such a short time was incredible—one hundred poems, fifty of which were published by the time she was twenty."[23] Here, the narrator identifies but does not detail the exact nature of the "different views." Rather, the narrator continues to focus on moments of renewed vigor in Wheatley memorialization: during the abolition movement, during the Harlem Renaissance, and finally during the civil rights movement of the mid-twentieth century.[24] With regard to the latter, the narrator emphasizes that "African Americans, still struggling for equality, saw the poet as a role model."[25] This statement reflects a deliberate omission of the negative interpretation offered by some African Americans during the 1960s and 1970s. Instead of discussing the political interpretations of certain aspects of Wheatley's life, the text uses ambiguity to frame controversy about Wheatley primarily as a specialized debate over the meaning of her poetry. The narrator at various points mentions that some people thought that Wheatley's poetry was "too limited" in topic, that "many historians have analyzed and discussed Wheatley's ability as a writer," and that "scholars still debate the meaning of Wheatley's poems."[26] This entire chapter gestures tentatively toward a historical understanding of Wheatley that is reflexive, fluid, and practical, yet the creators clearly decide not to deal with the messier aspects of political controversy about shared memory. The text admits a pluralism of memory, but it does not comment on the implications of that pluralism.

Other texts about Wheatley exhibit similar ambivalence. For example, the final chapter of Susan Gregson's 2002 biography, titled "The Gifts of Phillis Wheatley," begins by benignly mentioning that many people forgot about Wheatley's literary accomplishments after she died. Gregson's narrative, then, presents public memory not as a process of debate among various interpretations but as the attempt to ward off forgetfulness. This aspect of the narrative relies on the dualistic trope of forgetting/remembering that has been central to public discourse about memory.[27] Gregson's narrator explains that despite abolitionists' invocation of Wheatley's work as an example of what African Americans could accomplish, "people again forgot Phillis's accomplishments" once the institution of slavery had been abolished.[28] The narrator then points out that African Americans "rediscovered" Wheatley as they "explored their background" during the early twentieth century. Historical consensus about Wheatley is troubled in a callout box appearing a few pages later, which alludes to "some people" who "criticize Phillis for not taking a stronger stand against slavery."[29] This brief, vague comment gestures toward a certain absent moment in Wheatley's afterlife: critiques of her by some leaders of the Harlem Renaissance and, later, by those of the Black Power and Black Arts Movements. Although Gregson's narrator provides more substantive detail than Salisbury's, the text as a whole does not tackle the implications of controversies over public memory. Two features of the comment about "some people" lead to this conclusion: first, the criticism of Wheatley's poetry is typographically separated from the main body of the narrative; second, the comment does not contextualize the criticism of Wheatley within a certain time period or ascribe it to a particular group or individual. The creators of this text have attempted to accommodate multiple views while still unequivocally communicating to readers the creators' belief that Wheatley did not deserve criticism.

Ultimately, these concluding chapters and sections mix suggestions about a past in flux with authoritative conclusions about how Phillis Wheatley should be remembered in the future. (Such conclusions are typically constructed not as an imperative but as an indicative.) Creators combine articulations of historical continuity with lessons about how public memories change over time. Although the specific lessons can be unclear, the presence of such discussions marks a departure from previous narrative conventions and an implicit shift toward public memory as a salient frame for understanding the past, even for young readers.

Later biographies about Sojourner Truth also reflect this shift to public memory as a paradigm for understanding and representing the past. However, whereas recent Wheatley biographies try to address the various interpretations of Wheatley's poetry and the appropriate understanding of her life, many of the texts about Truth focus on the changing perceptions of their subject by highlighting official commemorations of her life, such as the issuing of postage stamps and the building of statues. Many texts about Truth also articulate a heavily presentist view on her life by reading it in terms of its influence on certain historical events or actions that have occurred since her death. These texts narrate history as a tale of continuity between past and present, one that is maintained through shared responsibility and communal activity. In several cases, the texts weave these features together in the concluding chapter, section, or paragraphs.

Texts published after 2000 also represent a consistent movement away from such singular, authoritative historical narratives toward the purported multiplicity, reflexivity, and accessibility of public memory. Whereas texts about Wheatley published during this same period tend to focus on the possibility of multiple interpretations of her poetry, texts about Truth highlight the meaning of commemorations of her life and the challenging task of documenting Truth's lifework. Many texts include lengthy descriptions of various commemorative acts and artifacts, suggesting that the way we collectively remember individuals is just as important as how we learn historical information about them.

These discussions of commemorative practice also provide an important conduit for audience engagement. For instance, after briefly describing Truth's death, Norma Jean Lutz's 2001 text reports that "more than 1,000 people attended her funeral, and white men carried her coffin." Lutz concluded the text with commentary from Truth's contemporary and fellow abolitionist Parker Pillsbury: "'The wondrous experiences of that most remarkable woman would make a library . . . could they all be gathered and spread before the world.' This is a fitting epitaph for a great American woman."[30] Although this conclusion is similar to those in earlier texts, the penultimate page offers something more: a callout box that details several of the commemorative activities in Battle Creek. Lutz explained: "Sojourner lived in Battle Creek the last 26 years of her life. In 1983, the citizens of Michigan inducted her into the Women's Hall of Fame in Lansing. The 200th anniversary of Sojourner's birth was celebrated in 1997. In September 1999, a 3,000-pound bronze sculpture of her was dedicated in the city. The Sojourner Truth Institute of Battle Creek is located in the downtown area of the city. There, the historical society houses the most extensive archives of Sojourner Truth artifacts and records in the United States."[31] In children's nonfiction texts, such callout boxes are used primarily to convey facts quickly in a manner that punctuates but does not interrupt the main narrative. Thus, the information lends support to the narrative, yet it also provides an alternative, more "factual" approach to the story being related throughout the text. In this case, the callout box also lends some documentary heft to the story by highlighting the grandeur of Truth memorialization. Readers hear, for example, of the massive "3,000-pound bronze statue" and the "most extensive archives," both located in Battle Creek. Even this brief and selective information encourages young readers to think of Truth as larger than life. Presented in this way, the facts are injected with an emotional resonance designed to elevate the projects of remembrance in children's minds.

Several other post-2000 texts offer variations on this theme. Joanne Mattern's 2003 photobiography presents information about the commemoration of Truth's life by using images, photo captions, and callout boxes.[32] The closing chapter, aptly titled "The Final Years," briefly describes Truth's death and funeral. The narrative concludes with this passage, which summarizes Truth's life for early readers and attempts to fix its subject in the memory of readers and the public: "Sojourner Truth fought for freedom for all people at a time when slavery was common. She also worked to get more rights for women and African Americans. Sojourner Truth will never be forgotten."[33] Included on this page spread are two visual examples of Truth commemorations: a photo of the Mars Rover *Sojourner* accompanied by a callout box and a captioned image of the U.S. stamp depicting Sojourner Truth that was issued in February 1986. Both are described as efforts to "honor" Sojourner Truth, which offers a particular take on the meaning of commemoration.[34]

All of these later texts exhibit varying levels of historical reflexivity for their readers: some transparently acknowledge lack of information about their subjects, and others obscure debates about certain aspects of their subjects' lives. The sometimes strange mixture of ideas, concepts, and conventions creates a picture of fragmentary change. There are still many children's biographies about Wheatley, Truth, and Chisholm that do not respond to critiques of historical objectivity, do not present historical narratives as multiple, and do not teach young readers about commemorative practices. The uneven nature of this transition is likely a result of the fact that, as the children's literature scholar Peter Hunt aptly put it, "the relationship between children's literature and the rest of history (and literature) is somewhat eccentric."[35] The relationship between these texts and their turn-of-the-millennium contexts may be eccentric, but this analysis makes clear that some texts display a shift—albeit in fits and starts—toward an understanding of history-making that aspires to be accessible, participatory, and democratic. Juvenile biographies published during this period began more seriously to treat children as future agents who would not simply idolize and imitate historical figures but who might critically engage their stories so that they could become resources for true, new rhetorical action.

Rethinking Public Memory and Agency in Rhetorical Studies

In 2001 the rhetorical critic James Jasinski observed that scholarship in rhetorical studies had begun to focus increasingly on what he called "concept-oriented criticism."[36] Following a half century wherein "method rule[d]" the practices of rhetorical criticism, the concept-oriented approach emerged in the last decade of the twentieth century as a means of mediating more smoothly between case studies and theoretical insights. "Concept-oriented criticism" employs theoretical concepts in order both to illuminate an object or set of objects and to advance understanding of the operative concept.[37] This book follows and advances this line of concept-oriented rhetorical scholarship. By examining the concepts of public memory and agency in tandem and at their intersection in the discursive objects, I have demonstrated not only how conceptual and critical work can illuminate each other but also how two interanimated concepts, by shedding light on each other, can more fully augment our understanding of a set of texts. This book has worked toward the following contributions in rhetorical studies.

First, this study demonstrated how the concept of public memory might be used to greater benefit as a critical tool in rhetorical studies. That is, I have argued that public memory, when understood as the rhetorical facet of history, can be used to illuminate the persuasive and constitutive functions of historical representation. Indeed, studies of public controversies that invoke the past have already begun implicitly to apply this approach to excellent effect.[38] With the exception of such scholarship, rhetorical analyses of public memory have often created or reified dichotomies between official "history" and vernacular "memory," categories of objects (that is, *this* is public memory, but *that* is not), or remembering and amnesia. Considering public memory as a hermeneutic concept highlights certain aspects of all of these topics by focusing on the rhetorical process of historical representation and circulation. In this way, the concept of public memory might be applied as a lens to revisit familiar texts of public address from a fresh perspective or more fully to comprehend the rhetorical repositioning of public individuals or debates at various moments in time. One might imagine, for example, a study of Barack Obama's first presidential inaugural address that focuses specifically on how the speech perpetuates and appropriates American public memory of Martin Luther King Jr. in a way that encourages U.S. citizens to do the same. Other possible studies might examine the strategic appropriation of certain individuals from the past for use in the controversies of the present, so that there is more work such as Cindy Koenig Richards's 2008 essay on the role played by memories about Sacagawea in woman suffrage efforts in the Pacific Northwest.[39]

Second, by outlining several features that characterize both public and academic usage of the term "memory," this study also showed how the very concept of memory in rhetorical studies depends on the concept of agency. These features include an emphasis on active, ongoing, and affective engagement with the past; a focus on fluidity and continuity across time; a preference for practical meaning; an emphasis on accessibility and visibility; and the possibility of multiple interpretations by both groups and individuals. An important thread running through these emphases is the idea that the process of creating public memory highlights, invites, and enables the exercise of human agency. Rather than decentering the human subject, as has happened in some academic discourses, discussions about how we remember the past frequently center the actions of individuals or groups. The present study, then, has shown how the term "memory" has been used and has adapted these observations into tools for rhetorical analysis. Because public memory, as a hermeneutic term and critical tool, has been fashioned from the mold of these discussions about memory and history, it possesses the unique capacity to highlight the marks that these discussions have left on discursive objects and texts. By focusing on the intersection of public memory and agency, this study has thus also contributed to scholarly debates about rhetorical agency. Karlyn Kohrs Campbell rightly pointed out that this term has had many meanings, both within the field of rhetoric and in the humanities more broadly.[40] The present study endeavors to retain some of this variety within the concept of agency while also making more explicit its function as an interpretive concept.

Third, this study developed the agential spiral as a critical tool to analyze how agency is performed and represented at three moments throughout the process of public remembrance. This book has argued, in part, that agency is a motivating force in the construction, reinterpretation, and uptake of public memory. Ricoeur's formulation integrates action, time, and narrative in a way that makes them legible as part of the process of creating public memory. Whereas Ricoeur concentrated primarily on the operations that occur at each moment—prefiguration, configuration, and refiguration—I also draw out the agent whose action shapes each moment: the agent acting in history, the agent(s) writing history, and the agent appropriating history. Each agent acts in ways that affect a continually evolving public memory. Human agency, specifically, figures prominently in what is recorded and passed down as history. Both groups and individual agents then revise and redeploy historical representations, which is part of the process of creating public memory. Finally, agents in the present draw upon certain representations of the past as resources for future judgment and action. As these actions are then recorded for posterity, they become the raw material needed for the construction of new histories and public memories. By looking both at the textual operations and at the various groups of people who affect those operations, we can gain a better understanding of how human actors, writers, speakers, and audiences become involved in creating public memory. Moreover, by employing the image of the agential spiral, I place these agents in a framework that highlights the ongoing, cyclical nature of the creation of public memory. The agential spiral enables critics to see the spiraling movement of textual production and interpretation that does not travel in precisely the same path but follows it in parallel, as one coil of a spring follows another.

By integrating Ricoeur, this book has demonstrated how his work can be fruitfully adapted to work in rhetorical criticism and theory, in part because of his preoccupation with the connection between texts and human action in the world. Although rhetorical scholars such as Michael Leff, Andreea Deciu Ritivoi, and Barbara Warnick have productively engaged his work, there has not been a sustained effort to incorporate his insights into the ongoing work of rhetorical analysis.[41] As Ritivoi has pointed out, there are many resonances between Ricoeur's work and rhetorical concerns. This study has touched on only some of these common themes, specifically as they relate to public memory and agency. Even so, this project is also part of a larger—albeit currently only intermittent—effort to interrogate the intersections between Ricoeur's work and the rhetorical tradition.

Fourth, this book has revived an old rhetorical idea that deserves further attention: the exemplar. Important work could be done on the concept of the exemplar, particularly as it has traveled into the postmodern landscape. As this study has made clear, the genre of biographies for children is built upon the idea of an exemplar, but what exactly this means to a contemporary public is not yet fully understood. The *Slate* article discussed earlier shows the apparent general contempt toward didactic children's texts that present glowing "role models" for young people. Looking more closely at these texts through the concept of the exemplar would likely yield more insight into how role models are presented to a public whose adults, at least, frequently reject the very idea.

Finally, this study enriches rhetorical studies of public memory by examining a significant but overlooked site of remembrance: children's biographies. The rhetorical power and significance of children's media is evident in the biographical sketches and nonfiction trade books that I have examined here. Although public memory already has been recognized as a powerful cultural form shaping action and determining policy, the way that public memories might first enter into circulation and into the consciousness of young people through children's literature and educational practices has received little critical attention. Scholars such as James Loewen and Joseph Moreau have examined how the past is represented in history textbooks, and Sara L. Schwebel has written about how historical fiction has been used in U.S. classrooms.[42] Yet children's nonfiction trade books have not been widely or deeply studied by critical scholars. In this project, I have shown how, in fact, children's nonfiction reflects the influence of deeply held values in U.S. public culture. Moreover, as an essential component of formal and informal history education, biographies for children possess a powerful capacity to transmit and reshape these values through the stories of figures from the past.

My examination of biographies of Phillis Wheatley, Sojourner Truth, and Shirley Chisholm also advances understanding of children's literature by, about, and/or for African Americans. As I have pointed out, much of this literature—especially that published early in the twentieth century—serves important rhetorical functions for its audience and community. Moreover, nonfiction texts about African American women are particularly compelling because of the ways in which they foreground the intersection of race and gender. I have noted how black leaders of the twentieth century have focused on the need for historical and biographical narratives about African American people, as a powerful resource both for correcting the whitewashed narrative of U.S. public memory and for developing a sense of communal pride and agency among African American youth.

The creators of books and periodicals such as the *Brownies' Book* recognized the potential of their creations, both for young readers and for the broader community. Some particularly savvy readers, such as the young Pocahontas Foster, also recognized the power of biographies. A letter from Foster that appeared in the May 1920 issue of the *Brownies' Book* declared, "I have never liked history because I always felt that it wasn't much good. Just a lot of dates and things that some men did, men whom I didn't know and nobody else whom I knew, knew anything about. Just something to take up one hour of the three hours left after school. But since I read the stories of Paul Cuffee, Blanche K. Bruce and Katy Ferguson, real colored people, whom I feel that I do know because they were brown people like me, I believe I do like history, and I think it is something more than dates." Foster explained that she had developed an appreciation for this history, in part because it narrated the lives of "people like [her]" and because it touched on "something more than dates." Her comments here attest to the rhetorical power of identification in making history meaningful for young readers. But her letter went beyond developing a simple appreciation of history to detail its potential for appropriation when she described her love of the story of Katy Ferguson, the first individual outlined in the magazine's biographical sketches. Foster concluded her letter, "I just love to think about that nice old lady and all she accomplished, although she began with nothing. When I think how much more happily colored girls start out in life now it seems to me we ought to be able to accomplish almost anything."[43] While nearly a century later we are still dealing with the effects of institutional racism and pervasive sexism, we should take to heart this young person's optimism about the power of memory to engage and equip people to imagine a better world.

Notes

Chapter One: Locating Memories *and* Agents in Children's Biographies

1. Laurie Halse Anderson, *Chains* (New York: Simon and Schuster, 2008).

2. Anderson, *Chains,* 268.

3. Anderson, *Chains,* 267–68.

4. Anderson, *Chains,* 268–69.

5. Karen Sánchez-Eppler, *Dependent States: The Child's Part in Nineteenth-Century American Culture* (Chicago: University of Chicago Press, 2005), xxi.

6. Chapter 3 examines sketches of Wheatley and Truth that were part of biographical collections published in the 1920s. No individual book-length biographies of these two women existed at that time.

7. This number also includes texts that were examined for the study but not cited in the analysis. They are listed in the bibliography of primary texts, which represents all of the juvenile biographies about these women published in the United States during this time. My list was generated by searching both the WorldCat and the Children's Literature Comprehensive Databases. With the exception of the 1968 and 2005 Childhood of Famous Americans biographies, this total includes neither different editions of the same text nor duplicate listings that appear without notable changes.

8. While the majority of texts examined in this analysis were authored, edited, illustrated, or consulted upon by women, both black and white, I include texts created by both white and black men as well. Most of these authors seem to understand themselves to be engaging in a progressive act by telling the stories of these women, but the precise nature of this act and how it might be interpreted as "progressive" varies depending on the creator's identity and historical position. On the predominance of female authors in children's publishing and children's literature criticism, see Peter Hunt, *An Introduction to Children's Literature* (New York: Oxford University Press, 1994), 6–7.

9. Vincent Carretta, *Phillis Wheatley: Biography of a Genius in Bondage* (Athens: University of Georgia Press, 2011), 45.

10. Basic biographical information on Phillis Wheatley is drawn from Carretta, *Genius in Bondage;* William H. Robinson, *Phillis Wheatley and Her Writings* (New York: Garland, 1984), 3–69; John C. Shields, "Phillis Wheatley's Struggle for Freedom in Poetry and Prose," in *The Collected Works of Phillis Wheatley,* ed. John C. Shields (New York: Oxford University Press, 1988), xxvii–xxxii.

11. I refer to this as a stand-alone biography in order to distinguish it from popular collective biographies, which include multiple individuals.

12. I refer to Sojourner Truth by that name after 1843. For events before that time, I refer to her as "Isabella." Where appropriate, I will employ other names as they are used by authors.

13. Biographical information drawn from Carleton Mabee and Susan Mabee Newhouse, *Sojourner Truth: Slave, Prophet, Legend* (New York: New York University Press, 1993); Nell Irvin

Painter, *Sojourner Truth: A Life, a Symbol* (New York: W. W. Norton, 1996); and Sojourner Truth with Frances W. Titus, *The Narrative of Sojourner Truth, with "Book of Life" and "A Memorial Chapter,"* ed. and with notes and introduction by Imani Perry (New York: Barnes and Noble Classics, 2005).

14. Truth with Titus, *Narrative,* 74.

15. Karlyn Kohrs Campbell, "Agency: Promiscuous and Protean," *Communication and Critical/Cultural Studies* 2:1 (2005): 3.

16. In referring to "intersecting identities," I am here drawing on the work of Kimberlé Crenshaw, who initially developed the concept of intersectionality in this essay: "Demarginalizing the Intersection of Race and Sex: A Black Feminist Critique of Antidiscrimination Doctrine, Feminist Theory, and Antiracist Politics," *University of Chicago Legal Forum* (1989): 139–67. www.heinonline.org (accessed December 23, 2016).

17. Roseann Mandziuk, "Commemorating Sojourner Truth: Negotiating the Politics of Race and Gender in the Spaces of Public Memory," *Western Journal of Communication* 67:3 (2003): 271–91; Painter, *Sojourner Truth,* 258–87.

18. Darlene Clark Hine, *Hine Sight: Black Women and the Re-Construction of American History* (Bloomington: Indiana University Press, 1994), 3–36; Henry Louis Gates Jr., *The Trials of Phillis Wheatley: America's First Black Poet and Her Encounters with the Founding Fathers* (New York: Basic Civitas Books, 2003), 70–82.

19. Roy Rosenzweig and David Thelen, *The Presence of the Past: Popular Uses of History in American Life* (New York: Columbia University Press, 1998), 191.

20. Rosenzweig and Thelen, *Presence of the Past,* 194.

21. Dianne Johnson, *Telling Tales: The Pedagogy and Promise of African American Literature for Youth* (New York: Greenwood Press, 1990), 79.

22. Ann W. Moore, "Setting the Bar for Biography," *School Library Journal* 51:11 (2005): 38; James Cross Gilbin, "Biography for the 21st Century," *School Library Journal* 48:2 (2002): 44–45.

23. See Hayden White, "The Question of Narrative in Contemporary Historical Theory," *History and Theory* 23:1 (1984): 3; Paul Ricoeur, *Memory, History, Forgetting* (Chicago: University of Chicago Press, 2004), 251–61. Perry Nodelman sees the education/entertainment question as inherent to the field of children's literature: Nodelman, *The Hidden Adult: Defining Children's Literature* (Baltimore: Johns Hopkins University Press, 2008), 36.

24. For an overview of the few studies of biography, see Peter C. Kunze, "What We Talk about When We Talk about Helen Keller: Disabilities in Children's Biographies," *Children's Literature Association Quarterly* 38:3 (2013): 306–7. Scholars such as Margery Fisher and Milton Meltzer have pointed out that the perception that children's literature is fundamentally didactic has especially been thought to compromise its legitimacy as a subject of serious academic inquiry; Margery Fisher, *Matters of Fact: Aspects of Non-Fiction for Children* (New York: Thomas Y. Crowell, 1972), 9; Milton Meltzer, "Notes on Biography," *Children's Literature Association Quarterly* 10:4 (1986): 175. On the shift in focus from didacticism to enjoyment, see Hunt, *An Introduction to Children's Literature,* 10–11, and Sánchez-Eppler, *Dependent States,* xviii.

25. Rob Wilson, "Producing American Selves: The Form of American Biography," *boundary 2* 18:2 (1991): 105, 113.

26. Timothy E. Cook, "The Newbery Award as Political Education: Children's Literature and Cultural Reproduction," *Polity* 17:3 (1985): 421.

27. Perry Nodelman, *The Pleasures of Children's Literature* (New York: Longman, 1992), 187.

28. Marc Aronson, *Beyond the Pale: New Essays for a New Era* (Lanham, Md.: Scarecrow Press, 2003), 72.

29. Gale Eaton, *Well-Dressed Role Models: The Portrayal of Women in Biographies for Children* (Lanham, Md.: Scarecrow Press, 2006); Gary Schmidt, *Making Americans: Children's Literature from 1930 to 1960* (Iowa City: University of Iowa Press, 2013), xxiv.

30. See Christina H. Dorr, "Searching for She-roes: A Study of Biographies of Historic Women Written for Children," *Children & Libraries: The Journal of the Association for Library Service to Children* 9:2 (2011): 42–49; Laura A. May, Teri Holbrook, and Laura E. Myers, "(Re) Storying Obama: An Examination of Recently Published Informational Texts," *Children's Literature in Education* 41:4 (2010): 273–90; John P. McCombe, "Picturing Jazz: Jazz Biography and Children's Literature," *Children's Literature Association Quarterly* 28:2 (2003): 68–80; Katie R. Peel, "'Strange Fruit': Representations of Julius and Ethel Rosenberg in Children's and Young Adult Nonfiction," *Children's Literature Association Quarterly* 36:2 (2011): 190–213; Ivy Linton Stabell, "Model Patriots: The First Children's Biographies of George Washington and Benjamin Franklin," *Children's Literature* 41 (2013): 91–114.

31. William H. Epstein, "Inducing Biography," *Children's Literature Association Quarterly* 12:4 (1987): 177–79; Marc Aronson, "Originality in Nonfiction," *School Library Journal* 52:1 (2006): 42–43; Gilbin, "Biography," 44–45; Moore, "Setting the Bar"; John E. Wills Jr., "Lives and Other Stories: Neglected Aspects of the Teacher's Art," *History Teacher* 26:1 (1992): 33–49.

32. John Bodnar, *Remaking America: Public Memory, Commemoration, and Patriotism in the Twentieth Century* (Princeton, N.J.: Princeton University Press, 1992), 13–14.

33. Hunt, *Introduction to Children's Literature,* 3.

34. Sánchez-Eppler, *Dependent States,* xx.

35. Gail Schmunk Murray, *American Children's Literature and the Construction of Childhood* (New York: Twayne, 1998), xv.

36. Nodelman, *The Hidden Adult,* 3.

37. Maria Nikolajeva has offered another evocative, if flippant, description of children's literature: "According to conventional genre definitions, all children's literature can be labeled as *bildungsroman*": Nikolajeva, *The Rhetoric of Character in Children's Literature* (Lanham, Md.: Scarecrow Press, 2002), ix.

38. Katharine Capshaw has observed that educational texts featuring African American historical figures "began to appear more frequently" beginning in 1945: Capshaw, *Civil Rights Childhood: Picturing Liberation in African American Photobooks* (Minneapolis: University of Minnesota Press, 2014), 69. Since it began keeping records, in 1985, the Cooperative Children's Book Center (CCBC) has charted an increase in books by and about black Americans: "Publishing Statistics on Children's Books about People of Color and First/Native Nations and by People of Color and First/Native Nations Authors and Illustrators," last modified October 11, 2016, http://ccbc.education.wisc.edu/books/pcstats.asp#black (accessed December 23, 2016). See also Beverly Lyon Clark, *Kiddie Lit: The Cultural Construction of Children's Literature in America* (Baltimore: Johns Hopkins University Press, 2003), xiii; Johnson, *Telling Tales,* 5.

39. Rudine Sims Bishop, *Free within Ourselves: The Development of African American Children's Literature* (Portsmouth, N.H.: Heinemann, 2007), xi–xii. I use the term "creators" to refer to all individuals whose ideas went into the creation of the text. Whereas the most significant of these are typically named (for example, author, illustrator, editor), others remain anonymous to readers. I choose this term to highlight the collective aspect of producing books for children and to mark the distance between perceived intentions of the author and the resulting text.

40. Wanda M. Brooks and Jonda C. McNair, eds., *Embracing, Evaluating, and Examining African American Children's and Young Adult Literature* (Lanham, Md.: Scarecrow Press, 2008), ix. Capshaw's *Civil Rights Childhood* includes a chapter on nonfiction picture books (65–119).

The CCBC provides the most comprehensive body of statistics about African American children's literature, tracking books *by* African American authors or illustrators beginning in 1985 and books both by and about African Americans beginning in 1994. The statistics since 1994 have created separate categories for books "by" and "about" members of various ethnic groups. While all of the texts I examine in this study are *about* African Americans, a smaller subset are by, about, *and* for African Americans.

41. Carole Blair, Greg Dickinson, and Brian L. Ott, "Introduction: Rhetoric/Memory/Place," in *Places of Public Memory: The Rhetoric of Museums and Memorials* (Tuscaloosa: University of Alabama Press, 2010), 2–3.

42. Michael Warner, *Publics and Counterpublics* (New York: Zone Books, 2002), 31.

43. For a useful overview of the 2,500-year-old discussion about contingency in the study and practice of rhetoric, see Dilip Parameshwar Gaonkar, "Contingency and Probability," in *Encyclopedia of Rhetoric,* ed. Thomas O. Sloane (New York: Oxford University Press, 2001), 151–66.

44. See Blair, Dickinson, and Ott, "Introduction," 5–22; Kendall R. Phillips, introduction to *Framing Public Memory* (Tuscaloosa: University of Alabama Press, 2004), 2; and Bradford Vivian, *Public Forgetting: The Rhetoric and Politics of Beginning Again* (University Park: Pennsylvania State University Press, 2010), 12–13.

45. On the rise of "memory" as an organizing concept, see Geoffrey Cubitt, *History and Memory* (New York: Manchester University Press, 2007), 1–3. On the linguistic turn as a cause of the increased interest in memory, see Kerwin Lee Klein, "On the Emergence of Memory in Historical Discourse," *Representations* 69 (Special Issue: Grounds for Remembering; Winter 2000): 127–50; and Gabrielle M. Spiegel, "Memory and History: Liturgical Time and Historical Time," *History and Theory* 41:2 (2002): 161–62.

46. David Gary Shaw, "Happy in Our Chains? Agency and Language in the Postmodern Age," *History and Theory* 40:4 (2001): 5. See also Elizabeth Deeds Ermarth, "Agency in the Discursive Condition," *History and Theory* 40:4 (2001): 34–58; Elías Palti, "The 'Return of the Subject' as a Historico-Intellectual Problem," *History and Theory* 43:1 (2004): 66–79; and William H. Sewell Jr., *Logics of History: Social Theory and Social Transformation* (Chicago: University of Chicago Press, 2005), 3.

47. For an insightful analysis of this "renewed and self-conscious interest in rhetoric," see Dilip Parameshwar Gaonkar, "Rhetoric and Its Double: Reflections of the Rhetorical Turn in the Human Sciences," in *The Rhetorical Turn: Invention and Persuasion in the Conduct of Inquiry,* ed. Herbert W. Simons (Chicago: University of Chicago Press, 1990), 341–66.

48. Although many scholars in memory studies also focus on individual or social memory, which are not necessarily "public," even these memories are treated as latently public: they possess the capacity to enter into the public narrative about the past, perhaps as a corrective or challenge to the dominant narrative. For one perspective on the differences among individual, social, collective, and public memory, see Edward S. Casey, "Public Memory in Place and Time," in *Framing Public Memory,* ed. Kendall R. Phillips (Tuscaloosa: University of Alabama Press, 2004), 17–44.

49. Shaw, "Happy in Our Chains?" 1.

50. Christian Lundberg and Joshua Gunn, "'Ouija Board, Are There Any Communications?' Agency, Ontotheology, and the Death of the Humanist Subject; or, Continuing the ARS Conversation," *Rhetoric Society Quarterly* 35:4 (2005): 83–105. For background on this discussion, see Joshua Gunn, "Refiguring Fantasy: Imagination and Its Decline in U.S. Rhetorical Studies," *Quarterly Journal of Speech* 89:1 (2003): 41–42; Ernest G. Bormann, John F. Cragan, and Donald C. Shields, "Defending Symbolic Convergence Theory from an Imaginary Gunn,"

Quarterly Journal of Speech 89:4 (2003): 366–72; Joshua Gunn, "Response," *Quarterly Journal of Speech* 89:4 (2003): 373; Joshua Gunn, "Refitting Fantasy: Psychoanalysis, Subjectivity, and Talking to the Dead," *Quarterly Journal of Speech* 90:1 (2004): 1–23; Christian Lundberg, "The Royal Road Not Taken: Joshua Gunn's 'Refitting Fantasy: Psychoanalysis, Subjectivity, and Talking to the Dead' and Lacan's Symbolic Order," *Quarterly Journal of Speech* 90:4 (2004): 495–500; Joshua Gunn, "On Dead Subjects: A Rejoinder to Lundberg on (a) Psychoanalytic Rhetoric," *Quarterly Journal of Speech* 90:4 (2004): 501–13. See also Cheryl Geisler, "How Ought We to Understand the Concept of Rhetorical Agency? Report from the ARS," *Rhetoric Society Quarterly* 34:3 (2004): 9–17; Cheryl Geisler, "Teaching the Post-Modern Rhetor: Continuing the Conversation on Rhetorical Agency," *Rhetoric Society Quarterly* 35:4 (2005): 107–13.

51. Campbell, "Agency," 1.

52. Daniel Rodgers discussed a similar phenomenon in his conceptual history of "republicanism." He argued that the elusive notion that greatly exercised historians in the 1980s was not an ideology, a tradition, or a paradigm. Rather, it was something much humbler yet much more powerful: an interpretive category that appeared in the right place at the right time. He concluded that "the gift of republicanism, as an explanatory concept, lay in its ability to do so much disparate interpretive work"; Rodgers, "Republicanism: The Career of a Concept," *Journal of American History* 79:1 (1992): 38.

53. Nick Turnbull, "Rhetorical Agency as a Property of Questioning," *Philosophy and Rhetoric* 37:3 (2004): 207.

54. For Taylor's discussion of the historical orientation of his project see *Sources of the Self: The Making of the Modern Identity* (Cambridge, Mass.: Harvard University Press, 1989), 199–207.

55. Taylor, *Sources of the Self,* 47–49, 286–89.

56. See also Spiegel, "Memory and History," 149–62.

57. Taylor, *Sources of the Self,* 351–52. For an example of another scholar who shares Taylor's views on the changing notions of temporality in Western modernity, see Benedict Anderson, *Imagined Communities,* rev. ed. (New York: Verso, 1991), 22–36.

58. Rosenzweig and Thelen, *Presence of the Past,* 6.

59. Charles Taylor, *Human Agency and Language: Philosophical Papers I* (Cambridge: Cambridge University Press, 1985), 5, 3. Taylor described the origins of this modern problem as part of what he called "affirmation of ordinary life," which he traced to the Protestant Reformation. Taylor argued that this pervasive idea creates much of the modern moral predicament, although in ways never remotely intended by the theologians who inspired the Reformation. The affirmation of ordinary life dissolves the "distinctions of worth" that had previously shaped moral agency and replaces them with a new idea that "the higher is to be found not outside of but as a *manner of living* ordinary life." In the context of this new, emancipatory theology, any life that aspired to give glory to God could be as good as any other, whether that life belonged to a dairy farmer or a deacon. Thus, when transposed into the secular realm, the affirmation of ordinary life introduced a leveling of moral distinctions, as well as a turn from outside standards to inner ones. See Taylor, *Sources of the Self,* 23.

60. Taylor, *Sources of the Self,* 498–99. For a more recent and somewhat differently inflected version of Taylor's ideas on the role of moral order in the modern social imaginary, see Charles Taylor, *Modern Social Imaginaries* (Durham, N.C.: Duke University Press, 2004), 3–22.

61. Taylor, *Sources of the Self,* 490. Paul Ricoeur used strikingly similar language to describe the function of the text, arguing that "a work opens up its readers and thus creates its own subjective vis-à-vis": Ricoeur, *From Text to Action: Essays in Hermeneutics II,* trans. Kathleen Blamey and John B. Thompson, 2nd ed. (Evanston, Ill.: Northwestern University Press, 2007), 87.

62. Taylor, *Sources of the Self,* 511–12. There is strong resonance here with Hannah Arendt's idea that the "who" of a political agent can be revealed only to others who are witnesses to and interpreters of that agent's actions: Arendt, *The Human Condition,* 2nd ed. (Chicago: University of Chicago Press, 1998), 40–58.

63. Allison James, "Agency," in *The Palgrave Handbook of Childhood Studies,* ed. Jens Qvortrop, William A. Corsaro, and Michael-Sebastian Honig (New York: Palgrave Macmillan, 2009), 34.

64. Robin Bernstein, *Racial Innocence: Performing American Childhood from Slavery to Civil Rights* (New York: New York University Press, 2011), 28–29.

65. Marah Gubar, "On Not Defining Children's Literature," *PMLA* 126:1 (2011): 209–16; Marah Gubar, "Risky Business: Talking about Children in Children's Literature Criticism," *Children's Literature Association Quarterly* 38:4 (2013): 450–57.

66. Marah Gubar, "The Hermeneutics of Recuperation: What a Kinship-Model Approach to Children's Agency Could Do for Children's Literature and Childhood Studies," *Jeunesse: Young People, Texts, Cultures* 8:1 (2016): 300.

67. Isocrates, "To Demonicus," in *Isocrates I,* trans. David C. Mirhady and Yun Lee Too (Austin: University of Texas Press, 2000), 19–21.

68. Rhetorical scholars disagree on how best to interpret Aristotle's works on the example. The debate cited here pivots on the question of whether the example is a form of inductive reasoning and, if so, how it serves to mediate between universal ideas and particular circumstances. See Gerard A. Hauser, "The Example in Aristotle's Rhetoric: Bifurcation or Contradiction?" *Philosophy and Rhetoric* 1:2 (1968): 78–90; William Lyon Benoit, "Aristotle's Example: The Rhetorical Induction," *Quarterly Journal of Speech* 66:2 (1980): 182–92; Gerard A. Hauser, "Aristotle's Example Revisited," *Philosophy and Rhetoric* 18:3 (1985): 171–80; William Lyon Benoit, "On Aristotle's Example," *Philosophy and Rhetoric* 20:4 (1987): 261–67; Gerard A. Hauser, "Reply to Benoit," *Philosophy and Rhetoric* 20:4 (1987): 268–73.

69. Timothy Hampton, *Writing from History: The Rhetoric of Exemplarity in Renaissance Literature* (Ithaca, N.Y.: Cornell University Press, 1990), 1–30; Samuel McCormick, "Mirrors for the Queen: A Letter from Christine de Pizan on the Eve of the Civil War," *Quarterly Journal of Speech* 94:3 (2008): 273–96.

70. Charles Taylor described Western "modernity" as the present social imaginary, which emerged after the Protestant Reformation and developed more fully in the seventeenth and eighteenth centuries. The imaginary is grounded in a moral order with four key features: first, the political order exists for mutual benefit between individuals; second, all individuals are entitled to seek certain benefits such as life and pursuit of life, security, and virtue; third, the order is meant to secure freedom (which is also a primary modern expression of "agency") and expresses itself in terms of rights; and fourth, these rights are envisioned within a horizon of equality among persons: Taylor, *Modern Social Imaginaries,* 19–22.

71. Sara C. VanderHaagen, "The 'Agential Spiral': Reading Public Memory through Paul Ricoeur," *Philosophy and Rhetoric* 46:2 (2013): 182–206.

72. Ricoeur, *Time and Narrative,* vol. 1, trans. Kathleen McLaughlin and David Pellauer (Chicago: University of Chicago Press, 1984), 53.

73. Schmidt, *Making Americans,* xxii.

74. Ricoeur's "emplotment" comes from Aristotle's *muthos;* Ricoeur, *Time and Narrative* 1: 31. Ricoeur's discussion of *muthos* and *mimesis* leans heavily toward what he described as the "poetic" and away from the "rhetorical." The discussion here is about narrative in general, including drama and fiction. However, Ricoeur later applied the foundational ideas developed here to historical narrative.

75. Ricoeur explained that these values are rooted in *doxa,* which he referred to as the "sedimented universe of ideas" or the background knowledge that serves as a premise for rhetorical argumentation; Ricoeur, "Rhetoric—Poetics—Hermeneutics," trans. Robert Harvey, in *Rhetoric and Hermeneutics in Our Time,* ed. Walter Jost and Michael J. Hyde (New Haven, Conn.: Yale University Press, 1997), 60–72. My use of the term here also reflects Andreea Deciu Ritivoi's paraphrase: "the sets of beliefs widely espoused by particular audiences": Ritivoi, *Paul Ricoeur: Tradition and Innovation in Rhetorical Theory* (Albany: State University of New York Press, 2006), 50.

76. Ricoeur, *Time and Narrative* 1: 33.

77. Ricoeur, *Time and Narrative* 1: 45.

78. Ricoeur, *Time and Narrative* 1: 53.

79. This is a take on Gadamer's hermeneutic circle. See Hans-Georg Gadamer, *Truth and Method,* 2nd rev. ed., trans. Joel Weinsheimer and Donald G. Marshall (New York: Continuum, 1998), 190–92, 265–66; Ricoeur, *Time and Narrative,* 1: 3–4.

80. Ricoeur, *Time and Narrative,* 1: 53.

81. Ricoeur's reference to a "poem" here marks his focus on poetic discourse in the section from which I am quoting. Ricoeur, *Time and Narrative,* 1: 71.

82. The philosopher David Carr also emphasized the importance of recognizing these "points of view" of the three main parties to storytelling. However, he emphasized, as I would, the way in which recognizing these various parties helps readers and critics better to understand the social meaning of historical understanding. He wrote, "Central to the analysis of stories and story-telling, apart from the temporal unfolding of events, is the relation among the points of view *on* those events belonging to characters in the story, the teller of the story, and the audience to whom the story is told. Further nuances involve distinctions between the real and implied narrator and the real and the implied audience of a story. While these notions will prove useful in elucidating the historical character of the individual's experience, they will also permit us to detach the crucial notions of *subject of a story*—and *teller of a story*—from the individual, and place both at the social level": Carr, *Time, Narrative, and History* (Bloomington: Indiana University Press, 1986), 5.

83. Aronson, *Beyond the Pale,* 69.

84. Arendt, *The Human Condition,* 9.

85. VanderHaagen, "The 'Agential Spiral,'" 202.

86. Courtney Weikle-Mills, *Imaginary Citizens: Child Readers and the Limits of American Independence, 1640–1868* (Baltimore: Johns Hopkins University Press, 2013), 1–9.

87. Chaim Perelman and Lucie Olbrechts-Tyteca, *The New Rhetoric: A Treatise on Argumentation,* trans. John Wilkinson and Purcell Weaver (Notre Dame, Ind.: University of Notre Dame Press, 1969), 52, 54.

88. Jerome S. Bruner, *Actual Minds, Possible Worlds* (Cambridge, Mass.: Harvard University Press, 1986), 123.

89. Bernstein, *Racial Innocence,* 29.

Chapter 2: Public Memory as a Rhetorical Hermeneutic

1. Kirt H. Wilson, "Debating the Great Emancipator: Abraham Lincoln and our Public Memory," *Rhetoric and Public Affairs* 13:3 (2010): 460.

2. *American Legends,* Rosen Publishing Group, 2015, http://www.rosenpublishing.com/index.php?page=shop.product_details&flypage=flypage.tpl&product_id=10817&category_id=770&option=com_virtuemart&Itemid=1 (accessed June 22, 2015).

3. Frances E. Ruffin, *Sojourner Truth* (New York: Rosen Publishing Group, 2002), 5. "Civil rights" and "legend" are boldfaced to indicate that they are included in the book's glossary.

4. Ruffin, *Sojourner Truth,* 6.
5. Ruffin, *Sojourner Truth,* 23.
6. Ruffin, *Sojourner Truth,* 7.
7. Carl Becker, "Everyman His Own Historian," *American Historical Review* 37:2 (1932): 223.
8. Becker, "Everyman," 229, 231, 232.
9. W. E. B. Du Bois, *Black Reconstruction in America: An Essay toward a History of the Part Which Black Folk Played in the Attempt to Reconstruct Democracy in America, 1860–1880,* ed. Henry Louis Gates Jr. (New York: Oxford University Press, 2007/1935), 591. Emphasis added.
10. Mary McLeod Bethune, "The Adaptation of the History of the Negro to the Capacity of the Child," *Journal of Negro History* 24:1 (1939): 9, 12.
11. Maurice Halbwachs, *On Collective Memory,* ed. Lewis A. Coser (Chicago: University of Chicago Press, 1992).
12. Hayden White, *Metahistory: The Historical Imagination in Nineteenth-Century Europe* (Baltimore: Johns Hopkins University Press, 1975).
13. On the influence of scholars such as Hayden White on the practices of cultural history around the same time as the emergence of memory, see Lloyd S. Kramer, "Literature, Criticism, and Historical Imagination: The Literary Challenge of Hayden White and Dominick LaCapra," in *The New Cultural History,* ed. Lynn Hunt (Berkeley: University of California Press, 1989), 97–128.
14. On the linguistic turn and the significance of agency, see Geoffrey Cubitt, *History and Memory* (New York: Manchester University Press, 2007), 61; Kerwin Lee Klein, "On the Emergence of Memory in Historical Discourse," *Representations* 69 (Special Issue: Grounds for Remembering; Winter 2000): 127–50; David Gary Shaw, "Happy in Our Chains? Agency and Language in the Postmodern Age," *History and Theory* 40:4 (2001): 5; Gabrielle M. Spiegel, "Memory and History: Liturgical Time and Historical Time," *History and Theory* 41:2 (2002): 161–62. On the question of agency, see Cornelia Hughes Dayton, "Rethinking Agency, Recovering Voices," *American Historical Review* 109:3 (2004): 827–43; Elizabeth Deeds Ermarth, "Agency in the Discursive Condition," *History and Theory* 40:4 (2001): 34–58; Walter Johnson, "On Agency," *Journal of Social History* 37:1 (2003): 113–24; Elías Palti, "The 'Return of the Subject' as a Historico-Intellectual Problem," *History and Theory* 43:1 (2004): 66–79; William H. Sewell Jr., *Logics of History: Social Theory and Social Transformation* (Chicago: University of Chicago Press, 2005), 3.
15. Joan Wallach Scott, *Gender and the Politics of History,* rev. ed. (New York: Columbia University Press, 1999), 17.
16. Natalie Zemon Davis, *The Return of Martin Guerre* (Cambridge, Mass.: Harvard University Press, 1983); Carlo Ginzburg, *The Cheese and the Worms: The Cosmos of a Sixteenth-Century Miller,* trans. John Tedeschi and Anne Tedeschi (Baltimore: Johns Hopkins University Press, 1980). For a summary of and response to this debate about narrative and history, see Hayden White, "The Question of Narrative in Contemporary Historical Theory," *History and Theory* 23:1 (1984): 1–33.
17. Klein, "On the Emergence of Memory," 127.
18. Klein, "On the Emergence of Memory," 128.
19. Cubitt, *History and Memory,* 1.
20. Alon Confino, "Collective Memory and Cultural History: Problems of Method," *American Historical Review* 102:5 (1997): 1386–403.
21. Cubitt, *History and Memory,* 2.
22. Cubitt, *History and Memory,* 35–36.
23. National Council on Public History, "What Is Public History?," 2016, http://ncph.org/what-is-public-history/about-the-field/ (accessed December 22, 2016).

24. David Glassberg, "Public History and the Study of Memory," *Public Historian* 18:2 (1996): 9. Other prominent historians, both public and academic and in between, responded to Glassberg's essay: Robert R. Archibald, "Memory and the Process of Public History," *Public Historian* 19:2 (1997): 61–64; Michael Kammen, "Public History and the Uses of Memory," *Public Historian* 19:2 (1997): 49–52; David Lowenthal, "History and Memory," *Public Historian* 19:2 (1997): 30–39. In her 1997 presidential address to the National Council on Public History, Diane F. Britton also cited the continuing influence of Carl Becker's 1931 speech: Britton, "Public History and Public Memory," *Public Historian* 19:3 (1997): 19.

25. Glassberg, "Public History," 10. Notably, Glassberg claimed in a footnote to this comment that "the new scholarship reflects the impact of communications theory."

26. Glassberg, "Public History," 14.

27. A search of U.S. newspapers on Lexis-Nexis reflects the exponential growth of terms such as "public memory" and "collective memory" in American public discourse. On November 4, 2014, a search for these two phrases yielded 14 articles in 1983, 85 in 1993, 220 in 2003, and 351 in 2013.

28. Roy Rosenzweig and David Thelen, *The Presence of the Past: Popular Uses of History in American Life* (New York: Columbia University Press, 1998), 3.

29. Joseph Moreau, *Schoolbook Nation: Conflicts over American History Textbooks from the Civil War to the Present* (Ann Arbor: University of Michigan Press, 2003), 3.

30. James W. Loewen, *Lies My Teacher Told Me: Everything Your American History Textbook Got Wrong* (New York: New Press, 1995).

31. Rosenzweig and Thelen, *Presence of the Past,* 181.

32. On the modes of narration endemic to the modern social imaginary, see Charles Taylor, *Modern Social Imaginaries* (Durham, N.C.: Duke University Press), 175–83.

33. See, for example, the following works: Charles E. Morris III, "My Old Kentucky Homo: Lincoln and the Politics of Queer Public Memory," in Kendall R. Phillips, ed., *Framing Public Memory* (Tuscaloosa: University of Alabama Press, 2004), 89–114; Merrill D. Peterson, *Lincoln in American Memory* (New York: Oxford University Press, 1994); Barry Schwartz, *Abraham Lincoln and the Forge of National Memory* (Chicago: University of Chicago Press, 2000); Schwartz, *Abraham Lincoln in the Post-Heroic Era: History and Memory in Late Twentieth-Century America* (Chicago: University of Chicago Press, 2009); Wilson, "Debating the Great Emancipator."

34. Ekaterina V. Haskins, *Popular Memories: Commemoration, Participatory Culture, and Democratic Citizenship* (Columbia: University of South Carolina Press, 2015), 3–4.

35. Germinal essays included Carole Blair, Marsha S. Jeppeson, and Enrico Pucci Jr., "Public Memorializing in Postmodernity: The Vietnam Veterans Memorial as Prototype," *Quarterly Journal of Speech* 77:3 (1991): 263–88; Stephen H. Browne, "Reading, Rhetoric, and the Texture of Public Memory," *Quarterly Journal of Speech* 81:2 (1995): 237–65; and Barbie Zelizer, "Reading the Past against the Grain: The Shape of Memory Studies," *Critical Studies in Mass Communication* 12:2 (1995): 214–39.

36. Browne, "Texture of Public Memory," 257.

37. A selection of journal articles will demonstrate the scope of study: Barbara A. Biesecker, "Remembering World War II: The Rhetoric and Politics of National Commemoration at the Turn of the 21st Century," *Quarterly Journal of Speech* 88:4 (2002): 393–409; Blair, Jeppeson, and Pucci, "Public Memorializing in Postmodernity," 263–88; Greg Dickinson, "Memories for Sale: Nostalgia and the Construction of Identity in Old Pasadena," *Quarterly Journal of Speech* 83:1 (1997): 1–27; Thomas R. Dunn, "'The Quare in the Square': Queer Memories, Sensibilities and Oscar Wilde," *Quarterly Journal of Speech* 100:2 (2014): 213–40; Ekaterina V. Haskins, "Between

Archive and Participation: Public Memory in a Digital Age," *Rhetoric Society Quarterly* 37:4 (2007): 401–22; Sara C. VanderHaagen and Angela G. Ray, "The Pilgrim-Critic at Places of Public Memory: Anna Dickinson's Southern Tour of 1875," *Quarterly Journal of Speech* 100:3 (2014): 348–74; Bradford J. Vivian, "Up from Memory: Epideictic Forgetting in Booker T. Washington's Cotton States Exposition Address," *Philosophy and Rhetoric* 45:2 (2012): 189–212; Carly S. Woods, Joshua P. Ewalt, and Sara J. Baker, "A Matter of Regionalism: Remembering Brandon Teena and Willa Cather at the Nebraska History Museum," *Quarterly Journal of Speech* 99:3 (2013): 341–63; and Elizabethada Wright, "Reading the Cemetery, *Lieu de Mémoire Par Excellance,*" *Rhetoric Society Quarterly* 33:2 (2003): 27–44. In addition to these essays, journals such as *Rhetoric and Public Affairs* (2005) and *Western Journal of Communication* (2010) have also run special issues devoted to the theme of memory. Prominent essay collections include Greg Dickinson, Carole Blair, and Brian L. Ott, eds., *Places of Public Memory: The Rhetoric of Museums and Memorials* (Tuscaloosa: University of Alabama Press, 2010); Charles E. Morris III, ed., *Remembering the AIDS Quilt* (East Lansing: Michigan State University Press, 2011); and Phillips, *Framing Public Memory.* Extended studies or monographs about public memory in rhetorical studies remain few, including M. Lane Bruner's *Strategies of Remembrance* (Columbia: University of South Carolina Press, 2002); Thomas R. Dunn's *Queerly Remembered: Rhetorics for Representing the GLBTQ Past* (Columbia: University of South Carolina Press, 2016); Haskins, *Popular Memories*; J. Christian Spielvogel, *Interpreting Sacred Ground: The Rhetoric of National Civil War Parks and Battlefields* (Tuscaloosa: University of Alabama Press, 2013); and Bradford Vivian's *Public Forgetting: The Rhetoric and Politics of Beginning Again* (University Park: Pennsylvania State University Press, 2010).

38. Frances A. Yates, *The Art of Memory,* 2nd ed. (Chicago: University of Chicago Press, 2001), 1–4.

39. Paul Ricoeur, *Memory, History, Forgetting* (Chicago: University of Chicago Press, 2004), 7–24.

40. On the treatment of memory as processual by communication scholars, see Todd Kelshaw and Jeffrey St. John, "Remembering 'Memory': The Emergence and Performance of an Institutional Keyword in Communication Studies," *Review of Communication* 7:1 (2007): 51; Zelizer, "Reading the Past against the Grain," 218–20. The historian Geoffrey Cubitt argued that "social memory" (his preferred term) ought to be thought of strictly as a process and not as a product; see Cubitt, *History and Memory,* 16. Ricoeur also has reminded us of the importance of distinguishing between memory as a process and memory as a product, although he did not necessarily suggest that one is fruitful and the other is not: Ricoeur, *Memory, History, Forgetting,* 22.

41. See Alison Landsberg, *Prosthetic Memory: The Transformation of Remembrance in the Age of Mass Culture* (New York: Columbia University Press, 2004), 16–19.

42. Thomas R. Dunn, "Remembering Matthew Shepard: Violence, Identity, and Queer Counterpublic Memories," *Rhetoric and Public Affairs* 13:4 (2010): 638.

43. See Carole Blair, Greg Dickinson, and Brian L. Ott, "Introduction: Rhetoric/Memory/Place," in Dickinson, Blair, and Ott, *Places of Public Memory,* 2–22; Phillips, *Framing Public Memory,* 3; and Vivian, *Public Forgetting,* 13.

44. Blair, Dickinson, and Ott, "Introduction: Rhetoric/Memory/Place," 1–54; Phillips, *Framing Public Memory,* 2; and Zelizer, "Reading the Past against the Grain," 17.

45. Philip Wander, "The Ideological Turn in Modern Criticism," *Central States Speech Journal* 34:1 (1983): 1–18; Raymie McKerrow, "Critical Rhetoric: Theory and Praxis," *Communication Monographs* 56:2 (1989): 91–111; Edwin Black, "The Second Persona," *Quarterly Journal of Speech* 56:2 (1970): 109–19.

46. In their search for evidence of power, critics can unwittingly produce studies that oversimplify their objects of analysis. Honest attempts to track the dynamics of power in different

discourses risk reifying unequal relationships between the powerful and powerless, rather than providing subtle analyses of how, when, where, and to what extent power relations shape understandings of the past. Scholars instead come to view discourses as either oppressive or oppressed, marginalized or central, manipulative or emancipatory. This happens, for example, in Haskins's analysis of the U.S. Postal Service's "Celebrate the Century" stamp collection. Although Haskins posited some fascinating arguments about the nature of collective memory in the context of postmodernity, the study ultimately flattened her objects of analysis by reducing the stamp collection to a state publicity project that catered to citizens' consumeristic tendencies: Haskins, "'Put Your Stamp on History': The USPS Commemorative Program Celebrate the Century and Postmodern Collective Memory," *Quarterly Journal of Speech* 89:1 (2003): 1–18.

47. See White, *Metahistory,* 349–50; Michel Foucault, *Language, Counter-Memory, Practice: Selected Essays and Interviews,* ed. Donald F. Bouchard (Ithaca, N.Y.: Cornell University Press, 1977), 113–98; John Bodnar, *Remaking America: Public Memory, Commemoration, and Patriotism in the Twentieth Century* (Princeton, N.J.: Princeton University Press, 1992), 13–20.

48. Zelizer, "Reading the Past against the Grain," 224–26.

49. Vivian has articulated a more nuanced view of the relationship between forgetting and remembering in "On the Language of Forgetting," *Quarterly Journal of Speech* 95:1 (2009): 89–104, and in *Public Forgetting.* Similarly, Kendall R. Phillips has argued, via a reading of classical texts, that "misremembering" is a more productive conceptual alternative to remembering than forgetting: Phillips, "The Failure of Memory: Reflections on Rhetoric and Public Remembrance," *Western Journal of Communication* 74:2 (2010): 208–23.

50. Paul Ricoeur provided a helpful, and hopeful, formulation of this problem of the "threat" of forgetting in *Memory, History, Forgetting.* He recognized that "forgetting indeed remains the disturbing threat that lurks in the background of the phenomenology of memory and the epistemology of history." Yet he advised his readers to view forgetting in two senses, one negative and one positive: "forgetting through the erasing of traces" and "backup forgetting," or "forgetting kept in reserve," respectively. Public memory can, in a crucial sense, give us recourse to the latter; see Ricoeur, *Memory, History, Forgetting,* 412–18.

51. Ricoeur, *Memory, History, Forgetting,* 21. This is not even to mention the significant issue of whether the concept of "trauma" should be applied to the collective level, given its therapeutic origins. On the role of trauma in rhetorical studies of public memory, see Ekaterina Haskins's review essay "Post-Traumatic Memories around the Globe," *Quarterly Journal of Speech* 95:3 (2009): 335–45.

52. Blair, Dickinson, and Ott, "Introduction: Rhetoric/Memory/Place," 18. In offering this different focus, I do not intend to suggest that projects focusing on recovery or the effects of trauma should be suspended. I think that such projects should continue, but not as the dominant modes of investigation in memory studies. They should be seen as only part of research in this area. Ricoeur speaks evocatively of a ghost of forgetting that "haunts" our efforts to remember: Ricoeur, *Memory, History, Forgetting,* 99.

53. Pierre Nora, "Between Memory and History: *Les Lieux de Mémoire,*" *Representations* 26 (Special Issue: Memory and Counter-Memory; Spring 1989): 12.

54. Halbwachs, *Collective Memory.*

55. Ruffin, *Sojourner Truth,* 6.

Chapter 3: "A World *of* Inspiration"

1. Audrey Wright, "The Jury," *Brownies' Book* 1:8 (August 1920): 256. The Tarbaby and Tomahawk: Race and Ethnic Images in Children's Literature: 1880–1939. http://childlit.unl.edu/brownies.192008.html (accessed December 21, 2016).

2. Mary McLeod Bethune, "Adaptation of the History of the Negro to the Capacity of the Child," *Journal of Negro History* 24:1 (1939): 10, 12. Rudine Sims Bishop described the purpose of historical literature by, about, and for African Americans slightly differently but no less compellingly: "This strong emphasis on African American history functions both as a corrective to the historical neglect, distortion, or omission of that history in school curricula and a manifestation of the belief that knowledge of their history will function as anchor, compass, and sail for African American children as they undertake their life journeys"; Bishop, *Free within Ourselves: The Development of African American Children's Literature* (Portsmouth, N.H.: Heinemann, 2007), 249.

3. Cary D. Wintz explained that most scholars view the Harlem Renaissance as "an event of the 1920s," but others "have either greatly expanded or sharply restricted the time span of the movement"; Wintz, "Series Introduction," *The Critics and the Harlem Renaissance* (New York: Garland, 1996), xiii. On the rhetorical implications of the debate over aesthetics, see chapter 6 of Eric King Watts, *Hearing the Hurt: Rhetoric, Aesthetics and Politics of the New Negro Movement* (Tuscaloosa: University of Alabama Press, 2012), 117–39.

4. "Introductory material" falls into the category that literature scholars have called "peritexts," which refer to "'peripheral features such as the cover, titlepage, table of contexts, chapter titles, epigraphs, postface, and above all illustrations." Margaret R. Higonnet observed that peritexts are especially significant to texts for children: Higonnet, "The Playground of the Peritext," *Children's Literature Association Quarterly* 15:2 (1990): 47.

5. I have excluded from this study Carter G. Woodson's *The Negro in Our History* (1922). Although this text includes some very brief biographical sketches, it functions primarily as a historical narrative rather than as a collection of life stories: Woodson, *The Negro in Our History* (Washington, D.C.: Associated Publishers, 1922). I have also excluded a collection of biographies about African Americans that, although advertised and endorsed in the February 1924 issue of the *Crisis,* appears to have been written by a white woman: Bessie Landrum, *Stories of Black Folk for Little Folk* (Atlanta: A. B. Caldwell, 1923).

6. Gary Schmidt, *Making Americans: Children's Literature from 1930 to 1960* (Iowa City: University of Iowa Press, 2013), xii–xiii.

7. Dianne Johnson, *Telling Tales: The Pedagogy and Promise of African American Literature for Youth* (New York: Greenwood Press, 1990), 5

8. Johnson, *Telling Tales,* 44; Katharine Capshaw Smith, *Children's Literature of the Harlem Renaissance* (Bloomington: Indiana University Press, 2004), xix, xx.

9. Johnson, *Telling Tales,* 12.

10. The *Brownies' Book* was predated by the periodical the *Ivy,* which was published briefly in 1887. There had also been Sunday School texts and etiquette books addressed to African American youth. Among these texts was L. A. Scruggs's rather unusual 1893 self-published collection of biographies, *Women of Distinction: Remarkable of Works and Invincible of Character* (Raleigh, N.C.: L. A. Scruggs, 1893). See also Bishop, *Free within Ourselves,* 21–43; and Jonda C. McNair, "A Comparative Analysis of *The Brownies' Book* and Contemporary African American Children's Literature Written by Patricia C. McKissack," in *Embracing, Evaluating, and Examining African American Children's and Young Adult Literature,* ed. Wanda M. Brooks and Jonda C. McNair (Lanham, Md.: Scarecrow Press, 2008), 3–7. For a discussion of the earliest history of African American children's literature, see Bishop, *Free within Ourselves,* 1–19.

11. Smith, *Harlem Renaissance,* 6.

12. W. E. B. Du Bois, "The True Brownies," *Crisis* 6 (1919): 285–86. The Tar Baby and the Tomahawk: Race and Ethnic Images in Children's Literature, 1880–1939, http://childlit.unl.edu/crisis.191910.html (accessed December 21, 2016). Significantly, Du Bois's October announcement followed one of the deadliest periods of antiblack violence in U.S. history—what

James Weldon Johnson termed the "Red Summer" of 1919—and it coincided with the beginning of the Harlem Renaissance. See Cameron McWhirter, *Red Summer: The Summer of 1919 and the Awakening of Black America* (New York: Henry Holt, 2011), 13.

13. Smith, *Harlem Renaissance,* 1.

14. Smith, *Harlem Renaissance,* 1.

15. Smith, *Harlem Renaissance,* xvi, 5.

16. Bishop, *Free within Ourselves,* 26; Johnson, *Telling Tales,* 44–45; Carolyn Wedin Sylvander, *Jessie Redmon Fauset, Black American Writer* (Troy, N.Y.: Whitson, 1981), 106. Katherine Capshaw Smith also claimed that Fauset "authored much of the magazine's unattributed or anonymous material": Smith, "*The Brownies' Book* and the Roots of African American Children's Literature," n.d. The Tar Baby and the Tomahawk: Race and Ethnic Images in American Children's Literature, 1880–1939, http://childlit.unl.edu/topics/edi.harlem.html (accessed December 23, 2016). All of this evidence leads me to conclude that Fauset should receive authorial credit for writing these biographies.

17. See the *Brownies' Book* 2:6 (June 1921), The Tar Baby and the Tomahawk: Race and Ethnic Images in Children's Literature, 1880–1939, http://childlit.unl.edu/brownies.192106.html (accessed December 21, 2016).

18. Iris Carlton-LaNey, "Elizabeth Ross Haynes: An African American Reformer of Womanist Consciousness, 1908–1940," *Social Work* 42:6 (1997): 575.

19. Mary McLeod Bethune, "Oswald Garrison Villard and Hallie Quinn Brown," *Chicago Defender,* October 15, 1949, p. 6.

20. Smith, *Harlem Renaissance,* xvii. On Du Bois's goals for the magazine, see also Bishop, *Free within Ourselves,* 23.

21. Bethune, "Adaptation of the History," 10.

22. Johnson, *Telling Tales,* 5.

23. Katharine Capshaw, *Civil Rights Childhood: Picturing Liberation in African American Photobooks* (Minneapolis: University of Minnesota Press, 2014), 155–211; Michelle H. Martin, *Brown Gold: Milestones of African American Children's Picture Books, 1845–2002* (New York: Routledge, 2004), 74.

24. See Laretta Henderson, *Ebony, Jr.! The Rise, Fall and Return of a Black Children's Magazine* (Lanham, Md.: Scarecrow Press, 2008).

25. On the effects of liberal multiculturalism on children's books, see Capshaw, *Civil Rights Childhood,* 221–23.

26. Lynn Neary, "To Achieve Diversity in Publishing, a Difficult Dialogue Beats Silence," *NPR News,* August 20, 2014, http://www.npr.org/blogs/codeswitch/2014/08/20/341443632/to-achieve-diversity-in-publishing-a-difficult-dialogue-beats-silence (accessed December 23, 2016).

27. Julia Des Jardins, *Women and the Historical Enterprise in America: Gender, Race, and the Politics of Memory, 1880–1945* (Chapel Hill: University of North Carolina Press, 2003), 146.

28. Bethune, "Adaptation of the History," 9–10; Julia Mickenberg, "Civil Rights, History, and the Left: Inventing the Juvenile Black Biography," *MELUS* 27:2 (2002): 70; Nancy Tolson, "Making Books Available: The Role of Early Libraries, Librarians, and Booksellers in the Promotion of African American Children's Literature," *African American Review* 32:1 (1998): 9, 15.

29. Du Bois, "The True Brownies," 285.

30. Elizabeth Ross Haynes, *Unsung Heroes* (New York: Du Bois and Dill, 1921), 7, https://archive.org/details/unsungheroesoohaynrich (accessed on December 21, 2016).

31. Josephine Turpin Washington, foreword to Hallie Quinn Brown, *Homespun Heroines and Other Women of Distinction* (Xenia, Ohio: Aldine, 1926), v, http://docsouth.unc.edu/neh/brownhal/brownhal.html (accessed on December 22, 2016).

32. Hallie Quinn Brown, *Homespun Heroines and Other Women of Distinction* (Xenia, Ohio: Aldine, 1926), vi.

33. Du Bois, "The True Brownies," 285.

34. Du Bois, "The True Brownies," 286.

35. Haynes, *Unsung Heroes,* 7.

36. Brown, *Homespun Heroines,* vii.

37. Du Bois, "The True Brownies," 286. Emphasis added.

38. Du Bois, "The True Brownies," 286.

39. Haynes, *Unsung Heroes,* 7.

40. Brown, *Homespun Heroines,* vii.

41. For discussions of this debate, see Hilene Flanzbaum, "Unprecedented Liberties: Re-Reading Phillis Wheatley," *MELUS* 18:3 (1993): 72–73; Gloria T. Hull, "Black Women Poets from Wheatley to Walker," *Negro American Literature Forum* 9:3 (1975): 91; M. A. Richmond, *Bid the Vassal Soar: Interpretive Essays on the Life and Poetry of Phillis Wheatley (ca. 1753–1784) and George Moses Horton (ca. 1797–1883)* (Washington, D.C.: Howard University Press, 1974), 53–66; and John C. Shields, *Phillis Wheatley's Poetics of Liberation: Backgrounds and Contexts* (Knoxville: University of Tennessee Press, 2008), 58–60.

42. Brown, *Homespun Heroines,* 5.

43. Brown, *Homespun Heroines,* 6.

44. Brown, *Homespun Heroines,* 6.

45. Brown, *Homespun Heroines,* 6.

46. Brown, *Homespun Heroines,* 6, 7, 6.

47. Brown, *Homespun Heroines,* 9–10.

48. Some contemporary books even go as far as to say that the Wheatleys—especially Mrs. Wheatley—actively resisted owning slaves. See Kathryn Kilby Borland and Helen Ross Speicher, *Phillis Wheatley: Young Revolutionary Poet,* ill. Cathy Morrison (Carmel, Ind.: Patria Press, 2005), 2.

49. Brown, *Homespun Heroines,* 5.

50. Brown, *Homespun Heroines,* 5.

51. In her very brief discussion of the *Brownies' Book* biographical sketches, Paula T. Connolly observed that a "focus on agency" appears in all of these sketches, especially as a means of revisioning the stories of passive slaves: Connolly, *Slavery in American Children's Literature, 1790–2010* (Iowa City: University of Iowa Press, 2013), 153.

52. Jessie Redmon Fauset, "The Story of Phillis Wheatley: A True Story," *Brownies' Book* 1:8 (August 1920): 251. The Tar Baby and the Tomahawk: Race and Ethnic Images in Children's Literature, 1880–1939, http://childlit.unl.edu/brownies.192008.html (accessed December 21, 2016).

53. Fauset, "The Story of Phillis Wheatley," 251–52.

54. Kenneth Burke, *A Grammar of Motives* (Berkeley: University of California Press, 1969), xv–xxiii.

55. Fauset, "The Story of Phillis Wheatley," 252. The spelling of Mrs. Wheatley's first name varies; I employ the spelling used by Phillis Wheatley's scholarly biographer Vincent Carretta.

56. Elizabeth Ross Haynes, "Phillis Wheatley," in *Unsung Heroes* (New York: Du Bois and Dill, 1921), 170, https://archive.org/details/unsungheroesoohaynrich (accessed on December 21, 2016).

57. Haynes, "Phillis Wheatley," 171.

58. Haynes, "Phillis Wheatley," 172.

59. Brown, *Homespun Heroines,* 7.

60. Fauset, "The Story of Phillis Wheatley," 252–53.

61. Haynes, *Unsung Heroes,* 174.
62. Brown, *Homespun Heroines,* 9.
63. Brown, *Homespun Heroines,* 10.
64. Brown, *Homespun Heroines,* 10.
65. The Wheatley scholar John C. Shields has taken a somewhat dimmer view of Brown's sketch, focusing on its presentation of Peters and grouping it—wrongly, I believe—with other negative assessments of Wheatley and her poetry from the Harlem Renaissance period: Shields, *Phillis Wheatley's Poetics of Liberation,* 58–59.
66. Brown, *Homespun Heroines,* 5. The poem received most critiques during the Harlem Renaissance and the Black Arts Movement. Because of these critiques, Henry Louis Gates Jr. called this poem the "most reviled poem in African-American literature": Gates, *The Trials of Phillis Wheatley: America's First Black Poet and Her Encounters with the Founding Fathers* (New York: Basic Civitas Books, 2003), 71. Although this poem was long criticized as accommodationist, more recent work has begun to read it as a complex and savvy negotiation of race and sex oppression; see Vincent Carretta, *Phillis Wheatley: Biography of a Genius in Bondage* (Athens: University of Georgia Press, 2011), 60–66.
67. Brown, *Homespun Heroines,* 5–6.
68. Fauset, "The Story of Phillis Wheatley," 251.
69. Haynes, "Phillis Wheatley," 167.
70. Haynes, "Phillis Wheatley," 168.
71. Connolly, *Slavery in American Children's Literature,* 160.
72. Connolly, *Slavery in American Children's Literature,* 150–51.
73. Haynes, "Phillis Wheatley," 167.
74. Haynes, "Phillis Wheatley," 176–77.
75. Brown, *Homespun Heroines,* 4.
76. Brown, *Homespun Heroines,* 8–9.
77. Fauset, "The Story of Phillis Wheatley," 253.
78. Fauset, "The Story of Phillis Wheatley," 253.
79. Although the antislavery movement certainly had implications for white Americans as well as black, these three authors explicitly represent Truth's antislavery work as a service to "her race," while they construe her efforts on behalf of woman suffrage as secondary. For this reason, I treat the sketches' representation of her antislavery work as a means of inviting readers to connect with Truth on the basis of racial identity.
80. Jessie Redmon Fauset, "A Pioneer Suffragette," *Brownies' Book* 1:4 (April 1920): 120. The Tar Baby and the Tomahawk: Race and Ethnic Images in Children's Literature, 1880–1939, http://childlit.unl.edu/brownies.192004.html (accessed December 21, 2016).
81. Fauset, "A Pioneer Suffragette," 120.
82. Fauset, "A Pioneer Suffragette," 121.
83. For an excellent discussion of how and why Gage's account came to be, see Nell Irvin Painter, *Sojourner Truth: A Life, a Symbol* (New York: W. W. Norton, 1996), 164–78.
84. Fauset, "A Pioneer Suffragette," 121.
85. Haynes's account appears to draw from the report by Marius Robinson, "Woman's Rights Convention," Salem (Ohio) *Anti-Slavery Bugle,* June 21, 1851, p. 4.
86. Elizabeth Ross Haynes, "The Suffragist," in *Unsung Heroes* (New York: Du Bois and Dill, 1921), 225, https://archive.org/details/unsungheroesoohaynrich (accessed on December 21, 2016).
87. Brown, *Homespun Heroines,* 16.
88. Brown, *Homespun Heroines,* 16; Haynes, "The Suffragist," 226.
89. Fauset, "A Pioneer Suffragette," 121.

90. Brown, *Homespun Heroines,* 15.
91. Haynes, "The Suffragist," 226.
92. Karlyn Kohrs Campbell, "Agency: Promiscuous and Protean," *Communication and Critical/Cultural Studies* 2:1 (2005): 3.
93. Later in the twentieth century, "self-determination" became a central principle in black feminist thought. While the phrase is not used by these authors, the message remains the same. I discuss at greater length how the narration of Truth's name change in contemporary biographies exhibits the marks of black feminist thought in Sara C. VanderHaagen, "Practical Truths: Black Feminist Agency and Public Memory in Biographies for Children," *Women's Studies in Communication* 35:1 (2012): 18–41.
94. Fauset, "A Pioneer Suffragette," 120. Fauset inaccurately dates the name change to 1837.
95. Sojourner Truth, with Frances W. Titus, *The Narrative of Sojourner Truth, with "Book of Life" and "A Memorial Chapter,"* ed. and with notes and introduction by Imani Perry (New York: Barnes and Noble Classics, 2005), 73.
96. Haynes, "The Suffragist," 220–21.
97. Brown, *Homespun Heroines,* 13.
98. Haynes, "The Suffragist," 215–18.
99. Haynes, "The Suffragist," 213.
100. Haynes, "The Suffragist," 213–15.
101. Haynes, "The Suffragist," 215–18.
102. Fauset, "A Pioneer Suffragette," 121.
103. Brown, *Homespun Heroines,* 14.
104. Brown, *Homespun Heroines,* 15–16.
105. Painter, *Sojourner Truth,* 161.
106. Fauset, "A Pioneer Suffragette," 120.
107. Brown, *Homespun Heroines,* 14–15.
108. Brown, *Homespun Heroines,* 13.
109. Brown, *Homespun Heroines,* 15.
110. Fauset, "A Pioneer Suffragette," 121; Haynes, "The Suffragist," 223.
111. Marc Aronson, *Beyond the Pale: New Essays for a New Era* (Lanham, Md.: Scarecrow Press, 2003), 72.
112. Johnson, *Telling Tales,* 44.
113. Carol Jones Collins, "African-American Young Adult Biography: In Search of the Self," in *African-American Voices in Young Adult Literature,* ed. Karen Patricia Smith (Metuchen, N.J.: Scarecrow Press, 1994), 6.
114. Gates, *Trials of Phillis Wheatley,* 68–85; and Painter, *Sojourner Truth,* 258–87. Other scholars have written about this phenomenon, including Gary Alan Fine, who coined the term "reputational entrepreneurship" to describe how individuals fashion and promote the reputation of individuals who have died: Fine, *Difficult Reputations: Collective Memories of the Evil, Inept, and Controversial* (Chicago: University of Chicago Press, 2001), 11–13. I exclude Chisholm here because her life ended too recently for there to have been significant changes in remembrance.
115. Both scholars have helpfully noted that the definition of "authenticity" is not fixed but changes over time, depending on the tone of public discourse.
116. See Gates, *Trials of Phillis Wheatley,* 76–78; Painter, *Sojourner Truth,* 271–72.
117. Painter, *Sojourner Truth,* 272.
118. Gates, *Trials of Phillis Wheatley,* 70–71. The text of the poem reads: "'Twas mercy brought me from my Pagan land, / Taught my benighted soul to understand / That there's a God, that there's a Saviour, too: / Once I redemption neither sought nor knew. / Some view

our sable race with scornful eye, / 'Their colour is a diabolic die.' / Remember, Christians, Negros, black as Cain, / May be refin'd, and join th' angelic train": Phillis Wheatley, *The Collected Works of Phillis Wheatley,* ed. John C. Shields (New York: Oxford University Press, 1988), 18.

119. Gates, *Trials of Phillis Wheatley,* 74.

Chapter 4: Prefiguration

1. See Edward S. Casey, "Public Memory in Place and Time," in *Framing Public Memory,* ed. Kendall R. Phillips (Tuscaloosa: University of Alabama Press, 2004), 24–39; Carole Blair, Greg Dickinson, and Brian L. Ott, "Introduction: Rhetoric/Memory/Place," in *Places of Public Memory: The Rhetoric of Museums and Memorials* (Tuscaloosa: University of Alabama Press, 2010), 6–7; and John R. Gillis, "Memory and Identity: The History of a Relationship," in *Commemorations: The Politics of National Identity,* ed. John R. Gillis (Princeton, N.J.: Princeton University Press, 1994), 3–4.

2. Deborah Kent, *Phillis Wheatley: First Published African-American Poet* (Chanhassen, Minn.: The Child's World, 2004), 6. For another example, see Susan R. Gregson, *Let Freedom Ring: Phillis Wheatley* (Mankato, Minn.: Bridgestone Books, 2002), 4.

3. Jacqueline McLendon, *Phillis Wheatley: A Revolutionary Poet* (New York: Rosen Publishing Group, 2003), 95–97; Cynthia Salisbury, *Phillis Wheatley: Legendary African-American Poet* (Berkeley Heights, N.J.: Enslow, 2001), 94; and Maryann N. Weidt, *Revolutionary Poet: A Story about Phillis Wheatley,* ill. Mary O'Keefe Young (Minneapolis: Carolrhoda Books, 1997), 59.

4. Although none of these authors compared the values of the two examples cited, one can easily consider the two artifacts—a manuscript of an individual poem and a copy of an early printing of Wheatley's book—as indications of the fact that Wheatley's "value" rose between 1984, when the book was sold for $2,000, and 1998, when the single manuscript was sold for $68,500.

5. This survey included nineteen books published after 1997; prior to 1997, there were no books that mentioned such facts. Strikingly, even Vincent Carretta prefaced his scholarly biography in this way, claiming, "Anyone whose correspondence is worth over $1,400 a word has more than enough cultural significance to deserve an authoritative biography": Carretta, *Phillis Wheatley: Biography of a Genius in Bondage* (Athens: University of Georgia Press, 2011), ix.

6. The PBS television series first aired in 1997. See "About ANTIQUES ROADSHOW," *Antiques Roadshow,* WGBH Boston. http://www.pbs.org//wgbh/roadshow/about/ (accessed December 23, 2016).

7. Wendy Brown, *Undoing the Demos: Neoliberalism's Stealth Revolution* (New York: Zone Books, 2015), 36.

8. Paul Ricoeur, *Time and Narrative,* vol. 1, trans. Kathleen McLaughlin and David Pellauer (Chicago: University of Chicago Press, 1984), 57.

9. Ricoeur, *Time and Narrative* 1: 54.

10. Ricoeur, *Time and Narrative* 1: 54–64.

11. Andreea Deciu Ritivoi, *Paul Ricoeur: Tradition and Innovation in Rhetorical Theory* (Albany: State University of New York Press, 2006), 50. The first sense of *doxa,* as an alternative to episteme, also pertains to the argument laid out in chapter 2. That is, because of its association with the discourse of memory, public memory has often been mapped onto the realm of the probable when the epistemic goals of academic history are believed to have fallen short.

12. Paul Ricoeur, "Rhetoric—Poetics—Hermeneutics," trans. Robert Harvey, in *Rhetoric and Hermeneutics in Our Time,* ed. Walter Jost and Michael J. Hyde (New Haven, Conn.: Yale University Press, 1997), 60–64.

13. See William H. Epstein, "Inducing Biography," *Children's Literature Association Quarterly* 12:4 (1987): 177–79; Rita Marcella, "The Role and Value of Biography for Children," in

Biography and Children: A Study of Biography for Children and Childhood in Biography, ed. Stuart Hannabuss and Rita Marcella (London: Library Association Publishing, 1993), 15–20; John E. Wills Jr., "Lives and Other Stories: Neglected Aspects of the Teacher's Art," *History Teacher* 26:1 (1992): 33–49.

14. Nigel Hamilton, *Biography: A Brief History* (Cambridge, Mass.: Harvard University Press, 2007), 2. Rob Wilson took a more critical view, calling biography "a supreme technology of Western selfhood": Wilson, "Producing American Selves: The Form of American Biography," *boundary 2* 18:2 (1991): 105.

15. Books from these series appearing in this analysis include Kathryn Kilby Borland and Helen Ross Speicher, *Phillis Wheatley: Young Colonial Poet,* ill. William K. Plummer, Childhood of Famous Americans (Indianapolis: Bobbs-Merrill, 1968); Kathryn Kilby Borland and Helen Ross Speicher, *Phillis Wheatley: Young Revolutionary Poet,* ill. Cathy Morrison, Young Patriots Series (Carmel, Ind.: Patria Press, 2005); Miriam Morris Fuller, *Phillis Wheatley: America's First Black Poetess,* ill. Victor Mays, Americans All (Champaign, Ill.: Garrard, 1971); Rick Burke, *Phillis Wheatley,* American Lives (Chicago: Heinemann Library, 2003); and Sneed B. Collard III, *Phillis Wheatley: She Loved Words,* American Heroes (Tarrytown, N.Y.: Marshall Cavendish Benchmark, 2010). Gary D. Schmidt has examined the Bobbs-Merrill series in the fourth chapter of *Making Americans: Children's Literature from 1930 to 1960* (Iowa City: University of Iowa Press, 2013), 95–122.

16. Wilson, "Producing American Selves," 113.

17. Timothy E. Cook, "The Newbery Award as Political Education: Children's Literature and Cultural Reproduction," *Polity* 17:3 (1985): 421.

18. As analysis of these texts will show, however, there is variation upon this general theme, particularly on the question of historical explanation. For example, biographers of Wheatley struggled to explain her declining fame, poverty, and, finally, death during the years following the publication of her book of poetry in 1773. Several biographers chose to make historical circumstance the primary causal agent behind this decline. See, for instance, Shirley Graham, *The Story of Phillis Wheatley, Poetess of the Revolution,* ill. Robert Burns, 12th ed. (1949; New York: Julian Messner, 1969), 8.

19. Gary Fertig, "Using Biography to Help Young Learners Understand the Causes of Historical Change and Continuity," *Social Studies* 99:4 (2008): 147.

20. Andrea Davis Pinkney, *Sojourner Truth's Step-Stomp Stride,* ill. Brian Pinkney (New York: Disney/Jump at the Sun Books, 2009), front book jacket.

21. Victoria Ortiz, *Sojourner Truth, a Self-Made Woman* (Philadelphia: J. B. Lippincott, 1974), 14.

22. Ortiz, *Sojourner Truth,* 29, 40.

23. Catherine Clinton, *Phillis's Big Test,* ill. Sean Qualls (Boston: Houghton Mifflin, 2008). For an influential example of the American cultural ideal of individual self-esteem and happiness, see Robert N. Bellah, *Habits of the Heart: Individualism and Commitment in American Life* (Berkeley: University of California Press, 1985). On the subject of teaching self-esteem in the public school classroom, see Maureen Stout, *The Feel-Good Curriculum: The Dumbing-Down of American Kids in the Name of Self-Esteem* (Cambridge, Mass.: Perseus Books, 2000).

24. Clinton, *Phillis's Big Test,* front book jacket.

25. Clinton explained Wheatley's refusal of John Wheatley's offer this way: "She would make her own way to the public hall where the most important men of the Massachusetts Bay Colony would examine her and settle the question once and for all: was she or was she not the author of her poems?" Clinton, *Phillis's Big Test,* 2.

26. Clinton, *Phillis's Big Test,* 1. In the larger passage that provides the context for this sentence, "consented" is the only textual clue to readers that Wheatley was not the sole actor in this particular drama.

27. Clinton, *Phillis's Big Test,* 14–15.

28. James Haskins, *Fighting Shirley Chisholm* (New York: Dial Press, 1975), 82; Nancy Hicks, *The Honorable Shirley Chisholm: Congresswoman from Brooklyn* (New York: Lion Books, 1971), 48; Jill S. Pollack, *Shirley Chisholm* (New York: Franklin Watts, 1994), 37; and Catherine Scheader, *Shirley Chisholm: Teacher and Congresswoman* (Hillside, N.J.: Enslow, 1990), 44, 124.

29. Hicks, *Honorable Shirley Chisholm,* 11.

30. Hicks, *Honorable Shirley Chisholm,* 12.

31. Hicks, *Honorable Shirley Chisholm,* 24.

32. Hicks, *Honorable Shirley Chisholm,* 24–25. Emphasis added.

33. On the significance of competition to neoliberal individualism, see Brown, *Undoing the Demos,* 36.

34. Hicks, *Honorable Shirley Chisholm,* 25.

35. Hicks, *Honorable Shirley Chisholm,* 48.

36. See Michael G. Kammen, *Mystic Chords of Memory: The Transformation of Tradition in American Culture* (New York: Knopf, 1991), 6, 45–47. Charles Taylor explained that the ideas of the Enlightenment encouraged among modern individuals a desire to play "a role in the chain of progress": Taylor, *Sources of the Self: The Making of the Modern Identity* (Cambridge, Mass.: Harvard University Press, 1989), 352.

37. Kent, *Phillis Wheatley,* 25.

38. Susan Taylor-Boyd, *Sojourner Truth: The Courageous Former Slave Whose Eloquence Helped Promote Human Equality* (Milwaukee: Gareth Stevens Children's Books, 1990), 6.

39. Pollack, *Shirley Chisholm,* 55.

40. Haskins, *Fighting Shirley Chisholm,* 118.

41. Taylor, *Sources of the Self,* 351–53, 510–11.

42. Wilson, "Producing American Selves," 106.

43. These texts could thus be said to traffic heavily in ideographs, as Michael Calvin McGee has understood the term. For McGee, an ideograph such as "liberty" served as a critical point of intersection between the study of rhetoric and the study of ideology: McGee, "The 'Ideograph': A Link between Rhetoric and Ideology," *Quarterly Journal of Speech* 66:1 (1980): 1–16. For an example of criticism using the ideograph, see John Louis Lucaites and Celeste Michelle Condit, "Reconstructing <Equality>: Culturetypal and Counter-Cultural Rhetorics in the Martyred Black Vision," *Communication Monographs* 57:1 (1990): 5–24.

44. Not all texts remain on such a general level. Many of these texts add layers to the readers' understanding of "freedom," particularly by exploring what might have been Truth's and Wheatley's mixed experiences of this complicated ideal.

45. Borland and Speicher, *Phillis Wheatley: Young Colonial Poet,* 137.

46. One could also argue that this conception of freedom minimized the significance of legal manumission, an issue that some texts engage. The reliance on such an extralegal conception of freedom might be explained by the fact that, unlike Sojourner Truth, Phillis Wheatley does not have an exciting "escape" story; see Paula T. Connolly, *Slavery in American Children's Literature, 1790–2010* (Iowa City: University of Iowa Press, 2013), 197.

47. David A. Adler, *A Picture Book of Sojourner Truth,* ill. Gershom Griffith (New York: Scholastic, 1994), 29; Edward Beecher Claflin, *Sojourner Truth and the Struggle for Freedom,* ill. Jada Rowland (Hauppage, N.Y.: Children's Press Choice, 1987), 43, 47; Kathleen Collins, *Sojourner Truth: Equal Rights Advocate* (New York: Rosen Publishing Group, 2004), 19; Julian

May, *Sojourner Truth: Freedom-Fighter,* ill. Phero Thomas (Chicago: Childrens Press, 1973), 19; Pinkney, *Sojourner Truth's Step-Stomp Stride,* 14–15; Peter Roop and Connie Roop, *Sojourner Truth* (New York: Scholastic, 2002), 41.

48. Pinkney, *Sojourner Truth's Step-Stomp Stride,* 14–15.

49. Pinkney, *Sojourner Truth's Step-Stomp Stride,* 16–17.

50. Pinkney, *Sojourner Truth's Step-Stomp Stride,* 22.

51. Hicks, *Honorable Shirley Chisholm,* 47.

52. Joan Wallach Scott, *Gender and the Politics of History,* rev. ed. (New York: Columbia University Press, 1999), xi.

53. Ricoeur, "Rhetoric—Poetics—Hermeneutics," 66.

54. In several cases, Wheatley does not even engage in the domestic work that one might expect to be commonplace in the life of an enslaved person. Some authors, in fact, have gone to great lengths to describe Wheatley as domestically inept. See, for instance, Borland and Speicher, *Phillis Wheatley: Young Colonial Poet,* 46–51.

55. Among the juvenile biographies about Wheatley and Truth, many that fall into the category of "history of a life" are picture books and early-reading texts. Since these books typically contain less text than their longer counterparts, it is possible that their creators chose to cut out complex historical context in order to streamline the narrative. It is also likely that texts for early readers are intended primarily to teach reading, with instruction in history a secondary objective. Examples of picture books and texts for early readers include Clinton, *Phillis's Big Test;* Helen Frost, *Sojourner Truth* (Mankato, Minn.: Capstone Press, 2003); Fuller, *Phillis Wheatley;* Garnet Nelson Jackson, *Phillis Wheatley, Poet,* ill. Cheryl Hanna (Cleveland, Ohio: Modern Curriculum Press, 1993); Suzanne Slade, *Sojourner Truth: Preacher for Freedom and Equality,* ill. Natascha Alex Banks (Minneapolis: Picture Window Books, 2008); and Pinkney, *Sojourner Truth's Step-Stomp Stride.*

56. Susan Brownmiller, *Shirley Chisholm* (New York: Doubleday, 1970); Fuller, *Phillis Wheatley;* Helen Stone Peterson, *Sojourner Truth: Fearless Crusader,* ill. Victor Mays (Champaign, Ill.: Garrard, 1972).

57. As Janet Beizer has pointed out, "Since the 1970s feminism has been not only reclaiming biographies of its own but also reclaiming biography after an earlier stage when graphing a woman's life would have inadmissibly rehearsed a tradition of patronizing women's works by conflating them with their days": Beizer, *Thinking through the Mothers: Reimagining Women's Biographies* (Ithaca, N.Y.: Cornell University Press, 2009), 25.

58. Fuller, *Phillis Wheatley,* 1–7.

59. Fuller, *Phillis Wheatley,* 1–7.

60. Fuller, *Phillis Wheatley,* 18.

61. Peterson, *Sojourner Truth,* 19.

62. Brownmiller, *Shirley Chisholm,* 13.

63. Fuller, *Phillis Wheatley,* 18–23. Although no one can know for sure what Wheatley's earliest poem was, most scholars agree that Wheatley's first published poem was the 1767 "On Messrs. Hussey and Coffin." According to Shields, this poem to King George was published in 1768: Phillis Wheatley, *The Collected Works of Phillis Wheatley,* ed. John Shields (New York: Oxford University Press, 1988), 337–38. Historical events and social movements are slightly more prominent in the Peterson text about Truth, in part because Truth's life story intersects more regularly with such events. Nonetheless, these are secondary to the development of Truth as the central character of her own story. One telling example describes the messages of Truth's early antislavery addresses (undated, though textual clues suggest the rough date to be 1850). Truth's fame as a speaker, the narrator explains, necessitates her adoption of Amy Post as an

"agent" of sorts. The narrator then tells readers that Truth was "the first black woman to give antislavery lectures in America" (55). Here, the text bends historical context into the service of Truth's life story in order to invest it with more historical significance. Although Truth was a pioneer in this regard, she was not strictly the "first." Another important example is Maria Miller W. Stewart, who addressed antislavery assemblies in New England as early as 1831. See Deborah F. Atwater, *African American Women's Rhetoric: The Search for Dignity, Personhood, and Honor* (Lanham, Md.: Lexington Books, 2009), 28–31.

64. Brownmiller, *Shirley Chisholm,* 67.

65. For more on this series, see Schmidt, *Making Americans,* 95–122.

66. Borland and Speicher, *Phillis Wheatley: Young Colonial Poet,* 150.

67. The basic narrative of Wheatley's life is, in fact, conducive to this approach. There are few primary-source accounts of her life and actions, which leaves the biographical author with greater room for invention. Moreover, Wheatley's early accomplishments and equally early death, at the age of thirty or thirty-one, make her an appropriate figure for a series that focuses on the *childhood* of great Americans. This is in stark contrast to Truth, whose most notable actions and speeches occurred after she was thirty years old.

68. Nell Irvin Painter observed that this reputation, although established during Truth's lifetime, was also highly fragmented; see Painter, *Sojourner Truth: A Life, a Symbol* (New York: W. W. Norton, 1996), 3–5, 258–80.

69. Claflin, *Sojourner Truth,* back cover.

70. Claflin, *Sojourner Truth,* 1.

71. On Lincoln, see Claflin, *Sojourner Truth,* v, 94–105; on the history of activism, see 59, 68, 97; on the victory of the Union, see 85–86, 102. The final example is particularly carefully portrayed in the text, as the author seemed to want to avoid a narrative of destiny. Thus, in the chapter "Prelude to War," the narrator deliberately reminds readers—by addressing them directly—that although the Civil War may seem "inevitable" to those of us with the benefit of hindsight, it did not appear that way to people living through that time period. This accomplishes two things. First, it educates the readers on historical understanding, how one should view events as if from within the perspective of the now-gone past. Second, it explicitly attempts to preserve the agential play or uncertainty of the protagonists of history. If one sees the war as inevitable, will one not also see the actions attempting to prevent it as undertaken in vain? However, the outcome of the Civil War is, strangely, portrayed as a foregone conclusion: all the efforts of the Confederacy are portrayed as regressions meant to "sink a fragile ship of liberty" (86) and the like.

72. Haskins, *Fighting Shirley Chisholm,* 3.

73. Haskins, *Fighting Shirley Chisholm,* 4.

74. Haskins, *Fighting Shirley Chisholm,* 5.

75. Haskins, *Fighting Shirley Chisholm,* 31.

76. Haskins, *Fighting Shirley Chisholm,* 34.

77. Haskins, *Fighting Shirley Chisholm,* 44, 46.

78. Clinton, *Phillis's Big Test,* 1. For additional examples, see Burke, *Phillis Wheatley,* 29; Kent, *Phillis Wheatley,* 6; Don McLeese, *Phillis Wheatley* (Vero Beach, Fla.: Rourke, 2005), 7.

79. Henry Louis Gates Jr., *The Trials of Phillis Wheatley: America's First Black Poet and Her Encounters with the Founding Fathers* (New York: Basic Civitas Books, 2003), 50.

80. See Claflin, *Sojourner Truth,* 1–3; Collins, *Sojourner Truth,* 28–29; Jennifer Blizin Gillis, *Sojourner Truth* (Chicago: Heinemann Library, 2006), 4–5; Margo McLoone, *Sojourner Truth: A Photo-Illustrated Biography* (Mankato, Minn.: Bridgestone Books, 1997), 4–5; Pinkney, *Sojourner Truth's Step-Stomp Stride,* 1; Taylor-Boyd, *Sojourner Truth,* 4–6. Several texts focus on one speech event or action and then describe Truth's career in more general, comprehensive terms.

81. Painter, *Sojourner Truth,* 115, 154, 201.

82. On the first case, see Carleton Mabee and Susan Mabee Newhouse, *Sojourner Truth: Slave, Prophet, Legend* (New York: New York University Press, 1993), 16–21; and Painter, *Sojourner Truth,* 32–35. On the slander case, see Mabee and Newhouse, *Sojourner Truth,* 37–40; and Painter, *Sojourner Truth,* 58. On the streetcar case, see Mabee and Newhouse, *Sojourner Truth,* 133–35; and Painter, *Sojourner Truth,* 210–11.

83. Roop and Roop, *Sojourner Truth,* 58; Norma Jean Lutz, *Sojourner Truth: Abolitionist, Suffragist, and Preacher* (Philadelphia: Chelsea House, 2001), 35; Joanne Mattern, *Sojourner Truth: Early Abolitionist* (New York: Rosen Publishing Group, 2003), 8. For other examples, see Adler, *Picture Book of Sojourner Truth,* 11; McLoone, *Sojourner Truth,* 13; and Frances E. Ruffin, *Sojourner Truth* (New York: Rosen Publishing Group, 2002), 14.

84. Frost, *Sojourner Truth,* 15; Taylor-Boyd, *Sojourner Truth,* 15. Emphasis added.

85. Previously, I noted the Peterson text's faulty claim that Truth was the first African American woman to speak against slavery. Another, much more recent text claims that Truth's 1850 *Narrative* was "the first book about a slave that was told in the words of a slave": Barbara R. Moore, *Sojourner Truth* (Boston: Houghton Mifflin, 2005), 10. This claim can easily be challenged on three counts. First, many other slave narratives were in circulation in the United States in 1850. Indeed, historians suggest that Frederick Douglass's successful 1845 autobiography inspired Truth to record her life story. See Painter, *Sojourner Truth,* 103. Second, Truth's amanuensis, Olive Gilbert, likely contributed many of her own words to the story that Truth dictated, and Gilbert was certainly not a slave. Third, Truth was no longer enslaved when she dictated her life story to Gilbert. Yet another text claims that Truth was "the first freedom rider": Gillis, *Sojourner Truth,* 5.

86. Brownmiller, *Shirley Chisholm,* 112–13; Haskins, *Fighting Shirley Chisholm,* 132, 164, 195; Hicks, *Honorable Shirley Chisholm,* 19, 77; Garnet Nelson Jackson, *Shirley Chisholm: Congresswoman,* ill. Thomas Hudson (Cleveland, Ohio: Modern Curriculum Press, 1994), 22; Pollack, *Shirley Chisholm,* 44; Lucia Raatma, *Shirley Chisholm* (New York: Marshall Cavendish, 2011), 34, 47, 73; Scheader, *Shirley Chisholm,* 77, 79, 110. Texts published prior to 1972 mention only the 1968 election; all later texts mention both achievements.

87. The one exception to this generalization was Selena Hastings, Countess of Huntingdon, who became a sponsor of Wheatley's poetry. Although she was not as famous as George Washington, Hastings was certainly prominent in eighteenth-century England.

88. See, for example, Collard, *Phillis Wheatley,* 16; Carol Greene, *Phillis Wheatley, First African-American Poet* (Chicago: Children's Press, 1995), 25–26; Kathryn Lasky, *A Voice of Her Own: The Story of Phillis Wheatley, Slave Poet,* ill. Paul Lee (Cambridge, Mass.: Candlewick Press, 2003), 24; Weidt, *Revolutionary Poet,* 24.

89. Borland and Speicher, *Phillis Wheatley: Young Colonial Poet,* 120–27; Lucille Arcola Chambers, *Negro Pioneers: Phillis Wheatley, Poetess,* ill. John Neal (New York: C & S Ventures, 1967), 11; Robin S. Doak, *Phillis Wheatley, Slave and Poet* (Minneapolis: Compass Point Books, 2006), 38; Bruce Fish and Becky Durost Fish, *Phillis Wheatley* (Chicago: Wright Group/McGraw-Hill, 2006), 17; Graham, *The Story of Phillis Wheatley,* 85; Lasky, *A Voice of Her Own,* 20; Weidt, *Revolutionary Poet,* 22.

90. See Gates, *Trials of Phillis Wheatley;* Clinton, *Phillis's Big Test;* Borland and Speicher, *Phillis Wheatley: Young Colonial Poet,* 93–96; Graham, *The Story of Phillis Wheatley,* 102–6; Weidt, *Revolutionary Poet,* 30.

91. Collard, *Phillis Wheatley,* 1; Fuller, *Phillis Wheatley,* 39; Graham, *The Story of Phillis Wheatley,* 105.

92. Gates, *Trials of Phillis Wheatley,* 29; Clinton, *Phillis's Big Test,* 30; Doak, *Phillis Wheatley,* 44.

93. Doak, *Phillis Wheatley,* 44.

94. The scholarly biographer Vincent Carretta has claimed that the British presence and a smallpox outbreak would have made an actual meeting in Cambridge unlikely. An April 1776 meeting in Providence, Rhode Island, was more likely, though not certain: Carretta, *Genius in Bondage*, 154–57.

95. The phrase "great poetical talents" is directly excerpted from the letter that Washington wrote to Phillis Wheatley upon receipt of her poem. Cited in Burke, *Phillis Wheatley,* 22. At least half a dozen other texts quote this phrase from Washington's letter.

96. Burke, *Phillis Wheatley,* 23.

97. Gregson, *Let Freedom Ring,* 31.

98. Lasky, *Phillis Wheatley,* 34. One text suggests that Washington's addressing Wheatley respectfully was not the result of a change of perspective on African Americans but could have resulted from Washington's assumption—having never met her—that Wheatley was in fact white. Of course, a later visit between Wheatley and the general would have disabused Washington of this notion. Salisbury, *Phillis Wheatley,* 70–71.

99. Doak, *Phillis Wheatley,* 74.

100. See Borland and Speicher, *Phillis Wheatley: Young Colonial Poet,* 184–91; Borland and Speicher, *Phillis Wheatley: Young Revolutionary Poet*, 117–18; Burke, *Phillis Wheatley,* 22–23; Chambers, *Negro Pioneers,* 19; Clinton, *Phillis's Big Test,* 30 (mentioned in epilogue); Collard, *Phillis Wheatley,* 28–29; Doak, *Phillis Wheatley,* 74; Fish and Fish, *Phillis Wheatley,* 26–27; Fuller, *Phillis Wheatley,* 55–67; Graham, *The Story of Phillis Wheatley,* 119–32; Greene, *Phillis Wheatley,* 35–39; Gregson, *Let Freedom Ring,* 30–31; Kent, *Phillis Wheatley,* 19; Lasky, *A Voice of Her Own,* 34; McLeese, *Phillis Wheatley,* 26–27; Laura Purdie Salas, *Phillis Wheatley: Colonial American Poet* (Mankato, Minn.: Capstone Press, 2006), 21–23; Salisbury, *Phillis Wheatley,* 68–71; Weidt, *Revolutionary Poet,* 47–48.

101. Ann Malaspina, *Phillis Sings Out Freedom: The Story of George Washington and Phillis Wheatley*, ill. Susan Keeter (Chicago, Ill.: Albert Whitman, 2010), 19.

102. Greene, *Phillis Wheatley,* 39.

103. Borland and Speicher, *Phillis Wheatley: Young Colonial Poet,* 190; Borland and Speicher, *Phillis Wheatley: Young Revolutionary Poet,* 118.

104. See Painter, *Sojourner Truth,* 3.

105. Painter, *Sojourner Truth,* 200–208; Matthew K. Samra, "Shadow and Substance: The Two Narratives of Sojourner Truth," *Midwest Quarterly* 38:2 (1997): 158–71.

106. The letter, originally addressed to Truth's friend Rowland Johnson, was published in the *National Anti-Slavery Standard* on December 17, 1864, less than two months after Truth's October 29 meeting with the president. The text of the letter can be found in Susan Pullon Fitch and Roseann M. Mandziuk, *Sojourner Truth as Orator: Wit, Story, and Song* (Westport, Conn.: Greenwood Press, 1997), 194–97.

107. Peterson, *Sojourner Truth,* 68–73. Many other texts that devote a chapter or special section to Truth's meeting with Lincoln also emphasize her rhetorical efficacy in that context, or at least her expectation that she would be heard by the president. These texts include Catherine Bernard, *Sojourner Truth: Abolitionist and Women's Rights Activist* (Berkeley Heights, N.J.: Enslow, 2001), 81; Claflin, *Sojourner Truth,* 94–105 ("Words for Lincoln"); Gillis, *Sojourner Truth,* 22–23 ("Meeting the President"); Aletha Jane Lindstrom, *Sojourner Truth: Slave, Abolitionist, and Fighter for Women's Rights*, ill. Paul Frame (New York: Julian Messner, 1980), 98–106 ("The Great Man and the Tragic Hour"); Taylor-Boyd, *Sojourner Truth,* 38 ("Advice to Lincoln").

108. Peterson, *Sojourner Truth,* 65.

109. Peterson, *Sojourner Truth,* 68.

110. Peterson, *Sojourner Truth,* 72. Truth's version of the meeting can be found in her "Book of Life"; Sojourner Truth, with Frances W. Titus, *The Narrative of Sojourner Truth, with "Book*

of Life" and "A Memorial Chapter," ed. and with notes and introduction by Imani Perry (New York: Barnes and Noble Classics, 2005), 130–34.

111. Peterson, *Sojourner Truth,* 72. The section of Truth's letter narrating this exchange reads: "He then showed me the Bible presented to him by the colored people of Baltimore, of which you have no doubt seen a description. I have seen it for myself, and it is beautiful beyond description. After I had looked it over, I said to him, This is beautiful indeed; the colored people have given this to the head of the government, and that government once sanctioned laws that would not permit its people to learn enough to enable them to read this book. And for what? Let them answer who can." Truth, *Narrative and "Book of Life,"* 131.

112. Raatma, *Shirley Chisholm,* 62.

113. Haskins, *Fighting Shirley Chisholm,* 187, 191; Scheader, *Shirley Chisholm,* 89, 93, 112.

114. Pollack, *Shirley Chisholm,* 51; Scheader, *Shirley Chisholm,* 115.

115. Brownmiller, *Shirley Chisholm,* 129; Haskins, *Fighting Shirley Chisholm,* 86–88; Hicks, *Honorable Shirley Chisholm,* 47; Raatma, *Shirley Chisholm,* 38.

116. This is true in another, more complex sense as well. One could adopt this perspective in order to argue that our knowledge of historical figures is largely arbitrary or coincidental: we know about certain people from the past only because they chanced to encounter others that hindsight and history have shown to be important (for example, Lincoln, Douglass, Washington). In other words, other historically notable black women lived during the eighteenth and nineteenth centuries, but Wheatley and Truth may be remembered because they ran into the right people.

117. For defenses of the role of biography in the classroom, see Beverly J. Boulware, Eula E. Monroe, and Bradley Ray Wilcox, "The 5L Instructional Design for Exploring Legacies through Biography," *Reading Teacher* 66:6 (2012), 487; Fertig, "Using Biography," 147; Hani Morgan, "Picture Book Biographies for Young Children: A Way to Teach Multiple Perspectives," *Early Childhood Education Journal* 37:3 (2009), 221; Carole Prendergast and Robin Klein, "Studying Heroes: Picture-Book Biographies and More," *Book Links* 15:4 (2006), 34; Wills, "Lives and Other Stories," 33–49.

Chapter 5: Configuration

1. Paul Ricoeur, *Time and Narrative,* vol. 1, trans. Kathleen McLaughlin and David Pellauer (Chicago: University of Chicago Press, 1984), 64–69.

2. In connecting the texts so closely with their creators, I am cognizant of the many critiques of authorship that have been articulated by literary and rhetorical theorists, among others. I agree with Ricoeur that in written discourse, "the author's intention and the meaning of the text cease to coincide"; Ricoeur, *From Text to Action: Essays in Hermeneutics II,* 2nd ed., trans. Kathleen Blamey and John B. Thompson (Evanston, Ill.: Northwestern University Press, 2007), 148. This does not mean, however, that we think of the text without an author; it means that one must exercise caution when drawing conclusions about the intention of an author and the ultimate import of a text for a given audience. I am focusing on an intermediary moment here, prior to the moment in which any supposed authorial intention might be achieved. See also Karlyn Kohrs Campbell, "Agency: Promiscuous and Protean," *Communication and Critical/Cultural Studies* 2:1 (2005): 5–6.

3. Debra Hawhee, "Kairotic Encounters," in *Perspectives on Rhetorical Invention,* ed. Janet M. Atwill and Janice M. Lauer (Knoxville: University of Tennessee Press, 2002), 24.

4. Sara L. Schwebel, *Child-Sized History: Fictions of the Past in U.S. Classrooms* (Nashville, Tenn.: Vanderbilt University Press, 2011), 160.

5. It should be noted that this body of texts includes books whose primary purpose is to help children learn to read. Several texts articulate this purpose explicitly. Literacy, of course,

provides a different interpretive framework that remains outside the scope of this project. Examples of such texts include Helen Frost, *Sojourner Truth* (Mankato, Minn.: Pebble Books, 2003); Joanne Mattern, *Sojourner Truth: Early Abolitionist* (New York: Rosen Publishing Group, 2003); Bruce Fish and Becky Durost Fish, *Phillis Wheatley* (Chicago: Wright Group/McGraw-Hill, 2006).

6. Jacqueline Bernard, *Journey toward Freedom: The Story of Sojourner Truth* (New York: W. W. Norton, 1967), x. In an introduction to a reprint of Bernard's biography, Nell Irvin Painter speculates that Bernard's "personal politics," particularly her feminism and "concern for racial justice," drew her toward Truth: Painter, introduction to *Journey toward Freedom: The Story of Sojourner Truth,* by Jacqueline Bernard (New York: Feminist Press, 1990), xxiii.

7. Bernard, *Journey toward Freedom,* x.

8. For examples of similar reflections on choice and purpose, see Shirley Graham, *The Story of Phillis Wheatley, Poetess of the Revolution,* 12th ed., ill. Robert Burns (1949; New York: Julian Messner, 1969), 7–9; and Ida R. Bellegarde, *Phillis Wheatley* (Pine Bluff, Ark.: Bell Enterprises, 1983), 9.

9. For a useful criticism of biography series, see Linda Walvoord Girard, "Series Thinking and the Art of Biography for Children," *Children's Literature Association Quarterly* 14:4 (1989): 187–92.

10. Susan Taylor-Boyd, *Sojourner Truth: The Courageous Former Slave Whose Eloquence Helped Promote Human Equality* (Milwaukee: Gareth Stevens Children's Books, 1990), back cover.

11. Instead of reporting that young Belle was sold away after the master died, as most narratives truthfully indicate, this one explains that she was sold because she was "headstrong" and "obstinate." Although it seems plausible to attribute these characteristics to Belle, most records of this transaction indicate that she was sold to pay off the debts of her owner's estate; Taylor-Boyd, *Sojourner Truth,* 7.

12. Miriam Morris Fuller, *Phillis Wheatley: America's First Black Poetess,* ill. Victor Mays (Champaign, Ill.: Garrard, 1971); Helen Stone Peterson, *Sojourner Truth: Fearless Crusader,* ill. Victor Mays (Champaign, Ill.: Garrard, 1972).

13. For a similar articulation of purpose and choice, see the description of the series titled *Henry Steele Commager's Americans: Profiles of Americans for Young People,* which can be found on the back cover of Edward Beecher Claflin's *Sojourner Truth and the Struggle for Freedom,* ill. Jada Rowland (Hauppage, N.Y.: Children's Press Choice, 1987).

14. Garnet Nelson Jackson, *Shirley Chisholm: Congresswoman,* ill. Thomas Hudson (Cleveland, Ohio: Modern Curriculum Press, 1994), unnumbered page; James Haskins, *Fighting Shirley Chisholm* (New York: Dial Press, 1975), front cover inside flap.

15. Haskins, *Fighting Shirley Chisholm,* unnumbered page.

16. Haskins, *Fighting Shirley Chisholm,* front cover inside flap.

17. Jackson, *Shirley Chisholm,* unnumbered page.

18. Although Haskins and Jackson did not state it explicitly, it seems plausible that these authors chose to highlight Chisholm's contributions to marginalized groups because of their commitment to the African American community. In their study of popular history-making in the United States, Rosenzweig and Thelen have found that African Americans responding to their survey placed much greater emphasis than whites on the history that they shared with members of their race. The survey found that, when asked to answer the question "Knowing about the past of which of the following four areas or groups is most important to you?" 26 percent of African American respondents chose "your racial or ethnic group," more than six times the 4 percent of whites who chose that response: Roy Rosenzweig and David Thelen, *The*

Presence of the Past: Popular Uses of History in American Life (New York: Columbia University Press, 1998), 149–51, 237.

19. Kathryn Lasky, *A Voice of Her Own: The Story of Phillis Wheatley, Slave Poet,* ill. Paul Lee (Cambridge, Mass.: Candlewick Press, 2003), 35.

20. Eric King Watts, "'Voice' and 'Voicelessness' in Rhetorical Studies," *Quarterly Journal of Speech* 87:2 (2001): 179–96.

21. Lasky, *A Voice of Her Own,* 35.

22. See also Anne Rockwell's author's note in *Only Passing Through: The Story of Sojourner Truth,* ill. R. Gregory Christie (New York: Knopf, 2000), 33. In explaining her choice to focus on only part of Truth's life, Rockwell said, "I've told her story only up to when her transformation takes place, for that part of the story moves me most." Biographical information identifies Lasky as a white Jewish woman, Lee as Asian American, and Anne Rockwell as a white woman.

23. Ricoeur, *Time and Narrative* 1: 65.

24. This aspect is akin to the transformation of the chronicle into the narrative, which Hayden White described in his work: White, *Metahistory: The Historical Imagination in Nineteenth-Century Europe* (Baltimore: Johns Hopkins University Press, 1975).

25. William H. Epstein argued that the genre of biography "has generally privileged the 'natural attitude' as the degree of discreteness that governs the generic relationship between 'event' and 'life.' Thus biographical recognition has usually treated 'events' as naturally discrete occurrences which are congruent with the space-time configurations of the biographical subject, delimited by the subject's birth and death." He also noted that a "more radical contemporary approach" to biography takes this relationship not as "natural" but as "naturalized." Although the latter approach is familiar in criticism and writing of biographies for the general adult audience, it is unusual in texts for children. See Epstein, *Recognizing Biography* (Philadelphia: University of Pennsylvania Press, 1987), 37–38.

26. See Lucy Jane Bledsoe, *Phillis Wheatley: First in Poetry* (Edgewood Cliffs, N.J.: Globe Books, 1989), 6–9 ("A Child Is Kidnapped from Africa"); Kathryn Kilby Borland and Helen Ross Speicher, *Phillis Wheatley: Young Colonial Poet,* ill. William K. Plummer (Indianapolis: Bobbs-Merrill, 1968), 11–14 (slave auction); Kathryn Kilby Borland and Helen Ross Speicher, *Phillis Wheatley: Young Revolutionary Poet,* ill. Cathy Morrison (Carmel, Ind.: Patria Press, 2005), 1–4 (slave auction); H. H. Cardigan, *The Light of One Candle,* ill. Cedric Lucas (New York: McGraw-Hill, n.d.), 2–3; Robin S. Doak, *Phillis Wheatley, Slave and Poet* (Minneapolis: Compass Point Books, 2006), 9 (slave auction); Fish and Fish, *Phillis Wheatley,* 7 (slave auction); Fuller, *Phillis Wheatley,* 7 (slave auction); Graham, *The Story of Phillis Wheatley,* 13–22 (Boston on "Market Day," when slaves were sold); Marilyn Jensen, *Phillis Wheatley: Negro Slave of Mr. John Wheatley of Boston* (Scarsdale, N.Y.: Lion Books, 1987), 7–12; J. T. Moriarty, *Phillis Wheatley: African American Poet* (New York: Rosen Publishing Group 2004), 4–10 ("Phillis's Early Years"); Maryann N. Weidt, *Revolutionary Poet: A Story about Phillis Wheatley,* ill. Mary O'Keefe Young (Minneapolis: Carolrhoda Books, 1997), 6 (slave auction/memory of mother).

27. Seventeen out of the thirty Wheatley biographies I reviewed include some version of this detail. See Borland and Speicher, *Phillis Wheatley: Young Colonial Poet,* 11; Rick Burke, *Phillis Wheatley* (Chicago: Heinemann Library, 2003), 7; Doak, *Phillis Wheatley,* 9; Fish and Fish, *Phillis Wheatley,* 7; Fuller, *Phillis Wheatley,* 7; Carol Greene, *Phillis Wheatley: First African-American Poet* (Chicago: Children's Press, 1995), 14; Susan R. Gregson, *Let Freedom Ring: Phillis Wheatley* (Mankato, Minn.: Bridgestone Books, 2002), 8; Jensen, *Phillis Wheatley,* 9; Deborah Kent, *Phillis Wheatley: First Published African-American Poet* (Chanhassen, Minn.: The Child's World, 2004), 7; Lasky, *Voice of Her Own,* 5; Ann Malaspina, *Phillis Sings Out Freedom: The Story of George Washington and Phillis Wheatley,* ill. Susan Keeter (Chicago: Albert

Whitman, 2010), 11–12; Jacquelyn McLendon, *Phillis Wheatley: A Revolutionary Poet* (New York: Rosen Publishing Group, 2003), 14–15; Moriarty, *Phillis Wheatley,* 8; Merle Richmond, *Phillis Wheatley: Poet* (New York: Chelsea House, 1988), 21; Cynthia Salisbury, *Phillis Wheatley: Legendary African-American Poet* (Berkeley Heights, N.J.: Enslow, 2001), 18; Victoria Sherrow, *Phillis Wheatley, Poet* (New York: Chelsea House, 1992), 9; Weidt, *Revolutionary Poet,* 6.

28. Burke, *Phillis Wheatley,* 4; Greene, *Phillis Wheatley,* 5–6; Lasky, *Voice of Her Own,* 2; Moriarty, *Phillis Wheatley,* 4–6; Weidt, *Revolutionary Poet,* 6.

29. Greene, *Phillis Wheatley,* 9–10.

30. Catherine Clinton, *Phillis's Big Test,* ill. Sean Qualls (Boston: Houghton Mifflin, 2008), 1 (publication of book/ "big test"); Sneed B. Collard III, *Phillis Wheatley: She Loved Words* (Tarrytown, N.Y.: Marshall Cavendish Benchmark, 2010), 1 (1772 examination); McLendon, *Revolutionary Poet,* 5 (publication of various poems); Richmond, *Phillis Wheatley,* 12–19 (meeting with Washington); Greg Roza, *"Guide My Pen": The Poems of Phillis Wheatley* (New York: Rosen Publishing Group, 2004), 7–9 (trip to England); Laura Purdie Salas, *Phillis Wheatley: Colonial American Poet* (Mankato, Minn.: Capstone Press, 2006), 4 (1772 examination); Salisbury, *Phillis Wheatley,* 5 (trip to England).

31. Jeri Ferris, *Walking the Road to Freedom: A Story about Sojourner Truth* (Minneapolis: Carolrhoda Books, 1988), 9; Julian May, *Sojourner Truth: Freedom-Fighter,* ill. Phero Thomas (Chicago: Childrens Press, 1973), 2; Patricia McKissack and Fredrick McKissack, *Sojourner Truth: A Voice for Freedom* (Berkeley Heights, N.J.: Enslow, 2002), 5–6; Barbara R. Moore, *Sojourner Truth* (Boston: Houghton Mifflin, 2005), 3; Peterson, *Sojourner Truth,* 6–14; Rockwell, *Only Passing Through,* 1–2; Lisa Trumbauer, *Let's Meet Sojourner Truth* (New York: Chelsea House, 2004), 4–5; Laura Hamilton Waxman, *Sojourner Truth* (Minneapolis: Lerner, 2008), 6–7.

32. May, *Sojourner Truth,* 2.

33. Other texts that begin with a scene in which Truth speaks to a crowd include Catherine Bernard, *Sojourner Truth: Abolitionist and Women's Rights Activist* (Berkeley Heights, N.J.: Enslow, 2001), 5–6 (Akron 1851); and Mary G. Butler, *Sojourner Truth: From Slave to Activist for Freedom* (New York: Rosen Publishing Group, 2003), 5–6 (Battle Creek 1863). Corona Brezina also began her text with the 1851 Akron speech. This entire text is framed by that address: Brezina, *Sojourner Truth's "Ain't I a Woman?" Speech: A Primary Source Investigation* (New York: Rosen Publishing Group, 2005), 5–6.

34. Katherine Krohn, *Sojourner Truth: Freedom Fighter* (Mankato, Minn.: Capstone Press, 2006), 4–5; Claflin, *Sojourner Truth,* 3.

35. Claflin, *Sojourner Truth,* 1.

36. Krohn, *Sojourner Truth,* 4–5.

37. Jennifer Blizin Gillis, *Sojourner Truth* (Chicago: Heinemann Library, 2006), 4–5 (streetcar incident); Taylor-Boyd, *Sojourner Truth,* 4–5 (streetcar incident).

38. Gillis, *Sojourner Truth,* 4.

39. Taylor-Boyd, *Sojourner Truth,* 5.

40. The texts that begin with a scene related to Chisholm's time in Barbados include Susan Brownmiller, *Shirley Chisholm* (New York: Doubleday, 1970), 11; Jackson, *Shirley Chisholm,* 1; Jill S. Pollack, *Shirley Chisholm* (New York: Franklin Watts, 1994), 8–9.

41. Brownmiller, *Shirley Chisholm,* 11.

42. Jackson, *Shirley Chisholm,* 1, 3.

43. Pollack, *Shirley Chisholm,* 8.

44. Brownmiller, *Shirley Chisholm,* 11; Jackson, *Shirley Chisholm,* 4; Pollack, *Shirley Chisholm,* 9.

45. Brownmiller, *Shirley Chisholm,* 11–12.

46. Ricoeur, *Time and Narrative* 1: 65. Ricoeur's concept of configuration resonates to some degree with the elements of the dramatistic pentad, as described by Kenneth Burke: Burke, *A Grammar of Motives* (Berkeley: University of California Press, 1969), xv.

47. See Vincent Carretta, *Phillis Wheatley: Biography of a Genius in Bondage* (Athens: University of Georgia Press, 2011), 96–108; Henry Louis Gates Jr., *The Trials of Phillis Wheatley: America's First Black Poet and Her Encounters with the Founding Fathers* (New York: Basic Civitas Books, 2003); Phillis Wheatley, *The Collected Works of Phillis Wheatley*, ed. John Shields (New York: Oxford University Press, 1988).

48. For representatives of these two extremes, see Bellegarde, *Phillis Wheatley*, and Salas, *Phillis Wheatley*, 4–15.

49. Karlyn Kohrs Campbell astutely described this balance in her first two propositions about rhetorical agency. She explained that "taken together these two propositions are designed to reject absolutely any binary that forces a choice between the autonomous individual and some form of determinism or to separate the individuals from culture and context." "At the same time," she continued, "agency manifests itself in the practices of individuals, practices linked to subject-positions and, hence, to agency." Campbell, "Agency," 5.

50. Borland and Speicher, *Phillis Wheatley: Young Colonial Poet,* 154; Borland and Speicher, *Phillis Wheatley: Young Revolutionary Poet,* 96–97; Lucille Arcola Chambers, *Negro Pioneers: Phillis Wheatley, Poetess,* ill. John Neal (New York: C & S Ventures, 1967), 13; Fuller, *Phillis Wheatley,* 31–35; Graham, *The Story of Phillis Wheatley,* 94–96.

51. Chambers, *Negro Pioneers,* 13.

52. Fish and Fish, *Phillis Wheatley,* 20; Burke, *Phillis Wheatley,* 16.

53. Greene, *Phillis Wheatley,* 26.

54. Kent, *Phillis Wheatley,* 10.

55. Kent, *Phillis Wheatley,* 12–13.

56. Collard, *Phillis Wheatley,* 17–18; Salisbury, *Phillis Wheatley,* 8.

57. Salas, *Phillis Wheatley,* 15; Weidt, *Revolutionary Poet,* 29–30.

58. Salas, *Phillis Wheatley,* 4–15.

59. Clinton, *Phillis's Big Test;* Lasky, *Voice of Her Own;* Malaspina, *Phillis Sings Out Freedom.*

60. Clinton, *Phillis's Big Test,* 20–21.

61. Lasky, *Voice of Her Own,* front inside cover.

62. Malaspina, *Phillis Sings Out Freedom,* 19, 28.

63. Jodi Melamed, *Represent and Destroy: Rationalizing Violence in the New Racial Capitalism* (Minneapolis: University of Minnesota Press, 2011), 14, 36, 229.

64. See Gates, *Trials of Phillis Wheatley,* 31; and John C. Shields, "Phillis Wheatley's Struggle for Freedom in Her Poetry and Prose," in *The Collected Works of Phillis Wheatley,* ed. John Shields (New York: Oxford University Press, 1988), 229.

65. Painter suggests that the name "expressed two of her . . . main preoccupations: transitoriness/permanence and distrust/credibility"; Nell Irvin Painter, "Representing Truth: Sojourner Truth's Knowing and Becoming Known," *Journal of American History* 81:2 (1994): 462. On the concept of *lieu de mémoire,* see Pierre Nora, "Between Memory and History: *Les Lieux de Mémoire,*" *Representations* 26 (Special issue: Memory and Counter-Memory; Spring 1989): 7–24.

66. Sojourner Truth and Frances W. Titus, *Narrative of Sojourner Truth with "Book of Life" and "A Memorial Chapter,"* ed. and with notes and introduction by Imani Perry (New York: Barnes and Noble Classics, 2005), 73–74.

67. In the *Narrative,* the name change is all but swallowed up by descriptions of the reasons and purposes of Truth's new mission. It says simply that "about an hour before she left, she informed Mrs. Whiting, the woman of the house where she was stopping, that her name was no

longer Isabella, but SOJOURNER; and that she was going east"; Truth and Titus, *Narrative,* 73. This tells us both something about original amanuensis Olive Gilbert's own nineteenth-century feminine interests in Christian missions and about the link between self-determination and responsibility that figures subsequent texts.

68. Bernard, *Journey toward Freedom,* 115–17.

69. Bernard, *Journey toward Freedom,* 120–21.

70. On the significance of self-determination in black feminist thought, see Sara C. VanderHaagen, "Practical Truths: Black Feminist Agency and Public Memory in Biographies for Children," *Women's Studies in Communication* 35:1 (2012): 25–29.

71. Jane Shumate, *Sojourner Truth* (Brookfield, Conn.: Millbrook Press, 1991), 14.

72. Laura Spinale, *Sojourner Truth* (Chanhassen, Minn.: The Child's World, 2000), 9.

73. Rockwell, *Only Passing Through,* 21.

74. Rockwell, *Only Passing Through,* 21.

75. Other texts that make the name change a pivotal moment in Truth's life narrative include David A. Adler, *A Picture Book of Sojourner Truth,* ill. Gershom Griffith (New York: Scholastic, 1994), 14–15; Krohn, *Sojourner Truth,* 16–17; Victoria Ortiz, *Sojourner Truth, a Self-Made Woman* (Philadelphia: J. B. Lippincott, 1974), 43–45; Frances E. Ruffin, *Sojourner Truth* (New York: Rosen Publishing Group, 2002), 18; Gwenyth Swain, *Sojourner Truth,* ill. Matthew Archambault (Minneapolis: Carolrhoda Books, 2005), 26–27; Taylor-Boyd, *Sojourner Truth,* 19–20; Waxman, *Sojourner Truth,* 22–23. With the exception of the Ortiz text, all of these were written in the 1990s or 2000s.

76. Hannah Arendt, *The Human Condition,* 2nd ed. (Chicago: University of Chicago Press, 1998), 192.

77. "Chisholm, Shirley Anita (1924–2005)," *History, Art & Archives, United States House of Representatives,* http://history.house.gov/People/Listing/C/CHISHOLM,-Shirley-Anita-%28C000371%29/ (accessed December 23, 2016).

78. Jackson, *Shirley Chisholm,* 19.

79. Jackson, *Shirley Chisholm,* 22.

80. On an articulation conceptualization of agency, see Kevin DeLuca, "Articulation Theory: A Discursive Grounding for Rhetorical Practice," *Philosophy and Rhetoric* 32:4 (1999): 334–48; Nathan Stormer, "Articulation: A Working Paper on Rhetoric and Taxis," *Quarterly Journal of Speech* 90:3 (2004): 257–84.

81. Brownmiller, *Shirley Chisholm,* 52–54; Haskins, *Fighting Shirley Chisholm,* 60–61; Pollack, *Shirley Chisholm,* 19; Lucia Raatma, *Shirley Chisholm* (New York: Marshall Cavendish, 2011), 18; Catherine Scheader, *Shirley Chisholm: Teacher and Congresswoman* (Hillside, N.J.: Enslow Publishers, 1990), 24.

82. Brownmiller, *Shirley Chisholm,* 52.

83. Brownmiller, *Shirley Chisholm,* 54.

84. Brownmiller, *Shirley Chisholm,* 85; Nancy Hicks, *The Honorable Shirley Chisholm: Congresswoman from Brooklyn* (New York: Lion Books, 1971), 17; Scheader, *Shirley Chisholm,* 57, 69.

85. Brownmiller, *Shirley Chisholm,* 89–91, 95; Haskins, *Fighting Shirley Chisholm,* 114–16; Hicks, *Honorable Shirley Chisholm,* 67; Pollack, *Shirley Chisholm,* 39; Raatma, *Shirley Chisholm,* 41; and Scheader, *Shirley Chisholm,* 74.

86. Brownmiller, *Shirley Chisholm,* 88; Hicks, *Honorable Shirley Chisholm,* 63–64; Haskins, *Fighting Shirley Chisholm,* 123.

87. Dennis Hevesi, "Nancy Hicks Maynard Dies at 61; A Groundbreaking Black Journalist," *New York Times,* September 23, 2008, A27.

88. Haskins, *Fighting Shirley Chisholm,* 123.

89. Hicks, *Honorable Shirley Chisholm,* 63.
90. Hicks, *Honorable Shirley Chisholm,* 63–64.
91. Brownmiller, *Shirley Chisholm,* 86.
92. Campbell, "Agency," 3–5.
93. Ricoeur, *Time and Narrative* 1: 65.
94. Ricoeur, *Time and Narrative* 1: 66.
95. Ricoeur, *Time and Narrative* 1: 66–67.
96. Penelope Lively, "Children and Memory," *Horn Book* 49:4 (1973): 400–407.
97. Bernard, *Journey toward Freedom,* 251.
98. Suzanne Slade, *Sojourner Truth: Preacher for Freedom and Equality,* ill. Natascha Alex Banks (Minneapolis: Picture Window Books, 2008), 21.
99. Kathleen Kudlinski, *Sojourner Truth: Voice for Freedom,* ill. Lenny Wooden (New York: Aladdin, 2003), 147.
100. Peter Roop and Connie Roop, *Sojourner Truth* (New York: Scholastic, 2002), 120.
101. Roop and Roop, *Sojourner Truth,* 120.
102. As Gabrielle Spiegel has argued, continuity is typically associated with memory. This would appear to contradict my argument about the effects of the discourse of memory upon these biographies. However, it seems that even the early texts, which would not have been affected by the turn to memory in the 1980s, emphasize continuity not only as something associated with memory but also as something associated with stories for children: Spiegel, "Memory and History: Liturgical Time and Historical Time," *History and Theory* 41:2 (2002): 149–62.
103. Brezina, *Sojourner Truth's "Ain't I a Woman?" Speech,* 49–50; Krohn, *Sojourner Truth,* 26.
104. Burke, *Phillis Wheatley,* 29; Doak, *Phillis Wheatley,* 90–95.
105. Hicks, *Honorable Shirley Chisholm,* 117; Raatma, *Shirley Chisholm,* 86; and Scheader, *Shirley Chisholm,* 124.

Chapter 6: Refiguration and Appropriation

1. Lawrence R. Sipe and Caroline E. McGuire have provided a helpful codification of young children's "resistant" responses to stories read aloud: intertextual ("That's not how the story goes."), preferential/categorical ("I don't like stories like that."), reality testing ("That's not the way life is."), engaged/kinetic ("That may be how life is, but it's too painful."), exclusionary ("I don't see myself—I am left out of this story."), and literary critical ("The author made a mistake—it's a bad story."): Sipe and McGuire, "Young Children's Resistance to Stories," *Reading Teacher* 60:1 (2006), 7. See also Holly Virginia Blackford, *Out of This World: Why Literature Matters to Girls* (New York: Teachers College Press, 2004); Sylvia Pantaleo, *Exploring Student Response to Contemporary Picturebooks* (Toronto: University of Toronto Press, 2008); and Lawrence R. Sipe, "Children's Response to Literature: Author, Text, Reader, Context," *Theory into Practice* 38:3 (1999): 120–29. Blackford applied reader-response theory in order to conduct ethnographic research on girls' responses to the books they read. Pantaleo analyzed North American elementary students' responses to contemporary picture books.
2. Paul Ricoeur, *From Text to Action: Essays in Hermeneutics II,* trans. Kathleen Blamey and John B. Thompson (Evanston, Ill.: Northwestern University Press, 2007), 37. See also David M. Kaplan, *Ricoeur's Critical Theory* (Albany: State University of New York Press, 2003), 53–54.
3. Paul Ricoeur, *Time and Narrative,* vol. 1, trans. Kathleen McLaughlin and David Pellauer (Chicago: University of Chicago Press, 1984), 70.
4. Ricoeur, *Time and Narrative* 1: 77. Ricoeur made this comment in order to characterize the common perspective of two different approaches to understanding the effects of texts: a theory of reading and a theory of reception. He bracketed the comparison of these approaches,

delaying it until volume 2 of *Time and Narrative*. It is a particularly useful comment for us, because it focuses attention on the text's capacity to "instruct" readers while not making universalizing comments about the precise outcomes of this instruction.

5. Hans-Georg Gadamer, *Truth and Method,* 2nd rev. ed., trans. Joel Weinsheimer and Donald G. Marshall (New York: Continuum, 1998), 30–31, 307–11.

6. Ricoeur, *Time and Narrative* 1: 77.

7. Ricoeur explained that mimesis$_3$ "marks the intersection of the world of the text and the world of the hearer or reader": Ricoeur, *Time and Narrative* 1: 71.

8. Ricoeur's argument here was a response to the dominant approach to literary studies, which viewed texts as self-contained fields of language with no relation to the "real." When *Time and Narrative* was originally written, this Derridean-inspired approach was indeed dominant. Although its influence has waned somewhat, its reverberations can still be powerfully felt in fields that center on the interpretation of texts, where there is still the general tendency to approach texts as products of something—culture, historical context, ideology—rather than as producers of something—actions, decisions, new ideas and practices.

9. Ricoeur, *Time and Narrative* 1: 81.

10. Karlyn Kohrs Campbell, "Agency: Promiscuous and Protean," *Communication and Critical/Cultural Studies* 2:1 (2005): 7.

11. According to Nodelman and others, including Beverly Lyon Clark, this makes the term "children's literature" "highly unusual as a category of literature." Perry Nodelman, *The Hidden Adult: Defining Children's Literature* (Baltimore: Johns Hopkins University Press, 2008), 3; see also Clark, *Kiddie Lit: The Cultural Construction of Children's Literature in America* (Baltimore: Johns Hopkins University Press, 2003), 14.

12. Chaim Perelman and Lucie Olbrechts-Tyteca, *The New Rhetoric: A Treatise on Argumentation,* trans. John Wilkinson and Purcell Weaver (Notre Dame, Ind.: University of Notre Dame Press, 1969), 19.

13. Edwin Black, "The Second Persona," *Quarterly Journal of Speech* 56:2 (1970): 109–19. Black described how this can be observed by those outside the text: "The critic can see in the auditor implied by a discourse a model of what the rhetor would have his real auditor become" (113). Maurice Charland further developed this idea in a 1987 essay. He combined the ideas articulated by Black with Louis Althusser's concept of interpellation. Using the example of the *Québécois,* Charland showed how discourses imagine an audience that already exists and an audience that the discourse will call into being. The idea of both addressing and constituting an audience also applies to the juvenile biographies surveyed here: Charland, "Constitutive Rhetoric: The Case of the *Peuple Québécois,*" *Quarterly Journal of Speech* 73:2 (1987): 133–50.

14. Most direct references to reader age occur in the peritextual material, such as the book cover or title page. For instance, the back cover of Edward Beecher Claflin's biography of Sojourner Truth indicates an audience of "young readers, ages 10–13": Claflin, *Sojourner Truth and the Struggle for Freedom,* ill. Jada Rowland (Hauppage, N.Y.: Children's Press Choice, 1987).

15. Clark, *Kiddie Lit,* 9.

16. Nodelman, *Hidden Adult,* 5.

17. Karen Sánchez-Eppler, *Dependent States: The Child's Part in Nineteenth-Century American Culture* (Chicago: University of Chicago Press, 2005), xvii.

18. Nodelman, *Hidden Adult,* 30–31. On the unique nature of character evolution in children's literature, see also Maria Nikolajeva, *The Rhetoric of Character in Children's Literature* (Lanham, Md.: Scarecrow Press, 2002), 131; Sánchez-Eppler, *Dependent States,* xvi.

19. James Haskins, *Fighting Shirley Chisholm* (New York: Dial Press, 1975), unnumbered page.

20. For another example of a text that specifies an African American audience, see Garnet Nelson Jackson, *Phillis Wheatley, Poet,* ill. Cheryl Hanna (Cleveland, Ohio: Modern Curriculum Press, 1992), and Jackson, *Shirley Chisholm: Congresswoman,* ill. Thomas Hudson (Cleveland, Ohio: Modern Curriculum Press, 1994). The "about the author" section of both volumes describes Jackson's "deep concern" for "African American students," for whom she has written her books.

21. "Army Hostess," *Chicago Defender,* May 9, 1942, p. 8; Maureen Honey, ed., *Shadowed Dreams: Women's Poetry of the Harlem Renaissance,* rev. ed. (Piscataway, N.J.: Rutgers University Press, 2006), 252.

22. For example, the sociologist Ronald L. Taylor provided a survey of both privately and publicly funded research demonstrating what he interpreted as a dramatic increase from the 1960s to the 1980s in the number of black youth who were "living in poverty, undereducated and unemployed, involved in crime and drug abuse, and having babies out of wedlock"; Taylor, "Black Youth in Crisis," *Humboldt Journal of Social Relations* 14:1&2 (1986–87): 106.

23. Ida R. Bellegarde, *Phillis Wheatley* (Pine Bluff, Ark.: Bell Enterprises, 1983), 5. Although many such prefatory remarks are scripted by an anonymous editor, these comments appear to come from Bellegarde herself. She is the sole author, editor, and publisher of all four texts in the series Black Heroes and Heroines, which makes it almost certain that she wrote the dedication.

24. Bellegarde, *Phillis Wheatley,* 9.

25. Bellegarde, *Phillis Wheatley,* 19.

26. This is a particularly peculiar statement for Bellegarde to have made, given that this supposedly ideal environment for pursuing personal goals was also a situation of enslavement. It is possible that Bellegarde hoped to emphasize the extreme nature of Wheatley's position as a slave and thereby encourage contemporary readers to view their own life circumstances in a more positive light. One can imagine Bellegarde saying to her readers, "Your life may be challenging, but at least you are not a slave."

27. Bellegarde, *Phillis Wheatley,* 51–53.

28. "Being young and uninformed, and not having the advice of her mistress, as might be expected Phillis became pregnant too soon, not only once but twice": Bellegarde, *Phillis Wheatley,* 52. Wheatley in fact became pregnant three times, all during her twenties. It is unclear whether the text has incorrect information or the third pregnancy should not be considered "too soon."

29. Insofar as Bellegarde's text uses Wheatley as a negative example rather than a positive one, it stands in stark contrast to the majority of contemporary biographies about Wheatley. But the Bellegarde text provides an instructive counterexample, primarily because it makes clear its role as a means of character formation for readers.

30. Many of the texts that market themselves as photobiographies include appendices and other peritexts that invite readers to participate in activities related to the stories. Readers are encouraged to do "further reading," to answer historical questions, and to try writing poetry. For examples of such appendices, see Deborah Kent, *Phillis Wheatley: First Published African-American Poet* (Chanhassen, Minn.: The Child's World, 2004), 31; Barbara R. Moore, *Sojourner Truth* (Boston: Houghton Mifflin, 2005), inside back cover; Jackson, *Phillis Wheatley,* inside front cover. Although these activities certainly attempt to address and thereby engage readers, the context is primarily pedagogical rather than narrative. That is, in these sections, readers are addressed primarily as students, not as readers encountering a story.

31. Throughout Andrea Davis Pinkney and Brian Pinkney's *Sojourner Truth's Step-Stomp Stride,* the narrator cultivates its own persona as a storyteller in the oral folk tradition. The

lyrical quality of the text, combined with the colloquial language, creates a mood for the reader, who is occasionally invoked as "child." The following passage demonstrates how this address is used: "In 1851, Sojourner step-stomped to a women's rights convention in a church in Akron, Ohio. There was no rain on the day of that convention, child. But, oh, there was *thunder*. What struck that spot was strong and loud. It was Sojourner's step-stomp stride" (25). The narrator uses a similar form of address in another part of the text (10–11). Although both examples use the word "child" to refer to an imagined reader who is likely to be a child, this term contains considerable ambiguity, mostly because it is a colloquialism commonly attributed to older African American women: Andrea Davis Pinkney, *Sojourner Truth's Step-Stomp Stride,* ill. Brian Pinkney (New York: Disney/Jump at the Sun Books, 2009).

32. Ricoeur, *Time and Narrative* 1: 64.

33. Rather than examine these texts in the chronological order of their publication, I examine them according to where the direct address appears in the text. For instance, in the Fish and Fish text, the address appears before the life narrative begins, whereas in Claflin's text the addresses appear throughout the narrative itself.

34. Bruce Fish and Becky Durost Fish, *Phillis Wheatley* (Chicago: Wright Group/McGraw Hill, 2006), 6.

35. Jackson, *Phillis Wheatley,* unnumbered page.

36. Jackson, *Shirley Chisholm,* unnumbered page.

37. Claflin, *Sojourner Truth,* 9.

38. Another example of inviting the reader's emotional engagement occurs when the narrator describes Isabella's experiences of the language barrier in the Neely household: "What would you do if you suddenly moved in with people who spoke a language you had never heard before? If they told you to do something, you wouldn't know where to begin or even what they were talking about. That was exactly Belle's situation with the Neelys": Claflin, *Sojourner Truth,* 14.

39. Claflin, *Sojourner Truth,* 58–59.

40. Aristotle, *On Rhetoric: A Theory of Civic Discourse,* trans. George A. Kennedy (New York: Oxford University Press, 1991), 244–46.

41. The narrator draws out the exercise of freedom of speech for its own sake, not necessarily for any specific changes in policy that such speech might produce: Claflin, *Sojourner Truth,* 141.

42. See, for example, Shirley Graham, *The Story of Phillis Wheatley: Poetess of the Revolution,* ill. Robert Burns, 12th ed. (1949; New York: Julian Messner, 1969), 13–14; Ann Rinaldi, *Hang a Thousand Trees with Ribbons: The Story of Phillis Wheatley* (Orlando, Fla.: Gulliver Books/ Harcourt, 1996), 1, 3–4.

43. Nikolajeva, *Rhetoric of Character,* 6. Nikolajeva noted that this generalization was based on research that indicated that children do empathize more with characters they perceive as "real." Even so, she said, creators of children's texts frequently misjudge the audience (6–7).

44. Nodelman, *Hidden Adult,* 20. Nikolajeva also described a process called "internal focalization," which enables an omniscient adult narrator to slip into a child protagonist's perspective and so to give the temporary impression that the narrative is being told from the child's point of view: Nikolajeva, "Imprints of the Mind: The Depiction of Consciousness in Children's Literature," *Children's Literature Association Quarterly* 26:4 (2002): 174.

45. Nodelman, *Hidden Adult,* 18.

46. Nikolajeva has noted a shift toward more psychologically complex characters in children's literature, which she traces back to the 1960s: Nikolajeva, *Rhetoric of Character,* x, 13.

47. See Nell Irvin Painter, *Sojourner Truth: A Life, a Symbol* (New York: W. W. Norton, 1996), 258–80; and Matthew K. Samra, "Shadow and Substance: The Two Narratives of Sojourner Truth," *Midwest Quarterly* 38:2 (1997): 158–71.

48. Nikolajeva recognized the importance of what she called the "real author-character" relationship in biographies, wherein the "author does not entirely 'invent' the character but is assumed to present a credible portrait based on facts." She went on to say that such texts are typically "used for educational and didactic purposes." Although she admitted the challenges these genres present to the formation of character, she supplied no further explanation and swiftly dismissed this issue simply because she was not interested in nonfiction for children. I do not fault Nikolajeva for trying to establish boundaries for her project. However, the fact that she explained her decision to ignore the character problems presented by nonfiction with what she seemed to view as a self-evident reason—that biographies have "educational" purposes—supports one of my arguments in this book: that juvenile biographies have been neglected by children's literature scholars when they should in fact be an important subject of critical scrutiny: Nikolajeva, *Rhetoric of Character,* 4.

49. Nikolajeva defined the "focalizer" as "the agency through whose eyes and/or mind we experience the events"; Nikolajeva, *Rhetoric of Character,* 5.

50. J. T. Moriarty, *Phillis Wheatley: African American Poet* (New York: Rosen Publishing Group, 2004), 8; Bellegarde, *Phillis Wheatley,* 17; Kathryn Kilby Borland and Helen Ross Speicher, *Phillis Wheatley: Young Colonial Poet,* ill. William K. Plummer (Indianapolis: Bobbs-Merrill, 1968), 11–12; Rick Burke, *Phillis Wheatley* (Chicago: Heinemann Library, 2003), 4, 7; Robin S. Doak, *Phillis Wheatley, Slave and Poet* (Minneapolis: Compass Point Books, 2006), 9, 15; Miriam Morris Fuller, *Phillis Wheatley: America's First Black Poetess,* ill. Victor Mays (Champaign, Ill.: Garrard, 1971), 7–8; Carol Greene, *Phillis Wheatley: First African-American Poet* (Chicago: Children's Press, 1995), 13, 17; Susan R. Gregson, *Let Freedom Ring: Phillis Wheatley* (Mankato, Minn.: Bridgestone Books, 2002), 8; Cynthia Salisbury, *Phillis Wheatley: Legendary African-American Poet* (Berkeley Heights, N.J.: Enslow, 2001), 5. To be fair, in one case this image of a fearful child is contradicted: one page after describing Wheatley as a "small frightened waif," Bellegarde's narrator oddly also says that she "did not seem to be intimidated as the older slaves were."

51. Jacqueline Bernard, *Journey toward Freedom: The Story of Sojourner Truth* (New York: W. W. Norton, 1967), x ("frightened, lonely, slave child"); Claflin, *Sojourner Truth,* 11 ("lost in private fears"); Katherine Krohn, *Sojourner Truth: Freedom Fighter* (Mankato, Minn.: Capstone Press, 2006), 9 ("Isabella worried that she would be sold"); Julian May, *Sojourner Truth: Freedom-Fighter,* ill. Phero Thomas (Chicago: Childrens Press, 1973), 2 ("A skinny black girl, eleven years old, stood trembling beside her mother."); Moore, *Sojourner Truth,* 3 (first line: "Belle and her brother were scared"); Susan Taylor-Boyd, *Sojourner Truth: The Courageous Former Slave Whose Eloquence Helped Promote Human Equality* (Milwaukee: Gareth Stevens Children's Books, 1990), 8 ("great agony" of Belle when leaving her parents). Enhancing the ominous mood, Bernard began her narrative by describing the mountainous, heavily wooded geography of the area: "In Sojourner's childhood their slopes seemed dangerous and black, for in those days, they were still covered with the dark hemlocks that had so frightened the superstitious early settlers and kept them from straying too far from the river": Bernard, *Journey toward Freedom,* 1.

52. Fuller, *Phillis Wheatley;* Helen Stone Peterson, *Sojourner Truth: Fearless Crusader,* ill. Victor Mays (Champaign, Ill.: Garrard, 1972).

53. Fuller, *Phillis Wheatley,* 7.

54. Fuller, *Phillis Wheatley,* 13.

55. For another example of the use of fear to characterize the young Phillis Wheatley, see Salisbury, *Phillis Wheatley,* 5–6. This text looks at Wheatley's arrival in Boston as a flashback from the perspective of her twenty-year-old self. Thus, it focuses even more on the contrast

between the "frightened, illiterate African child" and the confident young woman she had become.

56. Peterson, *Sojourner Truth,* 7.

57. Peterson, *Sojourner Truth,* 9–11.

58. Jackson, *Shirley Chisholm,* 1. Two other biographies provide a similar account of the trip: James Haskins, *Fighting Shirley Chisholm,* 9; and Catherine Scheader, *Shirley Chisholm: Teacher and Congresswoman* (Hillside, N.J.: Enslow, 1990), 8.

59. Lucia Raatma, *Shirley Chisholm* (New York: Marshall Cavendish, 2011), 7; Haskins, *Fighting Shirley Chisholm,* 11.

60. Scheader, *Shirley Chisholm,* 9; Raatma, *Shirley Chisholm,* 8.

61. Raatma, *Shirley Chisholm,* 8; Scheader, *Shirley Chisholm,* 9.

62. Scheader, *Shirley Chisholm,* 9.

63. Susan Brownmiller, *Shirley Chisholm* (New York: Doubleday, 1970), 11.

64. Haskins, *Fighting Shirley Chisholm,* 14; Jackson, *Shirley Chisholm,* 3; Jill S. Pollack, *Shirley Chisholm* (New York: Franklin Watts, 1994), 11; Raatma, *Shirley Chisholm,* 8.

65. Nodelman, *Hidden Adult,* 8–14.

66. Anna Mae Duane, introduction to *The Children's Table: Childhood Studies and the Humanities,* ed. Anna Mae Duane (Athens: University of Georgia Press, 2013), 5.

67. Kelly McDowell, "*Roll of Thunder, Hear My Cry:* A Culturally Specific, Subversive Concept of Child Agency," *Children's Literature in Education* 33:3 (2002): 224.

68. On Douglass's patronizing assessment of Truth, see Painter, *Sojourner Truth,* 96–98.

69. Borland and Speicher, *Phillis Wheatley: Young Colonial Poet,* 43–49.

70. As previously discussed, Bellegarde seems primarily interested in using Phillis Wheatley as both a model and a cautionary tale. She is a model for achieving literary greatness during a time of oppression of women and African Americans. She is a cautionary tale as someone who, despite her apparently strong (as Bellegarde has told it) recollection of her African past, allows her heritage to disintegrate, which ultimately leaves her lost and impoverished at the end of her short life. This complex and seemingly contradictory narrative begins early on, as the narrator develops a line of commentary about Wheatley's memories. After describing these "phantom" memories, the narrator explains that "black persons who spent most of their time and energies in performing their duties as servants and slaves in America did not forget their interests in art and their passion for the beautiful" (29). Here, Wheatley's memory of her past means memory of an African cultural and aesthetic past. By describing the respect for the beautiful that had been historically present in Africa, Bellegarde was able to attribute Phillis's own passions and gifts to this unacknowledged past. At first, this view provides an explanation of her poetic abilities. But later, readers learn that she allows herself to forget about her heritage. She becomes intolerant of other religions, with African paganism providing a central example (32). Through "little talks" with her mistress, Wheatley also "gradually released the brooding desire for Africa and spiritually felt that America was now home for her" (34). The narrator reports the poems that resulted after this but finds little redemptive material in the last years of Wheatley's life. Rather, she becomes the negative exemplar for what the text's creator deems bad choices: a bitter and haughty husband and then a pregnancy (51–53): Bellegarde, *Phillis Wheatley.*

71. Salisbury, *Phillis Wheatley,* 5.

72. Graham, *The Story of Phillis Wheatley,* 22.

73. See esp. Graham, *The Story of Phillis Wheatley,* 25–31. Graham's text emphasizes the association between Wheatley and nature more than texts published later, during a time when such associations might be perceived as stereotyping. As discussed earlier, Graham could make these

associations in part because many other African American authors for children during the 1930s and 1940s offered romanticized images of Africa. See also Katharine Capshaw Smith, *Children's Literature of the Harlem Renaissance* (Bloomington: Indiana University Press, 2004), 45–52.

74. Marah Gubar, "The Hermeneutics of Recuperation: What a Kinship-Model Approach to Children's Agency Could Do for Children's Literature and Childhood Studies," *Jeunesse: Young People, Texts, Cultures* 8:1 (2016): 294.

75. David A. Adler, *A Picture Book of Sojourner Truth,* ill. Gershom Griffith (New York: Scholastic, 1994), 3; Claflin, *Sojourner Truth,* 2, 19, 110, 140; Kathleen Collins, *Sojourner Truth: Equal Rights Advocate* (New York: Rosen Publishing Group, 2004), 4; Helen Frost, *Sojourner Truth* (Mankato, Minn.: Capstone Press, 2003), 9; Jennifer Blizin Gillis, *Sojourner Truth* (Chicago: Heinemann Library, 2006), 18; May, *Sojourner Truth,* 24; Margo McLoone, *Sojourner Truth: A Photo-Illustrated Biography* (Mankato, Minn.: Bridgestone Books, 1997), 5, 19; Peterson, *Sojourner Truth,* 8, 19; Anne Rockwell, *Only Passing Through: The Story of Sojourner Truth,* ill. R. Gregory Christie (New York: Knopf, 2000), 2; Frances E. Ruffin, *Sojourner Truth* (New York: Rosen Publishing Group, 2002), 10, 13; and Gwenyth Swain, *Sojourner Truth,* ill. Matthew Archambault (Minneapolis: Carolrhoda Books, 2005), 4–5, 14, 30, 47.

76. Gubar, "Hermeneutics of Recuperation," 299.

77. May, *Sojourner Truth,* 15.

78. Dianne Johnson, *Telling Tales: The Pedagogy and Promise of African American Literature for Youth* (New York: Greenwood Press, 1990), 44.

79. In the text, the narrator allusively suggests that Belle's connection to Dumont is an unhealthy example of what contemporary psychologists might call codependence. The complete passage reads: "Most of all, she missed her kind master, Dumont. It was true that the Bible said that her love for him had been a sin. But he was so handsome and kind! Belle still had not grown up" (19). This strange mention of her "love" for Dumont refers to a rumor, historically unsubstantiated, that Belle had a sexual relationship with John Dumont, which may have resulted in the birth of her first child. This suspicion is encouraged in May's text. When Belle is first sold to Dumont, the narrator indicates that Dumont "was the handsomest man Belle had ever seen" (8). Later, the narrator describes Belle's marriage to her husband, Thomas, and their subsequent children and encourages readers to consider the possibility of a sexual relationship between Belle and her master: Belle "had at least four children. Some of the slaves whispered that the children seemed too light-colored to be the offspring of Tom. Belle paid no attention to them. They were just jealous because she was treated so well. Her master was the kindest person in the world and she repaid him by working harder than any of the others" (10). By weaving the suggestion of Belle's illicit love in with the narrative about "growing up," the text implies a whole series of associations with adulthood, including health, self-respect, and freedom from exploitation. Such an implication is highly atypical in children's biographies about Truth: May, *Sojourner Truth.*

80. May, *Sojourner Truth,* 24.

81. See Charles Taylor, *Sources of the Self: The Making of the Modern Identity* (Cambridge, Mass.: Harvard University Press, 1989), 1–51.

82. On formal education, see Claflin, *Sojourner Truth,* 43, 71; choice and self-possession, 47; becoming an influential public person, 47–49; identifying virtue in others, 71; and political activism, 73.

83. Claflin, *Sojourner Truth,* 107.

84. Claflin, *Sojourner Truth,* 108.

85. Taylor, *Sources of the Self,* 351–54; see also Taylor, *Modern Social Imaginaries* (Durham, N.C.: Duke University Press, 2004), 163–74.

86. Brownmiller, *Shirley Chisholm*, 15, 28, 31; Haskins, *Fighting Shirley Chisholm*, 6–7, 14; Nancy Hicks, *Honorable Shirley Chisholm: Congresswoman from Brooklyn* (New York: Lion Books, 1971), 24–25, 29; Jackson, *Shirley Chisholm*, 7, 9; Pollack, *Shirley Chisholm*, 10, 12; Raatma, *Shirley Chisholm*, 13–14; Scheader, *Shirley Chisholm*, 13.
87. Haskins, *Fighting Shirley Chisholm*, 31, 34; Scheader, *Shirley Chisholm*, 20–21.
88. Haskins, *Fighting Shirley Chisholm*, 34.
89. Brownmiller, *Shirley Chisholm*, 33–42.
90. Brownmiller, *Shirley Chisholm*, 41.
91. Brownmiller, *Shirley Chisholm*, 42.
92. Haskins, *Fighting Shirley Chisholm*, 43.
93. Scheader, *Shirley Chisholm*, 21.
94. Shirley Chisholm, *Unbought and Unbossed: Expanded 40th Anniversary Edition* (1970; Washington, D.C.: Take Root Media, 2010), 25.
95. Haskins, *Fighting Shirley Chisholm*, 56; Raatma, *Shirley Chisholm*, 18; Scheader, *Shirley Chisholm*, 22. See also Pollack, *Shirley Chisholm*, 20.
96. Scheader, *Shirley Chisholm*, 22.
97. Haskins, *Fighting Shirley Chisholm*, 60.
98. Emma Uprichard, "Children as 'Being and Becomings': Children, Childhood, and Temporality," *Children and Society* 22:4 (2008): 306.
99. Clark, *Kiddie Lit*, 11.
100. Clark, *Kiddie Lit*, 12.
101. Ricoeur, *Time and Narrative* 1: 79.
102. On Taylor's concept of the repertory, see Taylor, *Modern Social Imaginaries*, 25.

Chapter 7: "Sanitize and Simplify"

1. Cate Plys and Robert Leighton, "All Presidents Are Above Average," *Slate.com*, February, 14, 2010, http://www.slate.com/articles/news_and_politics/politics/2010/02/all_presidents_are_above_average.html (accessed December 23, 2016). Plys and Leighton wrote a similar piece on biographies about baseball greats: Leighton and Plys, "Let's Read Two," *Slate.com*, April 5, 2010, http://www.slate.com/articles/sports/sports_nut/2010/04/lets_read_two.html (accessed January 9, 2018).
2. See Michael W. Apple and Linda K. Christian-Smith, eds., *The Politics of the Textbook* (New York: Routledge, 1991); James W. Loewen, *Lies My Teacher Told Me: Everything Your American History Textbook Got Wrong* (New York: New Press, 1995); Joseph Moreau, *Schoolbook Nation: Conflicts over American History Textbooks from the Civil War to the Present* (Ann Arbor: University of Michigan Press, 2004).
3. See, for example, James Loewen, "Why Do People Believe Myths about the Confederacy? Because Our Textbooks and Monuments Are Wrong," *Washington Post*, July 1, 2015, https://www.washingtonpost.com/posteverything/wp/2015/07/01/why-do-people-believe-myths-about-the-confederacy-because-our-textbooks-and-monuments-are-wrong/?utm_term=.ef8459c25ad1 (accessed December 23, 2016); and Russell Shorto, "How Christian Were the Founders?," *New York Times Magazine*, February 11, 2010, http://www.nytimes.com/2010/02/14/magazine/14texbooks-t.html?ref=magazine&ref=magazine (accessed December 23, 2016).
4. Alexandra Alter, "To Lure Young Readers, Nonfiction Writers Sanitize and Simplify," *New York Times*, October 7, 2014, A1.
5. Susan Taylor-Boyd, *Sojourner Truth: The Courageous Former Slave Whose Eloquence Helped Promote Human Equality* (Milwaukee: Gareth Stevens Children's Books, 1990), back cover. For examples of books that emphasize primary texts, see Corona Brezina, *Sojourner*

Truth's "Ain't I a Woman?" Speech: A Primary Source Investigation (New York: Rosen Publishing Group, 2005); Mary G. Butler, *Sojourner Truth: From Slave to Activist for Freedom* (New York: Rosen Publishing Group, 2003).

6. Ekaterina Haskins, *Popular Memories: Commemoration, Participatory Culture, and Democratic Citizenship* (Columbia: University of South Carolina Press, 2015), 119.

7. David Oswell, *The Agency of Children: From Family to Global Human Rights* (New York: Cambridge University Press, 2013), 3.

8. Haskins, *Popular Memories,* 4.

9. Jessie Redmon Fauset, "The Story of Phillis Wheatley," *Brownies' Book* 1:8 (August 1920): 253. The Tar Baby and the Tomahawk: Race and Ethnic Images in Children's Literature, 1880–1939, http://childlit.unl.edu/brownies.192008.html (accessed December 21, 2016).

10. Henry Louis Gates Jr., *The Trials of Phillis Wheatley: America's First Black Poet and Her Encounters with the Founding Fathers* (New York: Basic Civitas Books, 2003), 68–69.

11. Frances E. Ruffin, *Sojourner Truth* (New York: Rosen Publishing Group, 2002); Butler, *Sojourner Truth,* 76–82 ("The Legend Grows"). Another text that does the same things in a very different way is Brezina, *Sojourner Truth's "Ain't I a Woman?" Speech.* As the title indicates, this text is not a straightforward biography. However, because it communicates much the same information about Truth's life and legacy as other texts marketed as biographies, I include it in this project. The text employs the speech as a means of entering into Truth's life and into the process of historical research. This approach is in some ways similar to that of Catherine Clinton in *Phillis's Big Test,* a picture book that tells the story of Phillis Wheatley's life through a snapshot of her experience of being interviewed by eighteen Boston men in October 1772: Clinton, *Phillis's Big Test,* ill. Sean Qualls (Boston: Houghton Mifflin, 2008).

12. Of the texts that were published after 2000, roughly half include at least a paragraph of interpretive commentary after the life narrative has concluded. Some of these devote a full chapter or section to the "afterlife."

13. Lucia Raatma, *Shirley Chisholm* (New York: Marshall Cavendish, 2011), 74–87.

14. Raatma, *Shirley Chisholm,* 75.

15. Raatma, *Shirley Chisholm,* 75–76.

16. Raatma, *Shirley Chisholm,* 78.

17. Raatma, *Shirley Chisholm,* 82–83.

18. Raatma, *Shirley Chisholm,* 84.

19. Raatma, *Shirley Chisholm,* 86. Catherine Scheader also concluded her text with this quotation, though it is not fully contextualized but merely presented as part of a group of quotations at the end of the narrative: Scheader, *Shirley Chisholm: Teacher and Congresswoman* (Hillside, N.J.: Enslow, 1990), 124.

20. See Molly Aloian, *Phillis Wheatley: Poet of the Revolutionary Era* (New York: Crabtree, 2013), 41; Robin S. Doak, *Phillis Wheatley, Slave and Poet* (Minneapolis: Compass Point Books, 2006), 89–95; Susan R. Gregson, *Let Freedom Ring: Phillis Wheatley* (Mankato, Minn.: Bridgestone Books, 2002), 38–41; Jacqueline McLendon, *Phillis Wheatley: A Revolutionary Poet* (New York: Rosen Publishing Group, 2003), 93–99; Laura Purdie Salas, *Phillis Wheatley: Colonial American Poet* (Mankato, Minn.: Capstone Press, 2006), 24–26; Cynthia Salisbury, *Phillis Wheatley: Legendary African-American Poet* (Berkeley Heights, N.J.: Enslow, 2001), 90–100; and Maryann N. Weidt, *Revolutionary Poet: A Story about Phillis Wheatley,* ill. Mary O'Keefe Young (Minneapolis: Carolrhoda Books, 1997), 59–60.

21. Weidt, *Revolutionary Poet,* 59.

22. Salisbury, *Phillis Wheatley,* 90.

23. Salisbury, *Phillis Wheatley,* 93.

24. Salisbury, *Phillis Wheatley,* 95–98.

25. Salisbury, *Phillis Wheatley,* 97.

26. Salisbury, *Phillis Wheatley,* 93, 95, 98.

27. See Kendall R. Phillips, introduction to *Framing Public Memory*, ed. Kendall R. Phillips (Tuscaloosa: University of Alabama Press, 2004), 3–6, 10; Bradford Vivian, *Public Forgetting: The Rhetoric and Politics of Beginning Again* (University Park: Pennsylvania State University Press, 2010), 1–16; and Vivian, "On the Language of Forgetting," *Quarterly Journal of Speech* 95:1 (2009): 89–104.

28. Gregson, *Let Freedom Ring,* 38.

29. Gregson, *Let Freedom Ring,* 41. A "callout box" appears alongside but separate from the main body of the narrative text. It is typically distinguished from the narrative by being contained within a bounded area marked by a border, change of color, and often a title.

30. Norma Jean Lutz, *Sojourner Truth: Abolitionist, Suffragist, and Preacher* (Philadelphia: Chelsea House, 2001), 71.

31. Lutz, *Sojourner Truth,* 70. In the main text on this page, Lutz relates some of the anecdotes surrounding Truth's death. She includes the oft-repeated though likely apocryphal story about how, when a friend alluded to her imminent death, Truth corrected the friend's notion of death, saying, "I ain't gonna die, honey. I'm going home like a shooting star!" Nell Irvin Painter explained that this story was invented by Hallie Quinn Brown in *Homespun Heroines and Other Women of Distinction* (Xenia, Ohio: Aldine, 1926), 17, http://docsouth.unc.edu/neh/brownhal/brownhal.html (accessed December 22, 2016): Painter, *Sojourner Truth: A Life, a Symbol* (New York: W. W. Norton, 1996), 264–65.

32. Joanne Mattern, *Sojourner Truth: Early Abolitionist* (New York: Rosen Publishing Group, 2003), 18–21.

33. Mattern, *Sojourner Truth,* 20.

34. Other examples that address commemoration include Brezina, *Sojourner Truth's "Ain't I a Woman?" Speech,* 45–50; Kathleen Collins, *Sojourner Truth: Equal Rights Advocate* (New York: Rosen Publishing Group, 2004), 28–29; Katherine Krohn, *Sojourner Truth: Freedom Fighter* (Mankato, Minn.: Capstone Press, 2006), 26; Kathleen Kudlinski, *Sojourner Truth: Voice for Freedom,* ill. Lenny Wooden (New York: Aladdin, 2003), 146–48; Peter Roop and Connie Roop, *Sojourner Truth* (New York: Scholastic, 2002), 117–20.

35. Peter Hunt, *Children's Literature* (Oxford: Blackwell, 2001), 12.

36. James Jasinski, "The Status of Theory and Method in Rhetorical Criticism," *Western Journal of Communication* 65:3 (2001): 254.

37. Jasinski, "Status of Theory and Method," 254–55.

38. Some notable examples include Carole Blair and Neil Michel, "The AIDS Memorial Quilt and the Contemporary Culture of Public Commemoration," *Rhetoric and Public Affairs* 10:4 (2007): 595–626; Thomas R. Dunn, "Remembering 'A Great Fag': Visualizing Public Memory and the Construction of Queer Space," *Quarterly Journal of Speech* 97:4 (2011): 435–60; and Charles E. Morris III, "My Old Kentucky Homo: Lincoln and the Politics of Queer Public Memory," in *Framing Public Memory* Kendall R. Phillips, ed., (Tuscaloosa: University of Alabama Press, 2004), 89–114.

39. Cindy Koenig Richards, "Inventing Sacagawea: Public Women and the Transformative Potential of Epideictic Rhetoric," *Western Journal of Communication* 73:1 (2009): 1–22.

40. Karlyn Kohrs Campbell, "Agency: Promiscuous and Protean," *Communication and Critical/Cultural Studies* 2:1 (2005): 1.

41. Michael Leff, "The Habitation of Rhetoric," in *Argument and Critical Practice: Proceedings of the Fifth SCA/AFA Conference on Argumentation,* ed. Joseph Wenzel (Annandale,

Va.: Speech Communication Association, 1987), 1–9; Michael Leff, "Tradition and Agency in Humanistic Rhetoric," *Philosophy and Rhetoric* 36:2 (2003): 135–47; Andreea Deciu Ritivoi, *Paul Ricoeur: Tradition and Innovation in Rhetorical Theory* (Albany: State University of New York Press, 2006); Barbara Warnick, "A Ricoeurian Approach to Rhetorical Criticism," *Western Journal of Speech Communication* 51:3 (1987): 227–44.

42. Loewen, *Lies My Teacher Told Me;* Moreau, *Schoolbook Nation;* Sara L. Schwebel, *Child-Sized History: Fictions of the Past in U.S. Classrooms* (Nashville, Tenn.: Vanderbilt University Press, 2011).

43. Pocahontas Foster, "The Jury," *Brownies' Book* 1:5 (May 1920): 140. The Tar Baby and the Tomahawk: Race and Ethnic Images in Children's Literature, 1880–1939, http://childlit.unl.edu/brownies.192005.html (accessed December 21, 2016).

Bibliography

Biographies for Children and Young People and Other Primary Texts

Adler, David A. *A Picture Book of Sojourner Truth.* Ill. Gershom Griffith. New York: Scholastic, 1994.

Aloian, Molly. *Phillis Wheatley: Poet of the Revolutionary Era.* Understanding the American Revolution. New York: Crabtree, 2013.

Anderson, Laurie Halse. *Chains.* New York: Simon and Schuster, 2008.

Bellegarde, Ida R. *Phillis Wheatley.* Vol. 4, Black Heroes and Heroines. Pine Bluff, Ark.: Bell Enterprises, 1983.

Bernard, Catherine. *Sojourner Truth: Abolitionist and Women's Rights Activist.* Historical American Biographies. Berkeley Heights, N.J.: Enslow, 2001.

Bernard, Jacqueline. *Journey toward Freedom: The Story of Sojourner Truth.* New York: W. W. Norton, 1967.

Bledsoe, Lucy Jane. *Phillis Wheatley: First in Poetry.* Edgewood Cliffs, N.J.: Globe Books, 1989.

Bontemps, Arna. *Story of the Negro.* Ill. Ray Lufkin. 1948. 4th ed. New York: Knopf, 1955.

Borland, Kathryn Kilby, and Helen Ross Speicher. *Phillis Wheatley: Young Colonial Poet.* Ill. William K. Plummer. Childhood of Famous Americans. Indianapolis: Bobbs-Merrill, 1968.

——. *Phillis Wheatley: Young Revolutionary Poet.* Ill. Cathy Morrison. Young Patriots Series. Carmel, Ind.: Patria Press, 2005.

Brezina, Corona. *Sojourner Truth's "Ain't I a Woman?" Speech: A Primary Source Investigation.* Great Historic Debates and Speeches. New York: Rosen Publishing Group, 2005.

Brown, Hallie Quinn. *Homespun Heroines and Other Women of Distinction.* Xenia, Ohio: Aldine, 1926. http://docsouth.unc.edu/neh/brownhal/brownhal.html (accessed December 22, 2016).

Brownmiller, Susan. *Shirley Chisholm.* New York: Doubleday, 1970.

Burke, Rick. *Phillis Wheatley.* American Lives. Chicago: Heinemann Library, 2003.

Butler, Mary G. *Sojourner Truth: From Slave to Activist for Freedom.* Library of American Lives and Times. New York: Rosen Publishing Group, 2003.

Cardigan, H. H. *The Light of One Candle.* Ill. Cedric Lucas. New York: McGraw-Hill. N.d.

Chambers, Lucille Arcola. *Negro Pioneers: Phillis Wheatley, Poetess.* Ill. John Neal. New York: C & S Ventures, 1967.

Claflin, Edward Beecher. *Sojourner Truth and the Struggle for Freedom.* Ill. Jada Rowland. Henry Steele Commager's Americans: Profiles of Americans for Young People. Hauppage, N.Y.: Children's Press Choice, 1987.

Clinton, Catherine. *Phillis's Big Test.* Ill. Sean Qualls. Boston: Houghton Mifflin, 2008.

Collard, Sneed B., III. *Phillis Wheatley: She Loved Words.* American Heroes. Tarrytown, N.Y.: Marshall Cavendish Benchmark, 2010.

Collins, Kathleen. *Sojourner Truth: Equal Rights Advocate.* Primary Sources of Famous People in American History. New York: Rosen Publishing Group, 2004.

Doak, Robin S. *Phillis Wheatley, Slave and Poet.* Signature Lives: Revolutionary Era. Minneapolis: Compass Point Books, 2006.

Du Bois, W. E. B. "The True Brownies." *Crisis* 6 (October 1919): 285–286. The Tar Baby and the Tomahawk: Race and Ethnic Images in Children's Literature, 1880–1939. http://childlit.unl.edu/crisis.191910.html (accessed December 21, 2016).

Fauset, Jessie Redmon. "A Pioneer Suffragette." *Brownies' Book* 1:4 (April 1920): 120–21. The Tar Baby and the Tomahawk: Race and Ethnic Images in Children's Literature, 1880–1939. http://childlit.unl.edu/brownies.192004.html (accessed December 21, 2016).

——. "The Story of Phillis Wheatley: A True Story." *Brownies' Book* 1:8 (August 1920): 251–53. The Tar Baby and the Tomahawk: Race and Ethnic Images in Children's Literature, 1880–1939. http://childlit.unl.edu/brownies.192008.html (accessed December 21, 2016).

Ferris, Jeri. *Walking the Road to Freedom: A Story about Sojourner Truth.* Minneapolis: Carolrhoda Books, 1988.

Fish, Bruce, and Becky Durost Fish. *Phillis Wheatley.* Amazing Americans: Revolutionary Period, 1754–1790. Chicago: Wright Group/McGraw-Hill, 2006.

Foster, Pocahontas. "The Jury." *Brownies' Book* 1:5 (May 1920): 140. The Tar Baby and the Tomahawk: Race and Ethnic Images in Children's Literature, 1880–1939. http://childlit.unl.edu/brownies.192005.html (accessed December 21, 2016).

Frost, Helen. *Sojourner Truth.* Mankato, Minn.: Capstone Press, 2003.

Fuller, Miriam Morris. *Phillis Wheatley: America's First Black Poetess.* Ill. Victor Mays. Americans All. Champaign, Ill.: Garrard, 1971.

Gillis, Jennifer Blizin. *Sojourner Truth.* American Lives. Chicago: Heinemann Library, 2006.

Graham, Shirley. *The Story of Phillis Wheatley: Poetess of the American Revolution.* Ill. Robert Burns. 1949. 12th ed. New York: Julian Messner, 1969.

Greene, Carol. *Phillis Wheatley: First African-American Poet.* Chicago: Children's Press, 1995.

Gregson, Susan R. *Let Freedom Ring: Phillis Wheatley.* Mankato, Minn.: Bridgestone Books, 2002.

Haskins, James. *Fighting Shirley Chisholm.* New York: Dial Press, 1975.

Haynes, Elizabeth Ross. *Unsung Heroes.* New York: Du Bois and Dill, 1921. https://archive.org/details/unsungheroesoohaynrich (accessed December 21, 2016).

Hicks, Nancy. *The Honorable Shirley Chisholm: Congresswoman from Brooklyn.* New York: Lion Books, 1971.

Horn, Geoffrey M. *Sojourner Truth: Speaking Up for Freedom.* Voices for Freedom: Abolitionist Heroes. New York: Crabtree, 2010.

Jackson, Garnet Nelson. *Phillis Wheatley, Poet.* Ill. Cheryl Hanna. Cleveland, Ohio: Modern Curriculum Press, 1993.

——. *Shirley Chisholm: Congresswoman.* Ill. Thomas Hudson. Cleveland, Ohio: Modern Curriculum Press, 1994.

Jensen, Marilyn. *Phillis Wheatley: Negro Slave of Mr. John Wheatley of Boston.* Scarsdale, N.Y.: Lion Books, 1987.

Kent, Deborah. *Phillis Wheatley: First Published African-American Poet.* Our People: Spirit of America. Chanhassen, Minn.: The Child's World, 2004.

Krohn, Katherine. *Sojourner Truth: Freedom Fighter.* FactFinders Biographies. Mankato, Minn.: Capstone Press, 2006.

Kudlinski, Kathleen. *Sojourner Truth: Voice for Freedom.* Ill. Lenny Wooden. Childhood of Famous Americans. New York: Aladdin, 2003.

Landrum, Bessie. *Stories of Black Folk for Little Folk.* Atlanta: A. B. Caldwell, 1923.

Lasky, Kathryn. *A Voice of Her Own: The Story of Phillis Wheatley, Slave Poet.* Ill. Paul Lee. Cambridge, Mass.: Candlewick Press, 2003.

Lindstrom, Aletha Jane. *Sojourner Truth: Slave, Abolitionst, and Fighter for Women's Rights.* Ill. Paul Frame. New York: Julian Messner, 1980.

Lutz, Norma Jean. *Sojourner Truth: Abolitionist, Suffragist, and Preacher.* Famous Figures of the Civil War Era. Philadelphia: Chelsea House, 2001.

Malaspina, Ann. *Phillis Sings Out Freedom: The Story of George Washington and Phillis Wheatley.* Ill. Susan Keeter. Chicago: Albert Whitman, 2010.

Mattern, Joanne. *Sojourner Truth: Early Abolitionist.* Women Who Shaped History. New York: Rosen Publishing Group, 2003.

May, Julian. *Sojourner Truth: Freedom-Fighter.* Ill. Phero Thomas. Chicago: Childrens Press, 1973.

McKissack, Patricia, and Fredrick McKissack. *Sojourner Truth: A Voice for Freedom.* Great African Americans. Berkeley Heights, N.J.: Enslow, 2002.

McLeese, Don. *Phillis Wheatley.* Heroes of the American Revolution. Vero Beach, Fla.: Rourke, 2005.

McLendon, Jacqueline. *Phillis Wheatley: A Revolutionary Poet.* The Library of American Lives and Times. New York: Rosen Publishing Group, 2003.

McLoone, Margo. *Sojourner Truth: A Photo-Illustrated Biography.* Mankato, Minn.: Bridgestone Books, 1997.

Moore, Barbara R. *Sojourner Truth.* Boston: Houghton Mifflin, 2005.

Moriarty, J. T. *Phillis Wheatley: African American Poet.* Primary Sources of Famous People in American History. New York: Rosen Publishing Group 2004.

Ortiz, Victoria. *Sojourner Truth, a Self-Made Woman.* Philadelphia: J. B. Lippincott, 1974.

Peterson, Helen Stone. *Sojourner Truth: Fearless Crusader.* Ill. Victor Mays. Americans All. Champaign, Ill.: Garrard, 1972.

Pinkney, Andrea Davis. *Sojourner Truth's Step-Stomp Stride.* Ill. Brian Pinkney. New York: Disney/Jump at the Sun Books, 2009.

Pollack, Jill S. *Shirley Chisholm: A First Book.* New York: Franklin Watts, 1994.

Raatma, Lucia. *Shirley Chisholm.* Leading Women. New York: Marshall Cavendish, 2011.

Richmond, Merle. *Phillis Wheatley: Poet.* American Women of Achievement. New York: Chelsea House, 1988.

Rinaldi, Ann. *Hang a Thousand Trees with Ribbons: The Story of Phillis Wheatley.* Orlando, Fla.: Gulliver Books/Harcourt, 1996. Published with reader's guide in 2005.

Rockwell, Anne. *Only Passing Through: The Story of Sojourner Truth.* Ill. R. Gregory Christie. New York: Knopf, 2000.

Roop, Peter, and Connie Roop. *Sojourner Truth.* In Their Own Words. New York: Scholastic, 2002.

Roza, Greg. *"Guide My Pen": The Poems of Phillis Wheatley.* Great Moments in American History. New York: Rosen Publishing Group, 2004.

Ruffin, Frances E. *Sojourner Truth.* American Legends. New York: Rosen Publishing Group, 2002.

Salas, Laura Purdie. *Phillis Wheatley: Colonial American Poet.* Mankato, Minn.: Capstone Press, 2006.

Salisbury, Cynthia. *Phillis Wheatley: Legendary African-American Poet.* Berkeley Heights, N.J.: Enslow, 2001.

Scheader, Catherine. *Shirley Chisholm: Teacher and Congresswoman.* Contemporary Women Series. Hillside, N.J.: Enslow, 1990.

Scruggs, L. A. *Women of Distinction: Remarkable of Works and Invincible of Character.* Raleigh, N.C.: L. A. Scruggs, 1893.

Sherrow, Victoria. *Phillis Wheatley.* Junior World Biographies. New York: Chelsea House, 1992.

Shumate, Jane. *Sojourner Truth.* Brookfield, Conn.: Millbrook Press, 1991.

Slade, Suzanne. *Sojourner Truth: Preacher for Freedom and Equality.* Ill. Natascha Alex Banks. Minneapolis: Picture Window Books, 2008.

Spinale, Laura. *Sojourner Truth.* Chanhassen, Minn.: The Child's World, 2000.

Swain, Gwenyth. *Sojourner Truth.* Ill. Matthew Archambault. Minneapolis: Carolrhoda Books, 2005.

Taylor-Boyd, Susan. *Sojourner Truth: The Courageous Former Slave Whose Eloquence Helped Promote Human Equality.* People Who Have Helped the World. Milwaukee: Gareth Stevens Children's Books, 1990.

Trumbauer, Lisa. *Let's Meet Sojourner Truth.* New York: Chelsea House, 2004.

Waxman, Laura Hamilton. *Sojourner Truth.* History Maker Bios. Minneapolis: Lerner, 2008.

Weidt, Maryann N. *Revolutionary Poet: A Story about Phillis Wheatley.* Ill. Mary O'Keefe Young. Carolrhoda Creative Minds Biography. Minneapolis: Carolrhoda Books, 1997.

Whalin, W. Terry. *Sojourner Truth: American Abolitionist.* Philadelphia: Chelsea House, 1999.

Woodson, Carter G. *The Negro in Our History.* Washington, D.C.: Associated Publishers, 1922.

Wright, Audrey. "The Jury." *Brownies' Book* 1:8 (August 1920): 256. The Tar Baby and the Tomahawk: Race and Ethnic Images in Children's Literature, 1880–1939. http://childlit.unl.edu/brownies.192008.html (accessed December 21, 2016).

Scholarly Publications and Other Secondary Sources

"About ANTIQUES ROADSHOW." *Antiques Roadshow.* WGBH Boston. http://www.pbs.org/wgbh/roadshow/about.html (accessed December 23, 2016).

Alter, Alexandra. "To Lure Young Readers, Nonfiction Writers Sanitize and Simplify." *New York Times,* October 7, 2014, A1.

American Legends. Rosen Publishing Group. 2015. http://www.rosenpublishing.com.

Anderson, Benedict. *Imagined Communities.* Rev. ed. New York: Verso, 1991.

Apple, Michael W., and Linda K. Christian-Smith, eds. *The Politics of the Textbook.* New York: Routledge, 1991.

Archibald, Robert R. "Memory and the Process of Public History." *Public Historian* 19:2 (1997): 61–64.

Arendt, Hannah. *The Human Condition.* 2nd ed. Chicago: University of Chicago Press, 1998.

Aristotle. *On Rhetoric: A Theory of Civic Discourse.* Trans. George Kennedy. New York: Oxford University Press, 1991.

"Army Hostess." *Chicago Defender,* May 9, 1942, p. 8.

Aronson, Marc. *Beyond the Pale: New Essays for a New Era.* Lanham, Md.: Scarecrow Press, 2003.

———. "Originality in Nonfiction." *School Library Journal* 52:1 (2006): 42–43.

Atwater, Deborah F. *African American Women's Rhetoric: The Search for Dignity, Personhood, and Honor.* Lanham, Md.: Lexington Books, 2009.

Becker, Carl. "Everyman His Own Historian." *American Historical Review* 37:2 (1932): 221–36.

Beizer, Janet. *Thinking through the Mothers: Reimagining Women's Biographies.* Ithaca, N.Y.: Cornell University Press, 2009.

Bellah, Robert N. *Habits of the Heart: Individualism and Commitment in American Life.* Berkeley: University of California Press, 1985.

Benoit, William Lyon. "Aristotle's Example: The Rhetorical Induction." *Quarterly Journal of Speech* 66:2 (1980): 182–92.

——. "On Aristotle's Example." *Philosophy and Rhetoric* 20:4 (1987): 261–67.

Bernstein, Robin. *Racial Innocence: Performing American Childhood from Slavery to Civil Rights.* New York: New York University Press, 2011.

Bethune, Mary McLeod. "Adaptation of the History of the Negro to the Capacity of the Child." *Journal of Negro History* 24:1 (1939): 9–13.

——. "Oswald Garrison Villard and Hallie Quinn Brown." *Chicago Defender.* October 15, 1949, p. 6.

Biesecker, Barbara A. "Remembering World War II: The Rhetoric and Politics of National Commemoration at the Turn of the 21st Century." *Quarterly Journal of Speech* 88:4 (2002): 393–409.

Bishop, Rudine Sims. *Free within Ourselves: The Development of African American Children's Literature.* Portsmouth, N.H.: Heinemann, 2007.

Black, Edwin. "The Second Persona." *Quarterly Journal of Speech* 56:2 (1970): 109–19.

Blackford, Holly Virginia. *Out of This World: Why Literature Matters to Girls.* New York: Teachers College Press, 2004.

Blair, Carole, Marsha S. Jeppeson, and Enrico Pucci Jr. "Public Memorializing in Postmodernity: The Vietnam Veterans Memorial as Prototype." *Quarterly Journal of Speech* 77:3 (1991): 263–88.

Blair, Carole, and Neil Michel. "The AIDS Memorial Quilt and the Contemporary Culture of Public Commemoration." *Rhetoric and Public Affairs* 10:4 (2007): 595–626.

Bodnar, John. *Remaking America: Public Memory, Commemoration, and Patriotism in the Twentieth Century.* Princeton, N.J.: Princeton University Press, 1992.

Bormann, Ernest G., John F. Cragan, and Donald C. Shields. "Defending Symbolic Convergence Theory from an Imaginary Gunn." *Quarterly Journal of Speech* 89:4 (2003): 366–72.

Boulware, Beverly J., Eula E. Monroe, and Bradley Ray Wilcox. "The 5L Instructional Design for Exploring Legacies through Biography." *Reading Teacher* 66:6 (2012): 487–94.

Britton, Diane F. "Public History and Public Memory." *Public Historian* 19:3 (1997): 11–23.

Brooks, Wanda M., and Jonda C. McNair, eds. *Embracing, Evaluating, and Examining African American Children's and Young Adult Literature.* Lanham, Md.: Scarecrow Press, 2008.

Brown, Wendy. *Undoing the Demos: Neoliberalism's Stealth Revolution.* New York: Zone Books, 2015.

Browne, Stephen H. "Reading, Rhetoric, and the Texture of Public Memory." *Quarterly Journal of Speech* 81:2 (1995): 237–65.

Bruner, Jerome S. *Actual Minds, Possible Worlds.* Cambridge, Mass.: Harvard University Press, 1986.

Bruner, M. Lane. *Strategies of Remembrance.* Columbia: University of South Carolina Press, 2002.

Burke, Kenneth. *A Grammar of Motives.* Berkeley: University of California Press, 1969.

Campbell, Karlyn Kohrs. "Agency: Promiscuous and Protean." *Communication and Critical/Cultural Studies* 2:1 (2005): 1–19.

Capshaw, Katharine. *Civil Rights Childhood: Picturing Liberation in African American Photobooks.* Minneapolis: University of Minnesota Press, 2014.

Carlton-LaNey, Iris. "Elizabeth Ross Haynes: An African American Reformer of Womanist Consciousness, 1908–1940." *Social Work* 42:6 (1997): 573–83.

Carr, David. *Time, Narrative, and History.* Bloomington: Indiana University Press, 1986.

Carretta, Vincent. *Phillis Wheatley: Biography of a Genius in Bondage.* Athens: University of Georgia Press, 2011.

Casey, Edward S. "Public Memory in Place and Time." In *Framing Public Memory*, 24–39. Edited by Kendall R. Phillips. Tuscaloosa: University of Alabama Press, 2004.

Charland, Maurice. "Constitutive Rhetoric: The Case of the *Peuple Québécois*." *Quarterly Journal of Speech* 73:2 (1987): 133–50.

Chisholm, Shirley. *Unbought and Unbossed: Expanded 40th Anniversary Edition.* Washington, D.C.: Take Root Media, 2010. First published by Houghton Mifflin in 1970.

"Chisholm, Shirley Anita (1924–2005)." *History, Art & Archives, United States House of Representatives.* http://history.house.gov/People/Listing/C/CHISHOLM,-Shirley-Anita-%28C000371%29/ (accessed December 23, 2016).

Clark, Beverly Lyon. *Kiddie Lit: The Cultural Construction of Children's Literature in America.* Baltimore: Johns Hopkins University Press, 2003.

Collins, Carol Jones. "African-American Young Adult Biography: In Search of the Self." In *African-American Voices in Young Adult Literature,* 1–30. Edited by Karen Patricia Smith. Metuchen, N.J.: Scarecrow Press, 1994.

Confino, Alon. "Collective Memory and Cultural History: Problems of Method." *American Historical Review* 102:5 (1997): 1386–403.

Connolly, Paula T. *Slavery in American Children's Literature, 1790–2010.* Iowa City: University of Iowa Press, 2013.

Cook, Timothy E. "The Newbery Award as Political Education: Children's Literature and Cultural Reproduction." *Polity* 17:3 (1985): 421–45.

Crenshaw, Kimberlé. "Demarginalizing the Intersection of Race and Sex: A Black Feminist Critique of Antidiscrimination Doctrine, Feminist Theory, and Antiracist Politics." *University of Chicago Legal Forum* (1989): 139–67. www.heinonline.org (accessed December 23, 2016).

Cubitt, Geoffrey. *History and Memory.* New York: Manchester University Press, 2007.

Davis, Natalie Zemon. *The Return of Martin Guerre.* Cambridge, Mass.: Harvard University Press, 1983.

Dayton, Cornelia Hughes. "Rethinking Agency, Recovering Voices." *American Historical Review* 109:3 (2004): 827–43.

DeLuca, Kevin. "Articulation Theory: A Discursive Grounding for Rhetorical Practice." *Philosophy and Rhetoric* 32:4 (1999): 334–48.

Des Jardins, Julia. *Women and the Historical Enterprise in America: Gender, Race, and the Politics of Memory, 1880–1945.* Chapel Hill: University of North Carolina Press, 2003.

Dickinson, Greg. "Memories for Sale: Nostalgia and the Construction of Identity in Old Pasadena." *Quarterly Journal of Speech* 83:1 (1997): 1–27.

Dickinson, Greg, Carole Blair, and Brian L. Ott, eds. *Places of Public Memory: The Rhetoric of Museums and Memorials.* Tuscaloosa: University of Alabama Press, 2010.

Dorr, Christina H. "Searching for She-roes: A Study of Biographies of Historic Women Written for Children." *Children & Libraries: The Journal of the Association for Library Service to Children* 9:2 (2011): 42–49.

Du Bois, W. E. B. *Black Reconstruction in America: An Essay toward a History of the Part Which Black Folk Played in the Attempt to Reconstruct Democracy in America, 1860–1880.* Edited by Henry Louis Gates Jr. New York: Oxford University Press, 2007/1935.

Dunn, Thomas R. "'The Quare in the Square': Queer Memories, Sensibilities and Oscar Wilde." *Quarterly Journal of Speech* 100:2 (2014): 213–40.

———. *Queerly Remembered: Rhetorics for Representing the GLBTQ Past.* Columbia: University of South Carolina Press, 2016.

———. "Remembering 'A Great Fag': Visualizing Public Memory and the Construction of Queer Space." *Quarterly Journal of Speech* 97:4 (2011): 435–60.

——. "Remembering Matthew Shepard: Violence, Identity, and Queer Counterpublic Memories." *Rhetoric and Public Affairs* 13:4 (2010): 611–51.
Duane, Anna Mae, ed. *The Children's Table: Childhood Studies and the Humanities.* Athens: University of Georgia Press, 2013.
Eaton, Gale. *Well-Dressed Role Models: The Portrayal of Women in Biographies for Children.* Lanham, Md.: Scarecrow Press, 2006.
Epstein, William H. "Inducing Biography." *Children's Literature Association Quarterly* 12:4 (1987): 177–79.
——. *Recognizing Biography.* Philadelphia: University of Pennsylvania Press, 1987.
Ermarth, Elizabeth Deeds. "Agency in the Discursive Condition." *History and Theory* 40:4 (2001): 34–58.
Fertig, Gary. "Using Biography to Help Young Learners Understand the Causes of Historical Change and Continuity." *Social Studies* 99:4 (2008): 147–54.
Fine, Gary Alan. *Difficult Reputations: Collective Memories of the Evil, Inept, and Controversial.* Chicago: University of Chicago Press, 2001.
Fisher, Margery. *Matters of Fact: Aspects of Non-Fiction for Children.* New York: Thomas Y. Crowell, 1972.
Fitch, Susan Pullon, and Roseann M. Mandziuk. *Sojourner Truth as Orator: Wit, Story, and Song.* Westport, Conn.: Greenwood Press, 1997.
Flanzbaum, Hilene. "Unprecedented Liberties: Re-Reading Phillis Wheatley." *MELUS* 18:3 (1993): 71–81.
Foucault, Michel. *Language, Counter-Memory, Practice: Selected Essays and Interviews.* Edited by Donald F. Bouchard. Ithaca, N.Y.: Cornell University Press, 1977.
Gadamer, Hans-Georg. *Truth and Method.* 2nd rev. ed. Translated by Joel Weinsheimer and Donald G. Marshall. New York: Continuum, 1998.
Gaonkar, Dilip Parameshwar. "Contingency and Probability." In *Encyclopedia of Rhetoric,* 151–66. Edited by Thomas O. Sloane. New York: Oxford University Press, 2001.
——. "Rhetoric and Its Double: Reflections of the Rhetorical Turn in the Human Sciences." In *The Rhetorical Turn: Invention and Persuasion in the Conduct of Inquiry,* 341–66. Edited by Herbert W. Simons. Chicago: University of Chicago Press, 1990.
Gates, Henry Louis, Jr. *The Trials of Phillis Wheatley: America's First Black Poet and Her Encounters with the Founding Fathers.* New York: Basic Civitas Books, 2003.
Geisler, Cheryl. "How Ought We to Understand the Concept of Rhetorical Agency? Report from the ARS." *Rhetoric Society Quarterly* 34:3 (2004): 9–17.
——. "Teaching the Post-Modern Rhetor: Continuing the Conversation on Rhetorical Agency." *Rhetoric Society Quarterly* 35:4 (2005): 107–13.
Gilbin, James Cross. "Biography for the 21st Century." *School Library Journal* 48:2 (2002): 44–45.
Gillis, John R. "Memory and Identity: The History of a Relationship." In *Commemorations: The Politics of National Identity,* 3–24. Edited by John R. Gillis. Princeton, N.J.: Princeton University Press, 1994.
Ginzburg, Carlo. *The Cheese and the Worms: The Cosmos of a Sixteenth-Century Miller.* Translated by John Tedeschi and Anne Tedeschi. Baltimore: Johns Hopkins University Press, 1980.
Girard, Linda Walvoord. "Series Thinking and the Art of Biography for Children." *Children's Literature Association Quarterly* 14:4 (1989): 187–92.
Glassberg, David. "Public History and the Study of Memory." *Public Historian* 18:2 (1996): 7–23.

Gubar, Marah. "The Hermeneutics of Recuperation: What a Kinship-Model Approach to Children's Agency Could Do for Children's Literature and Childhood Studies." *Jeunesse: Young People, Texts, Cultures* 8:1 (2016): 291–310.

——. "On Not Defining Children's Literature." *PMLA* 126:1 (2011): 209–16.

——. "Risky Business: Talking about Children in Children's Literature Criticism." *Children's Literature Association Quarterly* 38:4 (2013): 450–57.

Gunn, Joshua. "On Dead Subjects: A Rejoinder to Lundberg on (a) Psychoanalytic Rhetoric." *Quarterly Journal of Speech* 90:4 (2004): 501–13.

——. "Refiguring Fantasy: Imagination and Its Decline in U.S. Rhetorical Studies." *Quarterly Journal of Speech* 89:1 (2003): 41–59.

——. "Refitting Fantasy: Psychoanalysis, Subjectivity, and Talking to the Dead." *Quarterly Journal of Speech* 90:1 (2004): 1–23.

——. "Response." *Quarterly Journal of Speech* 89:4 (2003): 373.

Halbwachs, Maurice. *On Collective Memory.* Edited by Lewis A. Coser. Chicago: University of Chicago Press, 1992.

Hamilton, Nigel. *Biography: A Brief History.* Cambridge, Mass.: Harvard University Press, 2007.

Hampton, Timothy. *Writing from History: The Rhetoric of Exemplarity in Renaissance Literature.* Ithaca, N.Y.: Cornell University Press, 1990.

Haskins, Ekaterina V. "Between Archive and Participation: Public Memory in a Digital Age." *Rhetoric Society Quarterly* 37:4 (2007): 401–22.

——. *Popular Memories: Commemoration, Participatory Culture, and Democratic Citizenship.* Columbia: University of South Carolina Press, 2015.

——. "Post-Traumatic Memories around the Globe." *Quarterly Journal of Speech* 95:3 (2009): 335–45.

——. "'Put Your Stamp on History': The USPS Commemorative Program *Celebrate the Century* and Postmodern Collective Memory." *Quarterly Journal of Speech* 89:1 (2003): 1–18.

Hauser, Gerard A. "Aristotle's Example Revisited." *Philosophy and Rhetoric* 18:3 (1985): 171–80.

——. "The Example in Aristotle's Rhetoric: Bifurcation or Contradiction?" *Philosophy and Rhetoric* 1:2 (1968): 78–90.

——. "Reply to Benoit." *Philosophy and Rhetoric* 20:4 (1987): 268–73.

Hawhee, Debra. "Kairotic Encounters." In *Perspectives on Rhetorical Invention,* 16–35. Edited by Janet M. Atwill and Janice M. Lauer. Knoxville: University of Tennessee Press, 2002.

Henderson, Laretta. *Ebony, Jr.! The Rise, Fall and Return of a Black Children's Magazine.* Lanham, Md.: Scarecrow Press, 2008.

Hevesi, Dennis. "Nancy Hicks Maynard Dies at 61; A Groundbreaking Black Journalist." *New York Times,* September 23, 2008, A27.

Higonnet, Margaret R. "The Playground of the Peritext." *Children's Literature Association Quarterly* 15:2 (1990): 47–49.

Hine, Darlene Clark. *Hine Sight: Black Women and the Re-Construction of American History.* Bloomington: Indiana University Press, 1994.

Honey, Maureen, ed. *Shadowed Dreams: Women's Poetry of the Harlem Renaissance.* Rev. ed. Piscataway, N.J.: Rutgers University Press, 2006.

Hull, Gloria T. "Black Women Poets from Wheatley to Walker." *Negro American Literature Forum* 9:3 (1975): 91–96.

Hunt, Peter. *Children's Literature.* Oxford: Blackwell, 2001.

——. *An Introduction to Children's Literature.* New York: Oxford University Press, 1994.

Isocrates. "To Demonicus." In *Isocrates I,* 19–21. Translated by David C. Mirhady and Yun Lee Too. Austin: University of Texas Press, 2000.

James, Allison. "Agency." In *The Palgrave Handbook of Childhood Studies,* 34–45. Edited by Jens Qvortrop, William A. Corsaro, and Michael-Sebastian Honig. New York: Palgrave Macmillan, 2009.

Jasinski, James. "The Status of Theory and Method in Rhetorical Criticism." *Western Journal of Communication* 65:3 (2001): 249–70.

Johnson, Dianne. *Telling Tales: The Pedagogy and Promise of African American Literature for Youth.* New York: Greenwood Press, 1990.

Johnson, Walter. "On Agency." *Journal of Social History* 37:1 (2003): 113–24.

Kammen, Michael G. *Mystic Chords of Memory: The Transformation of Tradition in American Culture.* New York: Knopf, 1991.

——. "Public History and the Uses of Memory." *Public Historian* 19:2 (1997): 49–52.

Kaplan, David M. *Ricoeur's Critical Theory.* Albany: State University of New York Press, 2003.

Kelshaw, Todd, and Jeffrey St. John. "Remembering 'Memory': The Emergence and Performance of an Institutional Keyword in Communication Studies." *Review of Communication* 7:1 (2007): 46–77.

Klein, Kerwin Lee. "On the Emergence of Memory in Historical Discourse." *Representations* 69 (Special Issue: Grounds for Remembering; Winter 2000): 127–50.

Kramer, Lloyd S. "Literature, Criticism, and Historical Imagination: The Literary Challenge of Hayden White and Dominick LaCapra." In *The New Cultural History,* 97–128. Edited by Lynn Hunt. Berkeley: University of California Press, 1989.

Kunze, Peter C. "What We Talk about When We Talk about Helen Keller: Disabilities in Children's Biographies." *Children's Literature Association Quarterly* 38:3 (2013): 304–18.

Landsberg, Alison. *Prosthetic Memory: The Transformation of Remembrance in the Age of Mass Culture.* New York: Columbia University Press, 2004.

Leff, Michael. "The Habitation of Rhetoric." In *Argument and Critical Practice: Proceedings of the Fifth SCA/AFA Conference on Argumentation,* 1–9. Edited by Joseph Wenzel. Annandale, Va.: Speech Communication Association, 1987.

——. "Tradition and Agency in Humanistic Rhetoric." *Philosophy and Rhetoric* 36:2 (2003): 135–47.

Leighton, Robert and Cate Plys. "Let's Read Two." *Slate.com,* April 5, 2010. http://www.slate.com/articles/sports/sports_nut/2010/04/lets_read_two.html (accessed December 23, 2016).

Lively, Penelope. "Children and Memory." *Horn Book* 49:4 (1973): 400–407.

Loewen, James W. *Lies My Teacher Told Me: Everything Your American History Textbook Got Wrong.* New York: New Press, 1995.

——. "Why Do People Believe Myths about the Confederacy? Because Our Textbooks and Monuments are Wrong." *Washington Post,* July 1, 2015. https://www.washingtonpost.com/posteverything/wp/2015/07/01/why-do-people-believe-myths-about-the-confederacy-because-our-textbooks-and-monuments-are-wrong/?utm_term=.ef8459c25ad1 (accessed December 23, 2016).

Lowenthal, David. "History and Memory." *Public Historian* 19:2 (1997): 30–39.

Lucaites, John Louis, and Celeste Michelle Condit. "Reconstructing <Equality>: Culturetypal and Counter-Cultural Rhetorics in the Martyred Black Vision." *Communication Monographs* 57:1 (1990): 5–24.

Lundberg, Christian. "The Royal Road Not Taken: Joshua Gunn's 'Refitting Fantasy: Psychoanalysis, Subjectivity, and Talking to the Dead' and Lacan's Symbolic Order." *Quarterly Journal of Speech* 90:4 (2004): 495–500.

Lundberg, Christian, and Joshua Gunn. "'Ouija Board, Are There Any Communications?' Agency, Ontotheology, and the Death of the Humanist Subject, or Continuing the ARS Conversation." *Rhetoric Society Quarterly* 35:4 (2005): 83–105.

Mabee, Carleton, and Susan Mabee Newhouse. *Sojourner Truth: Slave, Prophet, Legend.* New York: New York University Press, 1993.

Mandziuk, Roseann. "Commemorating Sojourner Truth: Negotiating the Politics of Race and Gender in the Spaces of Public Memory." *Western Journal of Communication* 67:3 (2003): 271–91.

Marcella, Rita. "The Role and Value of Biography for Children." In *Biography and Children: A Study of Biography for Children and Childhood in Biography,* 7–39. Edited by Stuart Hannabuss and Rita Marcella. London: Library Association, 1993.

Martin, Michelle H. *Brown Gold: Milestones of African American Children's Picture Books, 1845–2002.* New York: Routledge, 2004.

May, Laura A., Teri Holbrook, and Laura E. Myers. "(Re)Storying Obama: An Examination of Recently Published Informational Texts." *Children's Literature in Education* 41:4 (2010): 273–90.

McCombe, John P. "Picturing Jazz: Jazz Biography and Children's Literature." *Children's Literature Association Quarterly* 28:2 (2003): 68–80.

McCormick, Samuel. "Mirrors for the Queen: A Letter from Christine de Pizan on the Eve of the Civil War." *Quarterly Journal of Speech* 94:3 (2008): 273–96.

McDowell, Kelly. "*Roll of Thunder, Hear My Cry*: A Culturally Specific, Subversive Concept of Child Agency." *Children's Literature in Education* 33:3 (2002): 213–25.

McGee, Michael Calvin. "The 'Ideograph': A Link between Rhetoric and Ideology." *Quarterly Journal of Speech* 66:1 (1980): 1–16.

McKerrow, Raymie. "Critical Rhetoric: Theory and Praxis." *Communication Monographs* 56:2 (1989): 91–111.

McNair, Jonda C. "A Comparative Analysis of *The Brownies' Book* and Contemporary African American Children's Literature by Patricia McKissack." In *Embracing, Evaluating, and Examining African American Children's and Young Adult Literature,* 3–29. Edited by Wanda M. Brooks and Jonda C. McNair. Lanham, Md.: Scarecrow Press, 2008.

McWhirter, Cameron. *Red Summer: The Summer of 1919 and the Awakening of Black America.* New York: Henry Holt, 2011.

Melamed, Jodi. *Represent and Destroy: Rationalizing Violence in the New Racial Capitalism.* Minneapolis: University of Minnesota Press, 2011.

Meltzer, Milton. "Notes on Biography." *Children's Literature Association Quarterly* 10:4 (1986): 172–75.

Mickenberg, Julia. "Civil Rights, History, and the Left: Inventing the Juvenile Black Biography." *MELUS* 27:2 (2002): 65–71.

Morgan, Hani. "Picture Book Biographies for Young Children: A Way to Teach Multiple Perspectives." *Early Childhood Education Journal* 37:3 (2009): 219–27.

Moore, Ann W. "Setting the Bar for Biography." *School Library Journal* 51:11 (2005): 38–39.

Moreau, Joseph. *Schoolbook Nation: Conflicts over American History Textbooks from the Civil War to the Present.* Ann Arbor: University of Michigan Press, 2004.

Morris III, Charles E. "My Old Kentucky Homo: Lincoln and the Politics of Queer Public Memory." In *Framing Public Memory,* 89–114. Edited by Kendall R. Phillips. Tuscaloosa: University of Alabama Press, 2004.

Morris III, Charles E., ed. *Remembering the AIDS Quilt.* East Lansing: Michigan State University Press, 2011.

Murray, Gail Schmunk. *American Children's Literature and the Construction of Childhood.* New York: Twayne, 1998.

National Council on Public History. "What Is Public History?" 2016. http://ncph.org/what-is-public-history/about-the-field/ (accessed December 22, 2016).

Neary, Lynn. "To Achieve Diversity in Publishing, a Difficult Dialogue Beats Silence." *NPR News,* August 20, 2014. http://www.npr.org/blogs/codeswitch/2014/08/20/341443632/to-achieve-diversity-in-publishing-a-difficult-dialogue-beats-silence (accessed December 23, 2016).

Nikolajeva, Maria. "Imprints of the Mind: The Depiction of Consciousness in Children's Literature." *Children's Literature Association Quarterly* 26:4 (2002): 173–87.

——. *The Rhetoric of Character in Children's Literature.* Lanham, Md.: Scarecrow Press, 2002.

Nodelman, Perry. *The Hidden Adult: Defining Children's Literature.* Baltimore: Johns Hopkins University Press, 2008.

——. *The Pleasures of Children's Literature.* New York: Longman, 1992.

Nora, Pierre. "Between Memory and History: *Les Lieux de Mémoire.*" *Representations* 26 (Special Issue: Memory and Counter-Memory; Spring 1989): 7–25.

Oswell, David. *The Agency of Children: From Family to Global Human Rights.* New York: Cambridge University Press, 2013.

Painter, Nell Irvin. Introduction to *Journey toward Freedom: The Story of Sojourner Truth,* by Jacqueline Bernard, xv–xxv. New York: Feminist Press, 1990.

——. "Representing Truth: Sojourner Truth's Knowing and Becoming Known." *Journal of American History* 81:2 (1994): 461–92.

——. *Sojourner Truth: A Life, a Symbol.* New York: W. W. Norton, 1996.

Palti, Elías. "The 'Return of the Subject' as a Historico-Intellectual Problem." *History and Theory* 43:1 (2004): 57–82.

Pantaleo, Sylvia. *Exploring Student Response to Contemporary Picturebooks.* Toronto: University of Toronto Press, 2008.

Peel, Katie R. "'Strange Fruit': Representations of Julius and Ethel Rosenberg in Children's and Young Adult Nonfiction." *Children's Literature Association Quarterly* 36:2 (2011): 190–213.

Perelman, Chaim, and Lucie Olbrechts-Tyteca. *The New Rhetoric: A Treatise on Argumentation.* Translated by John Wilkinson and Purcell Weaver. Notre Dame, Ind.: University of Notre Dame, 1969.

Peterson, Merrill D. *Lincoln in American Memory.* New York: Oxford University Press, 1994.

Phillips, Kendall R., ed. *Framing Public Memory.* Tuscaloosa: University of Alabama Press, 2004.

——. "The Failure of Memory: Reflections on Rhetoric and Public Remembrance." *Western Journal of Communication* 74:2 (2010): 208–23.

Plys, Cate, and Robert Leighton. "All Presidents Are Above Average." *Slate.com,* February 14, 2010. http://www.slate.com/articles/news_and_politics/politics/2010/02/all_presidents_are_above_average.html (accessed December 23, 2016).

Prendergast, Carole, and Robin Klein. "Studying Heroes: Picture-Book Biographies and More." *Book Links* 15:4 (2006): 34–38.

"Publishing Statistics on Children's Books about People of Color and First/Native Nations and by People of Color and First/Native Nations Authors and Illustrators." *Cooperative Children's Book Center.* Last modified October 11, 2016, http://ccbc.education.wisc.edu/books/pcstats.asp#black (accessed December 23, 2016).

Richards, Cindy Koenig. "Inventing Sacagawea: Public Women and the Transformative Potential of Epideictic Rhetoric." *Western Journal of Communication* 73:1 (2009): 1–22.

Richmond, M. A. *Bid the Vassal Soar: Interpretive Essays on the Life and Poetry of Phillis Wheatley (ca. 1753–1784) and George Moses Horton (ca. 1797–1883).* Washington, D.C.: Howard University Press, 1974.

Ricoeur, Paul. *From Text to Action: Essays in Hermeneutics II.* Translated by Kathleen Blamey and John B. Thompson. 2nd ed. Evanston, Ill.: Northwestern University Press, 2007.

——. *Memory, History, Forgetting.* Translated by Kathleen Blamey and David Pellauer. Chicago: University of Chicago Press, 2004.

——. "Rhetoric—Poetics—Hermeneutics." Translated by Robert Harvey. *Rhetoric and Hermeneutics in Our Time,* 60–72. Edited by Walter Jost and Michael J. Hyde. New Haven, Conn.: Yale University Press, 1997.

——. *Time and Narrative,* vol. 1. Translated by Kathleen McLaughlin and David Pellauer. Chicago: University of Chicago Press, 1984.

Ritivoi, Andreea Deciu. *Paul Ricoeur: Tradition and Innovation in Rhetorical Theory.* Albany: State University of New York Press, 2006.

Robinson, William H. *Phillis Wheatley and Her Writings.* New York: Garland, 1984.

Rodgers, Daniel. "Republicanism: The Career of a Concept." *Journal of American History* 79:1 (1992):11–38.

Rosenzweig, Roy, and David Thelen. *The Presence of the Past: Popular Uses of History in American Life.* New York: Columbia University Press, 1998.

Samra, Matthew K. "Shadow and Substance: The Two Narratives of Sojourner Truth." *Midwest Quarterly* 38:2 (1997): 158–71.

Sánchez-Eppler, Karen. *Dependent States: The Child's Part in Nineteenth-Century American Culture.* Chicago: University of Chicago Press, 2005.

Schmidt, Gary D. *Making Americans: Children's Literature from 1930 to 1960.* Iowa City: University of Iowa Press, 2013.

Schwartz, Barry. *Abraham Lincoln and the Forge of National Memory.* Chicago: University of Chicago Press, 2000.

——. *Abraham Lincoln in the Post-Heroic Era: History and Memory in Late Twentieth-Century America.* Chicago: University of Chicago Press, 2009.

Schwebel, Sara L. *Child-Sized History: Fictions of the Past in U.S. Classrooms.* Nashville, Tenn.: Vanderbilt University Press, 2011.

Scott, Joan Wallach. *Gender and the Politics of History.* Rev. ed. New York: Columbia University Press, 1999.

Sewell, William H., Jr. *Logics of History: Social Theory and Social Transformation.* Chicago: University of Chicago Press, 2005.

Shaw, David Gary. "Happy in Our Chains? Agency and Language in the Postmodern Age." *History and Theory* 40:4 (2001): 1–9.

Shields, John C. *Phillis Wheatley's Poetics of Liberation: Backgrounds and Contexts.* Knoxville: University of Tennessee Press, 2008.

——. "Phillis Wheatley's Struggle for Freedom in Her Poetry and Prose." In *The Collected Works of Phillis Wheatley,* 229-70. Edited by John Shields. New York: Oxford University Press, 1988.

Shorto, Russell. "How Christian Were the Founders?" *New York Times Magazine,* February 11, 2010. http://nytimes.com/2010/02/14/magazine/14textbooks-t.html (accessed January 9, 2018).

Sipe, Lawrence R. "Children's Response to Literature: Author, Text, Reader, Context." *Theory into Practice* 38:3 (1999): 120–29.

Sipe, Lawrence R., and Caroline E. McGuire. "Young Children's Resistance to Stories." *Reading Teacher* 60:1 (2006): 6–13.

Smith, Katharine Capshaw. "*The Brownies' Book* and the Roots of African American Children's Literature." N.d. The Tar Baby and the Tomahawk: Race and Ethnic Images in American Children's Literature, 1880–1939, http://childlit.unl.edu/topics/edi.harlem.html (accessed December 23, 2016).

——. *Children's Literature of the Harlem Renaissance.* Bloomington: Indiana University Press, 2004.

Spiegel, Gabrielle M. "Memory and History: Liturgical Time and Historical Time." *History and Theory* 41:2 (2002): 149–62.

Spielvogel, J. Christian. *Interpreting Sacred Ground: The Rhetoric of National Civil War Parks and Battlefields.* Tuscaloosa: University of Alabama Press, 2013.

Stabell, Ivy Linton. "Model Patriots: The First Children's Biographies of George Washington and Benjamin Franklin." *Children's Literature* 14 (2013): 91–114.

Stormer, Nathan. "Articulation: A Working Paper on Rhetoric and Taxis." *Quarterly Journal of Speech* 90:3 (2004): 257–84.

Stout, Maureen. *The Feel-Good Curriculum: The Dumbing-Down of American Kids in the Name of Self-Esteem.* Cambridge, Mass.: Perseus Books, 2000.

Sylvander, Carolyn Wedin. *Jessie Redmon Fauset, Black American Writer.* Troy, N.Y.: Whitson, 1981.

Taylor, Charles. *Human Agency and Language: Philosophical Papers I.* Cambridge: Cambridge University Press, 1985.

——. *Modern Social Imaginaries.* Durham, N.C.: Duke University Press, 2004.

——. *Sources of the Self: The Making of the Modern Identity.* Cambridge, Mass.: Harvard University Press, 1989.

Taylor, Ronald L. "Black Youth in Crisis." *Humboldt Journal of Social Relations* 14:1&2 (1986–87): 106–33.

Tolson, Nancy. "Making Books Available: The Role of Early Libraries, Librarians, and Booksellers in the Promotion of African American Children's Literature." *African American Review* 32:1 (1998): 9–16.

Truth, Sojourner, with Frances W. Titus. *The Narrative of Sojourner Truth, with "Book of Life" and "A Memorial Chapter."* Edited by and with introduction and notes by Imani Perry. *Narrative and "Book of Life"* originally published in 1878; *"A Memorial Chapter"* originally published in 1884. New York: Barnes and Noble Classics, 2005.

Turnbull, Nick. "Rhetorical Agency as a Property of Questioning." *Philosophy and Rhetoric* 37:3 (2004): 207–22.

Uprichard, Emma. "Children as 'Being and Becomings': Children, Childhood, and Temporality." *Children and Society* 22:4 (2008): 303–13.

VanderHaagen, Sara C. "The 'Agential Spiral': Reading Public Memory through Paul Ricoeur." *Philosophy and Rhetoric* 46:2 (2013): 182–206.

——. "Practical Truths: Black Feminist Agency and Public Memory in Biographies for Children." *Women's Studies in Communication* 35:1 (2012): 18–41.

VanderHaagen, Sara C., and Angela G. Ray. "The Pilgrim-Critic at Places of Public Memory: Anna Dickinson's Southern Tour of 1875." *Quarterly Journal of Speech* 100:3 (2014): 348–74.

Vivian, Bradford J. "On the Language of Forgetting." *Quarterly Journal of Speech* 95:1 (2009): 89–104.

——. *Public Forgetting: The Rhetoric and Politics of Beginning Again.* University Park: Pennsylvania State University Press, 2010.

——. "Up from Memory: Epideictic Forgetting in Booker T. Washington's Cotton States Exposition Address." *Philosophy and Rhetoric* 45:2 (2012): 189–212.

Wander, Philip. "The Ideological Turn in Modern Criticism." *Central States Speech Journal* 34:1 (1983): 1–18.

Warner, Michael. *Publics and Counterpublics.* New York: Zone Books, 2002.

Warnick, Barbara. "A Ricoeurian Approach to Rhetorical Criticism." *Western Journal of Speech Communication* 51:3 (1987): 227–44.

Watts, Eric King. *Hearing the Hurt: Rhetoric, Aesthetics and Politics of the New Negro Movement.* Tuscaloosa: University of Alabama Press, 2012.

——. "'Voice' and 'Voicelessness' in Rhetorical Studies." *Quarterly Journal of Speech* 87:2 (2001): 179–96.

Weikle-Mills, Courtney. *Imaginary Citizens: Child Readers and the Limits of American Independence, 1640–1868.* Baltimore: Johns Hopkins University Press, 2013.

Wheatley, Phillis. *The Collected Works of Phillis Wheatley.* Edited by John C. Shields. New York: Oxford University Press, 1988.

White, Hayden. *Metahistory: The Historical Imagination in Nineteenth-Century Europe.* Baltimore: Johns Hopkins University Press, 1975.

——. "The Question of Narrative in Contemporary Historical Theory." *History and Theory* 23:1 (1984): 1–33.

Wills, John E., Jr. "Lives and Other Stories: Neglected Aspects of the Teacher's Art." *History Teacher* 26:1 (1992): 33–49.

Wilson, Rob. "Producing American Selves: The Form of American Biography." *boundary 2* 18:2 (1991): 104–29.

Wilson, Kurt H. "Debating the Great Emancipator: Abraham Lincoln and Our Public Memory." *Rhetoric and Public Affairs* 13:3 (2010): 455–79.

Wintz, Cary D. "Series Introduction." In *The Critics and the Harlem Renaissance,* xiii–xvi. Edited by Cary D. Wintz. New York: Garland, 1996.

Woods, Carly S., Joshua P. Ewalt, and Sara J. Baker. "A Matter of Regionalism: Remembering Brandon Teena and Willa Cather at the Nebraska History Museum." *Quarterly Journal of Speech* 99:3 (2013): 341–63.

Wright, Elizabethada. "Reading the Cemetery, *Lieu de Mémoire Par Excellance.*" *Rhetoric Society Quarterly* 33:2 (2003): 27–44.

Yates, Frances A. *The Art of Memory.* 2nd ed. Chicago: University of Chicago Press, 2001.

Zelizer, Barbie. "Reading the Past against the Grain: The Shape of Memory Studies." *Critical Studies in Mass Communication* 12:2 (1995): 214–39.

Index